Superyacht
X-Rated

CW00427882

Superyacht X-Rated

Marc Wilder

JOHN BLAKE

Published by John Blake Publishing Ltd,
3 Bramber Court, 2 Bramber Road,
London W14 9PB, England

www.johnblakepublishing.co.uk

First published in paperback in 2010

ISBN: 978 1 84454 970 2

All rights reserved. No part of this publication may be reproduced, stored in a
retrieval system, or in any form or by any means, without the prior permission in
writing of the publisher, nor be otherwise circulated in any form of binding or
cover other than that in which it is published and without a similar condition
including this condition being imposed on the subsequent publisher.

British Library Cataloguing-in-Publication Data:

A catalogue record for this book is available from the British Library.

Design by www.envydesign.co.uk

Printed in Great Britain by CPI Bookmarque, Croydon CR0 4TD

1 3 5 7 9 10 8 6 4 2

© Text copyright Marc Wilder, 2010

Papers used by John Blake Publishing are natural, recyclable products made from
wood grown in sustainable forests. The manufacturing processes conform to the
environmental regulations of the country of origin.

Every attempt has been made to contact the relevant copyright-holders,
but some were unobtainable. We would be grateful if the appropriate people
could contact us.

This book is dedicated to the good, the bad and the ugly that I've sailed the seas with throughout the years. Without experiencing your energy – good or bad, this book would not have been possible. Also dedicated to 'Shiner', RIP. You put a smile on everyone's face. Last but by no means least, to my fiancée, who is the love of my life, my best friend and soul mate. Without you in my life nothing would matter.

ACKNOWLEDGEMENTS

It was looking out at this very statue of
Captain Cook in Whitby, North Yorkshire
that I got the inspiration to head out to sea.
This is where my life story began.

(Photo courtesy of Howard from www.beautifulbritain.co.uk)

CONTENTS

INTRODUCTION

My name is Marc Wilder, age 37, and I'm a qualified Master Mariner. I've spent nearly two action-packed decades at sea, working on a multitude of different ships. This has included working as a Navigation Officer on government ships, on square-rigged sailing ships that take the handicapped to sea, huge cruise ships and a millionaires' private yacht, to name but a few.

I decided to go to sea after having what can only be described as an epiphany one day, as I sat down overlooking the ocean and the Captain Cook's statue in Whitby, North Yorkshire. Since then I have travelled, worked and played all over the world. I started as a Merchant Navy officer cadetship with the Ministry of Defence in the early nineties, aged 18.

Recently, one of my more enjoyable times was spent working as Chief Officer on a large private motor yacht based in Monte Carlo. My job as second in command was to run the deck department and manage the crew for the

Captain whilst the yacht sailed around some of the most luxurious destinations of the world, such as the French and Italian Riviera. I've witnessed a lot while I've been working at sea – from exclusive private parties to drug-fuelled orgies, Russian gangsters to the most gorgeous escorts money can buy – and shared the experiences with a crew full of interesting characters. Every story in *Superyacht X-Rated* is based on true events, but I've condensed it down to one of the dirtiest, sexiest, most rock 'n' roll charters imaginable. Obviously the real names and the character's involvement in the shenanigans described within the book have been changed to protect identities. I hope you enjoy the ride... I sure have.

My favourite things are travelling, extra leg room, eating meat, going to music festivals, playing with my boy, drinking Guinness and fine malt whisky in large quantities, and spending quality time with my beautiful partner.

When I was a young boy, a well-known clairvoyant once told me that in the years to come I'd write a book that would result in fame and fortune. This is my first book... let's see if she was right.

CHAPTER 1
THE CRAZY GANG

'Chicken nuggets? You've got to be kidding!' shouts Tom. It's clear that Tom is a little upset by the request.

'Sorry, mate, the Captain has just told me,' I say, trying to calm him down.

He's upset because it's nearly the end of his shift and he now has to transfer a box of chicken nuggets by boat to the owner's multi-million-dollar mega-yacht lying in Monaco.

'I don't fucking believe these twats. They hire a state-of-the-art mega-yacht for $250,000 a week and what do they eat... shit!' Tom throws his hands in the air. 'What a pair of dickheads!'

'I'm pretty sure it's for their kid, mate,' I say, still trying my best to calm things down. 'Foie gras and lobster must upset his stomach, I guess.'

'I'll upset the little fucker when I bury my size ten boot up his arse. And I'll tell you another thing, boss – his bloody dad upset me watching him play football last weekend; fucking stupid haircut as well. How many

1

millions is he supposed to be worth? What a fucking joke!'

Tom was always straight to the point, and his sentences usually contained enough expletives to make a sailor blush. He was a great guy and everyone always knew where they stood with him. He'd been travelling around the world, usually by himself, living life to the full for years. He'd spent quite a lot of time recently backpacking in Bolivia. He'd been living an alternative lifestyle and being a reprobate. He got into working on millionaires' mega-yachts because his ferret business took a nosedive when his prize ferret apparently turned gay and wouldn't screw the females any more. He still curses the critter for letting him down, and he once explained that he lost patience with it one day and decided to take it out of its cage and put a shotgun to its head. 'Are you telling me that you shot your prize ferret because you thought it had turned fruit?'

'Nah, mate, that would have been too cruel,' he said in a softer voice.

'Oh, that's all right then,' I said, feeling a little better.

'So I drowned it!' Tom added before taking a big drag of his cigarette.

This was one of many conversations I had with Tom during his time aboard the yacht. He'd have me laughing my arse off on an hourly basis. I liked him a lot because he wasn't your average guy. He had never become affected by the bullshit and one-up-manship that surrounds the yachting world, and he never tried to be someone he wasn't. I was his boss and fairly frequently I had to give him a bollocking for one thing or another but I found it really difficult to get upset with him for long. Solid as a rock was Tom, and I respected him for that.

Another character aboard the yacht was a strapping Scotsman called Jock. He was born and bred in the poorer part of Glasgow. He had a heart of gold but he had very few social graces – especially after a few beers. The term 'social hand grenade' suited Jock completely and he was a bit of local colour. Jock had grown up on a tough housing estate, where even the rats don't walk down the streets after sunset. He was from a broken family and his dad used to come back pissed and either beat his mum or Jock if he got in the way. He did what he could in those days to survive, including stealing cars and selling rave tickets to gullible students.

He used to print off thousands of tickets for an organised outdoor rave. He'd then borrow his mate's banged-up Escort van and drive around the country selling them. We are talking thousands of tickets here for around £10 a ticket (this was the 1990s). He used to blag his way into a student bar and sell them to naïve, spotty students at half price – provided they bought a minimum of 20 or so. He'd pocket the cash and tell the buyer to wait outside a particular phone box at a certain time to be arranged. The buyer could then expect a call telling the pumped-up partygoers where the rave was. The only thing was, the phone call never used to come, and by the time the kids knew what had happened, Jock would be flying down the motorway to scam another city – thousands of pounds richer!

He got away with this and other ingenious scams for a long while until he underestimated a particular shady character in a northern city. For God's sake, he should've known when he got the go-ahead to meet the guy in his local where he did business. Jock turned up with 3,000 tickets and was greeted by a man the size of a pie shop with a face that looks like it'd had regular panel beating. There were three vicious-looking pit bulls terriers and three equally hard-looking sidekicks. They were all wearing dark jackets, even darker shades and pug expressions. Jock should have realised that when he walked in to this scenario he should listen to the little voice in his head that's screaming 'Don't fuck with these guys!' In situations like this you disregard what it's saying at your peril.

Typically, Jock decided that he wasn't going to listen. He did the deal and high-tailed it like all the times before. All went well until the night of the supposed phone call. He was at a nightclub before heading off to scam another city when he met a girl of dubious morals. He figured out that if he hung around and put the verbal spadework in, he wouldn't be sleeping on his own that night and he'd leave the city in the morning on a high note. Ten o'clock passed and he hadn't made the call, for obvious reasons. Eleven o'clock passed and still no call. By this time Mr Scary had realised that he'd been shafted. He'd a lot of explaining to do to the other gangsters he'd sold tickets to, as well as a couple of thousand party-hungry clubbers. He'd lost face and a shitload of cash, and he was obviously pissed off, to say the least. Loss of face + loss of cash = disaster area for our Jock!

Meanwhile everything seemed to be going well with Jock and Miss Slack-knickers and at around one in the morning, after sucking face with her, he decided to get a taxi back to her pad for some fun between the sheets. Jock likes to call it 'slimy pump-pump action'. As he was leaving the club, Mr Nasty arrived with his entourage. Jock was immediately

4

spotted and greeted with 'I'm gonna rip your fucking face off!' by one of the henchmen. Jock immediately ejected the 38G blonde from the taxi and pleaded with the driver to put his foot on the pedal. Mr Nasty jumped in to another taxi in hot pursuit. Jock threw a handful of cash at the driver and told him to head down a country lane and slow down enough so he could jump out and leg it across a field. The driver grudgingly agreed, Jock threw himself out and the taxi carried on. The only problem was, Mr Nasty and the gang had seen him. They stopped their taxi and chased after Jock on foot, fuelled by adrenaline and anger.

Jock ran and jumped like a gazelle over rocks, fences, hedges and other various obstacles, not to mention fields of bulls. He was being pursued by a psychotic mob and an enraged Aberdeen Angus. Running as hard as he could, he managed to create a gap between them of a hundred yards or so. Jumping in to a ditch, he took refuge in a pipe that took water under the road, and decided to crawl along it on his hands and knees until he was safely out of the area. He stayed there all night until he climbed out of a manhole at around ten the following morning in the middle of a busy high street, still dressed in his clubbing gear. He opened the manhole cover, climbed out, calmly stretched and yawned, and told an astonished passing pedestrian that he lived down there to save money on poll tax. Then he walked across the road and into a McDonald's for brunch. Priceless, and typical Jock antics.

Then there's Robbie. Robbie was the quiet one of the yacht's crew, but you know what they say about watching the quiet ones. He'd pretty much keep himself to himself but he'd absorb everything around him. He wasn't sensible by any means but he just wasn't as loud as Jock. Then again, who was? He was a man of very few words but when he did come out with something it was usually really funny or really philosophical and you'd be thinking about it all day. He was just an ordinary guy, but he was too intelligent for his own good and that would sometimes get him into trouble. He had quit school early because lessons bored him, probably because intellectually he was way ahead of the others. He was probably ahead of the teachers, come to think of it. He didn't stay at school long enough to take any exams and left with no formal qualifications.

He had a problem with substance abuse back then, probably for escapism. Nothing really heavy, just pills, weed and drink. He once worked in an old folks' home to make ends meet and he noticed at Christmas dinner that none of the inmates were talking. Most of them looked like they wanted to die. In a moment of madness the silly sod took pity on the poor old folk and wondered what he could do to give them a bit of party atmosphere. Sometimes he just lets emotions rule his head without really thinking about the consequences of his actions, and he laced the old folks' chocolate cake with a little speed.

Half an hour later, one granddad was bouncing around like a kiddie on a pogo stick, laughing his wrinkly old face off. Everyone else was chatting away like crazy people and he couldn't get a word in edgeways. The two resident spaniels, which had also had some of the cake, were going ballistic, running round like lunatics chasing their tails and barking the walls down. The place was in complete fucking mayhem. Robbie felt genuinely great that the atmosphere had picked up and everyone was enjoying themselves. He was feeling happy that he he'd brought a few moments of pleasure into otherwise dreary and dishevelled lives.

He decided to sit down with a few of the old boys, put some music on and share a joint with them. Everyone was having a blinding time until the manager walked in and discovered Albert buzzing his arse off and the normally orderly dining room had turned into a place that smelled like a Moroccan hashish den. That was the end of Robbie's career caring for the elderly. He swears blind that whilst shopping in town one day he bumped into one of the old boys who tried to score some hash off him.

'By crikey, it was cracking stuff that, son. Took all my aches and pains away! You wouldn't have any more, would you?'

It was a bloody silly thing to do, although everybody was fine. However, it does make you ponder the subject of narcotic substances. Robbie and I come from the same basic background as far as work and travel are concerned. We've both travelled extensively and worked in most of the countries around the globe. Robbie once gave me his thoughts on the use of party prescriptions over a few pints in the pub one night and it made remarkable sense to me. Robbie believed that the use of certain things in small quantities in a safe environment can help free your mind, drop your guard and make you very creative. One thing he noticed whilst travelling was that most countries and cultures have one thing in common, amongst other things: they all have some method of getting high!

Somebody famous once said that the only way to discover the limits of the possible is to go beyond them into the impossible. Somebody else said they believed in a prolonged displacement of the senses to attain the unknown. Robbie believes a quote from William Blake: 'When the doors of perception are cleansed, things will appear as they truly are – infinity!'

* * * *

The yacht was a beautiful, state of the art, top-of-the-range beauty. She weighed several hundred tonnes and was about half the length of a football field. She had teak decks, stainless steel, and very tasteful and expensive furnishings. There was space for twelve guests, and she carried twelve to thirteen crew who looked after their every whim in utmost luxury. The upper deck, or sun deck, had a large Jacuzzi, a barbeque and a bar. She also carried two rigid inflatable speed boats capable of carrying six to eight people. These were used for taking the guests waterskiing, fishing and wakeboarding. She had a stern garage, otherwise known as the lazarette, where the crew kept all the 'toys'. These included two immensely powerful 1300cc jet skis, scuba gear, a sailing dinghy and inflatable water toys.

Walking into the crew room on board the yacht, I find the crew sat around the table. 'You'd better keep out of the way of the Captain today, everyone,' I warn them. 'He's definitely not in the best of moods.'

Robbie sighs. 'Tell me something new. That man was born an arsehole and just grew bigger.'

'What's the matter with Thrush today, then?' Jock joins

in. 'Thrush' is Jock's nickname for the Captain, because just like thrush he's an irritating cunt. The first time Jock told me that, I was in the middle of drinking tea. I laughed so much I burnt myself.

The Captain was a cold, skinny, sour-faced man in his late fifties, with no sense of warmth and no idea about man management or how to treat people. He'd just joined this yacht because the owner of his last yacht died. That yacht was notorious because it was common knowledge that the owner liked to spread his seed into anyone or anything that moved. It was said that he would 'fuck the crack of dawn if he could get up early enough... he'll shag anything with two legs or sometimes four.' It was also alleged that he'd try it on with the crew – especially the officers.

Tom used to tell a great story, imagining Thrush working on his previous yacht. 'I bet his arsehole looked like it had gone through a bloody mincing machine by the time he'd left! I bet the owner used to make him turn up at his cabin every day, trousers folded neatly over the forearm and then tell him to assume the position.'

Thrush had no enthusiasm or passion for anything other than putting people down or being a general arsehole. He was just a cold-hearted businessman. A captain can earn a fortune on mega-yachts. Obviously, the bigger the yacht the more money they get, but most command salaries of £5,000 to £15,000 a month, tax free, and most of their expenses paid. There are lots of fringe benefits, including tips from the guests – if it's a charter yacht – which can be anything from five to twenty per cent of the total bill for the charter, usually around $200,000 a week. The food bill and the fuel bill and other costs are added to that. The crew are usually salaried but also get tips – also tax free.

A good captain will share out the tips equally amongst the crew, but some captains take a larger cut for themselves. Often they are the only ones who see the final bill, so nobody really knows how much tip is received – every way you look at it, the captains are on fortunes.

Captains also deal with most of the accounting, so only they really know what comes in and what goes out. Depending on the yacht, the captain will buy the ship's food, fuel and stores from their own supplier. If they do this they get kickbacks of say five to ten per cent on what they spend. Again, all this extra cash adds up. I asked to be kept abreast of expenses but was basically told to fuck off, for obvious reasons. The Captain was on the make *big time* and he wasn't sharing the wealth.

The crew hated the Captain and this sometimes made my job difficult. He was shacked up with a Polish stewardess called Olga, and everyone hated her, too. When he wasn't around she was his eyes and ears. If you were chatting amongst yourselves and she walked in and overheard what you were saying, you could pretty much guarantee it would get back to the Captain. The crew thought that he'd met her on an 'East European brides' website. She'd pamper his every whim when he was around and call him 'Puppy', much to the crew's amusement.

CHAPTER 2

WHITE SUITS AND BLACK MONEY

One of the things you can guarantee about anyone hiring a mega-yacht for a charter is they are stinking rich. We are not just talking people with a couple of million in the bank, we are talking people with a couple of hundred million or even a few billion in the bank. You often find that many of them are crooks in some way, shape or form. Sure, there are the legitimate businessmen and showbiz personalities, but sometimes they come from dubious backgrounds.

For the next charter we picked up a bunch of Russians and Japanese in the port of Nice. The crew had just spent the past twenty-four hours working really hard to get the yacht in pristine condition to create the right impression. This included washing, sponging and leathering the entire exterior by hand. Then we had to wash and treat the wood decks, polish the stainless steel and scrub the white speedboats. If we had just finished doing it and it rained that awful red sandy rain that comes off the Sahara, then we'd have to do it again. It was a ball-ache of a job! We'd just changed into fresh uniforms and were stood by the passerelle, which is yacht jargon for the gangplank, waiting for the guests to arrive. It was a beautiful sunny day and Jock already had a sweepstake going on what tip we were going to get at the end of the charter.

Zecky, the Chief Stewardess, is gorgeous and great fun. She was 'one of the lads', a head-banger in her time off but very professional when she had to be. She'd partied around the world and she was a legend. She first came into yachting thinking the sea air would sort her head out from years of clubbing… bless her.

Zecky radios from the hired limo that she'd met the guests from the airport and they would be with us in ten minutes. 'Oh and by the way, they're not what you were expecting.'

'What do you mean?' I say, intrigued.

'You'll see, but there's some eye candy for you boys.'

Two new, black limos edge round the corner and slowly pull up to the yacht. The doors open and huge bodyguards wearing designer suits and shades climb out. They give the area a quick 360-degree scan, then lean back into the car and give whoever it is the go ahead to get out. The crew watches silently with baited breath, waiting to see who it is that needs this sort of security. The crew have been told that no cameras are allowed onboard. Clearly, whoever it is doesn't want any evidence that he's been here with the other guests.

First, a shiny, high-heeled shoe steps out. Then a beautifully toned and waxed leg, and then another emerges from a second limo. Two stunning women walk towards the yacht. One is blonde and blue-eyed and looks like a taller and classier Pamela Anderson. The other is a black Latin American with wavy jet black hair, long legs and that South American sexiness you just can't put into words. Both are so beautiful they could bring traffic to a halt.

Robbie's mouth is wide open, like a goldfish at feeding time. 'Close your mouth, mate – you look like a gormless twat,' I say quietly.

'Ha! Sorry, mate, it's just…' says Rob, jumping back into work mode.

'I know, I know. Give your marks out of ten, then – what would you give them?'

'Marks out of ten – I'd give 'em one!' Rob grins.

'I guess I walked into that one. Seriously though, what do you reckon?'

'Well, put it this way boss. I'd crawl ten thousand miles through scorching desert, along a winding pathway, over broken glass, *naked,* just so I could put matchsticks in her shit!' he whispers.

I find this hilarious and have to try to control myself at the worst possible moment. However, the thing with me is that I just can't help my eyes. They have a really nasty habit of dropping me in the shit every time. The two girls walk up to the yacht and I greet them with a warm handshake.

The blonde leans forward and she smells divine. She kisses me on each cheek. 'I'm very pleased to meet you,' she says in an East European accent, giving me a cheeky wink.

Next, the dark girl walks up to me and does the whole supermodel strut that they use on the catwalk. I really don't know how they make their hips move like that but it's a delight to see. She struts towards me like a panther and she also leans forward and plants two kisses, but instead of moving on she stops for a chat. She gives me a polite two-handed shake, and in typical South American fashion, stands so close that if she gets any nearer I'll end up needing a condom.

She chats away in a husky Brazilian accent, looking at me with huge, chocolate brown eyes while stroking my forearm. Then the most embarrassing thing happens to me. 'Oh fuck! No fucking way... not now!' I scream silently to myself. I'm getting an erection, because she's just my type and there's nothing I can do about it. I just wish she'd stop looking at me that way and stroking my arm. Well, consciously and logically I want that, but subconsciously I'm thinking, 'Let's get naked'.

I'm trying to concentrate on what she's saying, as well as thinking as much as I can about dead puppies nailed to trees to help stem the flow of blood to my groin. Let's face it though, chaps, men have difficulty doing two things at once at the best of times – never mind with a boner! You know what they say: when there is a boil-up in the loins there is a freeze-up in the brain. (Jock says he has given his dick a name because he doesn't want a stranger making all the decisions for him.) She eventually moves on, but to my horror the main guest – who we came to refer to as 'Mr Big' – is now standing right behind her.

In all the excitement I didn't even notice him walk up. I'm now totally flustered and with an ever-filling hard-on as he greets me with a handshake.

'I'd gladly sell my soul to the Devil right now if I could only stop what is happening in my pants,' I say to myself.

Mr Big is dressed in a pristine white suit and he has a huge cigar in his mouth. He's wearing enough gold to put Mr T from the A-Team to shame, and it's a pretty vulgar display of wealth. He nods me a pleasantry and quickly walks on by.

'Thank God for small mercies,' I think. That's three guests down and about a half dozen to go. One more walks past and then another one. I'm thinking I'm going to get away with it before my hard-on grows too prominent, but the last guest is taking his time getting his stuff out of the car and my bulge is growing ever bigger as the last bodyguard finally walks up the passerelle. I'm signalling at him to walk past me so I can make my escape. Unfortunately, he stops right in front of me. Then he bends forward to put his briefcase down so he can shake my hand and as he does so he notices the bulge in my pants. He momentarily stays in the half-bent position with my boner only a few inches from his face. I'm still silently screaming 'DEAD PUPPIES!' to myself, but it's no use.

The bodyguard slowly stands up and takes his shades off, before giving me a very strange and uneasy look. He fixes me with a steely stare and decides not to shake my hand after all. Instead, he asks in a very stern manner to be taken to the ship's safe. If only God would have the mercy to open up the ground and swallow me up I would be eternally grateful.

I turn to Jock, who is also looking at me very strangely. My beetroot-red face and pained eyes say it all. 'Escort this gentleman to the Captain's cabin, please,' I say, putting on a firm, professional voice in a vain attempt to hide the incident.

'If you'd like to follow me, sir,' says Jock, ushering him

towards the passageway. As soon as the guest's back is turned I turn sharply around and head for the other passageway leading to the toilet. I'm walking in a slightly hunched position, for obvious reasons. I'm almost around the corner and into safety when the blonde suddenly comes out from nowhere and points to the suitcases next to the steps. 'You help me, please?'

I desperately look around for someone to give the job to but there is nobody. This can't be fucking happening! Having no other option, I turn around and grab a suitcase in each hand. She goes first and when she gets to the bottom of the stairs leading to her cabin, she turns around to see how I'm getting on. Her line of sight is directly in line with my crotch as she watches me come down the stairs, and a big grin spreads across her face.

'Fuck! That's two guests and Jock who've noticed it,' I think to myself. 'I'll not be able to keep this quiet.' I give the suitcases to the interior staff so they can unpack, then I get out and quickly make my way to the toilet, closing the door behind me. As soon as my knees hit the floor I put my fist in my mouth and let out and almighty 'Ahhhhhhhhhhhhhhh!' of embarrassment.

* * * *

It turns out that the guy in the white suit has brought around $450,000 in cash on board with him. It doesn't take a genius to figure out this is more than likely 'black' money and the Captain would soon be rubbing his hands at the sight of it all. It's not unusual in this game for this sort of thing to happen. These people usually have a disregard for money and it runs through their hands like sand. Once settled

16

aboard, the guests give directions to start the engines and head for St Tropez, where they wish to anchor off the beach until morning.

St Tropez is the destination of the rich and famous and 'the want to be looked at'. In the summer dozens of gleaming white mega-yachts are moored in the harbour and anchored off the beach. There is a real party atmosphere and it's a great place for celebrities, party heads, wannabes and fashion junkies. Cafes and bars line the busy beach. One of most famous of these is Club 55, where you can smell the money.

People go crazy for money around here, but I still have my feet grounded. As far as I'm concerned, all I want is enough to buy a few simple pleasures. I learned a long time ago that money alone will not make you happy. I've stacked shelves at supermarkets earning around £100 a week when things were bad. I've also had one of the top ten jobs in the world earning fantastic tax-free cash on private yachts, and after some serious soul-searching, I've found that my overall happiness was not directly proportional to the amount of money in my account.

When I was a young guy in my twenties, growing up and trying to figure the world out, one of the things I believed was that money was *all* you needed to be happy. Now that I've experienced money at both ends of the spectrum I know that is complete and utter bullshit. I've worked with and known some billionaires who were depressed because they have nothing to strive for. They are like caged wild animals that aren't free and are given everything they need without working for it. After a while the fire goes from behind their eyes and their soul starts to die. Many of the seriously rich people I've witnessed fall into the trap of sex and drugs to help relieve the tedium of life. It's a classic case of escapism.

I once had a chat with the owner of the yacht about his life and how money had changed him. The owner is worth about £800 million pounds or so. When I had got to know him well, I asked him if it had changed him in a negative sense as well as a positive sense. He lit a cigarette and took a deep drag, looked me straight in the eye and said: 'More than you'll ever know, mate.'

'Why's that, sir?' I asked.

'If you wanted to acquire money simply to make yourself happy you've lost the plot. Sometimes it's a fucking menace. Every day I have problems trying to find out the intentions of people and if they're fleecing me. I'm always aware of it and I find it very difficult to trust people. My life has actually got more stressful *because* of money. You end up having to mix with people who are constantly trying to outdo each other and it gets really petty. I get hassled all day. A few years ago, before I got really wealthy, all I wanted to do was make a million pounds. After a couple of years I made that, then it was ten million then fifty million. I call it the Del Boy Effect. Do you remember at the end of the series on that TV comedy called *Only Fools and Horses*?'

'I think so, but just remind me.'

'Del had been wheeling and dealing all his life and then he finally made it big. His saying back then was, "Rodney, this time next year we'll be millionaires!"'

'Oh yes, I remember.'

'When he got it he didn't know what to do with it. Next

he's telling his brother, "This time next year we'll be *billionaires*."'

'So where does it end and what's the secret of happiness?'

'The key to happiness is to appreciate and find pleasure in the simple things life has to offer you. Find the exotic in everyday life and you won't go far wrong.'

'Like what?'

'I don't know – the smell of a flower, the setting sun, the wind through your hair, the sound of the ocean, or the smile of your girlfriend. Living life for the moment and having the freedom to have as much variety in your life as possible. I watched a film once and it had this fantastic explanation in it about what we are talking about. I think it was called *American Beauty*. It basically said that you should have fantasies but make sure they are impossible to attain because the day you get what you're wanting and fantasising about, you can't and won't want it any more.

'It isn't the fantasy you've been fantasising about; it's the fantasy of the fantasy! This is because your desire makes you long for fantasies that are crazy, so we're only really happy when we're daydreaming about happiness in the future. It's sick, but true. Remember this: the hunt is much sweeter than the kill, so be careful what you wish for and fantasise about. Appreciate every second of your life and don't chase fool's gold.'

I ponder all this before answering. 'Does that mean I can have your cash, then, boss?' I say, joking.

'Fuck off, the wife would kill me! I'm not kidding you, mate. I lost my bank card the other day and I seriously considered *not* reporting it to the police.'

'Why?' I ask him, looking confused.

'Because, whoever finds the card and uses it will probably spend less than the wife.'

We shared a laugh before I questioned him again.

'What does it all mean, then?'

'Think of it this way. The key to happiness can be easily imagined if you hold your hand out in front of you. Just like the five digits on your hand, you need five things for complete happiness. Sure, you can do without a finger or a thumb but your hand won't be a hundred per cent healthy – just like your life. You can do without one of these things I'm about to mention but I doubt your happiness will be complete. The five "musts" for me personally are health, wealth, variety, companionship and peace of mind. Have all of these and you'll have happiness. Think about each one of them and imagine what your life would be like without them.'

'Fairly crap, I'd say.'

'Well put, mate. Enduring good and bad times in equal measures is a sure way of finding that elusive thing called happiness. Just like the tides, happiness and pain go in and out. There is no good without bad. The hardest thing in the world is not so much getting what you want, but it is appreciating what you've got when you've got it! They really are vitamins and minerals for the soul. Whatever you remember from what people tell you, promise me you'll remember that.'

'Yeah, OK. It seems like valuable advice to me.'

'Believe me, if you listen to what I've just told you, your *soul* will be richer than any bank account that I have.'

* * * *

The yacht is just out of the port of Nice, en route to St Tropez, and the two stunners are on the sun deck rubbing baby oils into their surgically enhanced bodies. They sit on the side of the Jacuzzi when I escort Mr Big to join them. He's dressed in nothing but very tight white Speedos and I'm thinking if he sneezes he'll cut himself clean in two.

'Can I get you anything?' asks Zecky.

'Three bottles of Cristal,' he replies. His eyes are firmly planted on the girls as they beckon him over.

'Will that be all, sir?' I say.

'Yes, for now,' he answers in a thick Russian accent. Ten minutes later Zecky joins me in the crew lounge and tells me that all three of them are at it like rabbits. I look at her with a grin like a Cheshire cat.

'What, all three of them?!'

'Yeah, I couldn't fucking believe it. Ménage à trois, I believe it's called.'

'What happened, then?' I ask, barely able to control my curiosity.

'Well, I went down to the fridge to get him the champagne and some strawberries and when I came back our friend Vladimir is shagging the blonde in the Jacuzzi and snogging the other. They are getting passed around like peace pipes!'

Jock seizes this opportunity to fire into me. 'You aren't going to get another boner, are you mate?'

Tact and diplomacy weren't Jock's strong points. 'Let's never talk about this again, Jock,' I tell him, joking. 'Go on, Zecky, carry on. I'm bloody dying here.'

'Well, I walked up on the sun deck and caught them at it and I didn't know where to put myself.'

'Didn't you join in, Zecky?' Jock shouts over. 'Thought you might be into gangbangs. Who wouldn't want to be the meat in that sandwich?'

'For fuck's sake, Jock!' I say, apologising for him.

'Second thoughts, I know you've got a packet of condoms with my name on it, darling,' says Jock, beaming and stroking her shoulder.

'What, Durex Extra Small?' Zecky fires back.

Jock does this every time Zecks is around. It's all good-natured banter on his part but Zecks puts him down every time with a witty comment. Jock seems to love it, though.

Zecky continues her story. 'Anyway, I put the tray down where the dark girl is pointing on the table right next to them. Then she looks sideways at me and gives me a wink. All this happens and he's still shagging the other. They all knew I was there but none of them gave a shit!'

'Some people, eh?' says Jock.

'Bloody hell, this is going to be an eventful charter,' I say.

Jock slips away and I take a stroll up to the wheelhouse and tell the Captain that everything is in order. Thankfully, he doesn't know about the explosion in my pants earlier on the passerelle. Well, not yet he doesn't, anyway.

'Have you seen Jock anywhere?' I ask him.

'I'm far too busy up here to keep an eye on your crew,' he shrugs.

I turn around and walk away from the spineless goon. I haven't really got the energy for another argument with him at the moment. I head down to the Jacuzzi pump room where the heating and lighting is controlled because I want to check everything is perfect for the guests. Not that the

Jacuzzi needs heating up, considering the action that is going on up there at the moment. As I walk in I can't believe my eyes. Jock is sat down in a chair with his back to me. He's looking through the underwater Jacuzzi window at the rampant trio getting up to mischief and he's having a wank.

'For fuck's sake, put it away, you dirty bastard,' I say, putting my hand over my eyes and turning away.

'Just give me a minute, mate,' he gasps urgently.

'What?'

'When am I ever going to get another opportunity like this without having to pay for it?' he says, looking over his shoulder and laughing. Jock really is one crazy fucker!

CHAPTER 3

BLEARY EYED AND BATTERED

Next morning the yacht is anchored a few hundred metres off the beach at St Tropez. The guests had an almighty party last night – pretty normal for the first night of a charter. Whoever is on deck-cleaning duty gets up a couple of hours before the guests surface from their slumber and makes sure the exterior guest areas are cleared and cleaned. This means scrubbing the decks, polishing the stainless steel, rearranging or washing the cushions and uncovering the seats.

Tom and Robbie get up at 5.30am, a little earlier than normal because they don't really know what they might find. They sort out the barbeque deck first. This is the area where the guests usually congregate, because it's the most comfortable and it offers easy access to the bar and lounge. They can also watch the huge plasma TV screen there. The crew always make sure that they approach this area in the morning with extreme caution. A couple of times they've found half-naked guests curled up on the sofa after a heavy night, or they've walked in on a guest snorting coke off the coffee table. It can be embarrassing for all concerned. We certainly don't condone the guests taking drugs, but we don't pretend that it doesn't happen. You can't really tell a guest who has paid around $250,000 for a charter that he can't snort a line of coke or smoke a spliff if he wants to. At the end of the day, money talks and theoretically speaking these guests are treated like a 500kg gorilla – they do what they want.

The clean and clear up doesn't take too long and the place is shipshape after a couple of hours. The worst they find was a little bit of vomit on the sunbed. It's no big deal in the whole scheme of things. All they do is bite their tongue, hold their nose and think of the gratuity.

We're still trying to figure out who these guys and girls are. I usually run the guests' names through Google, but I get nothing this time. I also ask around the yachting fraternity if anyone knows anything, but again come up with nothing. One thing is for sure though: whoever the main man is, he is off the map and untraceable. He's probably a drug lord or Russian gang boss, or something along those lines.

The guests finally start to wander out onto the sun patio around midday and amazingly their breakfast consists of ice-cold vodka and lines of coke. All of them are at it, with the exception of the bodyguards. I heard somewhere that 'the road to excess leads to the palace of wisdom.' If that's the case, then this bunch must be fucking Einsteins!

I tell the boys to make themselves scarce and stand down on the lower deck, but to make sure they keep an eye and an ear on what is going on. Tom tells me that the guests want to go jet skiing this morning so I take them out the lazarette. I tell Tom about the Jacuzzi incident last night and he has a good chuckle.

'What are they doing now?' Tom asks.

'Snorting coke and necking vodka shots.'

'They haven't even had breakfast yet!'

'That *is* their breakfast, mate.'

'Pretty hardcore bunch, eh?'

'And then some,' I tell him, raising my eyebrows. 'I think we're going to have our hands full this charter, so I'd keep on your toes, mate.'

'So have you discovered anything about this lot, then?' Robbie asks me.

'Yes, I caught one of the bodyguards checking himself out and flexing his muscles in the mirror last night.'

'You're kidding? Me too! The one with the swallow tattoo on the side of his neck?' says Robbie, looking surprised.

'Yeah.'

'I caught him talking to himself whilst he was combing his hair on the sun deck'

'What was he saying?'

'He was combing his hair whilst looking at himself in his pocket mirror and saying "very nice" or something like it.'

'Hey Rob, he's so vain, I bet he shouts his *own* name when he comes!'

'Probably,' Rob says, joining in the laughter.

'I've got a feeling they'll want to go on the jet skis to wake up, so we'd better get them in the water and check the engines. Hopefully they'll be OK, but I'll have to give them a safety demonstration on how to handle them.'

'Rather you than me, mate. Calming down a bunch of coked-up, bleary-eyed and battered Russian gangsters who only speak pigeon English isn't going to be child's play!'

It's the same story every time the male guests get on these powerful machines. They forget everything they've just been told and within seconds of putting their fingers on the throttle, they're out of control or going way too fast. It's a mixture of the male ego, excitement and testosterone surges... or a shitload of coke. The machines have 1300cc engines and they accelerate like missiles. It's the same-sized engine as a small car but they weigh next to nothing. They're lethal in the wrong hands, and even in the right hands if you push the envelope of safety.

I get the machines in the water and Mr Big spots them from the barbeque deck. The next thing he's running down the outside steps with the South American hooker in tow. He jogs up to me, reeking of booze, and his pupils are huge and black.

'We go now!' he says, jabbing his finger at the jet ski.

'Certainly, sir, but first I must give you a very quick safety brief,' I say. It falls on deaf ears.

'No... no... we go now. I know, I know!' he says impatiently.

I'm thinking I should've put a bet on this happening. I've been here before, though. It's my balls on the chopping board if I let him go on and there is an accident or, worse, he kills himself. In his state, it's very probable. I take his arm and tell him as politely as possible that I don't want anything to happen to his precious girlfriend, so I must give him the brief. I can't tell from his eyes if he understands what I'm saying or if he's going to shoot me, because his eyes have no soul.

They both come with me back up to the barbeque deck and I grab the lifejackets on the way up. All of the guests are out and the music is pretty loud. The bodyguards are just changing into their swimming shorts to accompany their boss and the other hooker is making out with one of Mr Big's entourage. I apologise and turn down the music so I can be heard. Robbie is stood next to me, trying his best to model the life jacket like an air stewardess.

'Excuse me, please. Sorry for disturbing you. If I could just take a few moments of your time,' I say to them. 'We've got the jet skis out as you requested and they're ready for you. They're very powerful and there are a few local laws around this beach you have to obey, so I'll just quickly explain them to you.'

The hooker is still making out with the guy, eagerly watched by Robbie, and I don't think any of them are paying attention or understand any more than ten per cent of what I'm saying. I'm about a minute into my speech, pointing out the safety features of the lifejacket, when I notice that Mr Big and the girl have vanished. I turn to Robbie and quietly ask where the other two are, but he's got his blinkers on.

'Robbie!' I say, a little louder to wake him from his dirty daydream.

I'm still met with silence.

'Robbie, where are the other two guests?'

'Oh sorry… what other two?' he says, turning towards me, startled.

'The *other* two!' I shout urgently.

Robbie is barely through his 'but they were here a minute ago speech' when there is a roar and the jet ski speeds away from the yacht with Mr Big and the girl on the back. She's holding on for dear life. Everyone stops what they are doing to watch. They start giving Mr Big further encouragement by yelling and whistling. Mr Big loves it and he's flying around like a man possessed. He's doing doughnuts, zigzagging and circling the yacht at speed. She's laughing hysterically and holding on to his hairy pot belly. Robbie and I look at each other and we can see that to carry on would be futile so we just leave them to it and hope for the best.

'Well, that went well, don't you think, Rob?' I say sarcastically.

'I don't think they understood a word.'

'Yeah, I know. It doesn't help that they're coked off their tits. You'd better get the boat in the water as a safety measure.'

'Right, mate. I'll be on the radio,' says Rob.

I walk up to the bridge to grab a pair of binoculars so I can see where they're heading. As I open the door the Captain has already heard the commotion and he has beaten me to them. The jet ski is flying along only a few metres from the beach, running parallel to it at full speed. This is really dangerous because of swimmers and children, not to mention the noise it makes. Bad news all round!

'Didn't you tell him about keeping his distance?' says Thrush.

'I tried, but he vanished before I could finish,' I say innocently.

'So, you *didn't* finish the safety brief,' he says in a condescending way.

I can tell by the tone of his voice that Thrush is in one of his moods again. There's a saying that you have to kiss a little ass before you can kick it, but unfortunately I'm not made that way. I hold back the impulse to grab the scissors off the chart table and drive them through the back of his head. This kind of thing really annoys me about this prick: he makes out that he's the blue-eyed boy and never makes any mistakes but in reality he's the most incompetent, mealy-mouthed, passionless dickhead I've ever had the misfortune to meet.

I take a deep breath and slowly let it out to help me keep calm, but I can feel my fist tightening uncontrollably. I nearly call him 'Thrush' out of habit, but I remember just in time. 'Listen, Captain, when we first arrived on deck this morning they started snorting coke and drinking vodka shots virtually immediately. I don't even think they've sobered up from last night.'

'If he crashes the jet ski or hurts anyone I will hold you fully responsible,' Thrush tells me.

'Now hang on a minute. You told me, and I quote, "Give them anything they want at any time. They are paying a lot of money for this charter so whatever they want, they get." Did you or did you not tell me that yesterday?' I say, losing my calm.

There is a short silence, then, still looking through his binoculars, Thrush just says, 'That will be all.'

I storm out of the door and I need to vent my anger before I knock a wall down or something. I decide to take it out on the punchbag in the crew quarters. I imagine the bag is Thrush's ribs and after five minutes punching at an intensity that would put Mike Tyson to shame, I feel just about human again.

Jock's heard the noise and pops his head round the corner. 'Don't worry about the skipper, boss – he's not worth it. Everyone knows he's a prick!'

I turn around with red knuckles and face him. 'Oh... hi mate, I'm just venting off a bit of anger.'

'I do that all the time, boss.'

'I didn't know you come down here, Jock?' I say, a little puzzled.

'I don't. I've barely got enough energy to eat my dinner at the end of my day.'

'So how do you vent your anger then?'

'I've got a much better way,' Jock smiles.

'What?'

'Special coffee.'

'Eh?'

'Special coffee. He's always fucking telling me to go make him a coffee, so that's exactly what I go and do. It helps me in ways I can't explain. It's twice as good as wasting energy punching the shit out of that bloody thing.'

'I'm not with you, mate. How does making the old man a coffee make you feel better?'

'Because, my dear buddy, before I pour the coffee in the cup I pull my foreskin back and rub the end of my dick around the rim of the cup.'

I look at him unable to control my laughter. 'You sick fucker!'

'I prefer to make him frothy cappuccinos if I can persuade him to have one, because you can hide so much more in it.'

'Go on, then,' I say, not sure if I really want to hear it.

'The foam, for example. I can make the foam out of

anything really. Spit, phlegm, spunk or all three if he really pisses me off,' Jock explains with a poker face expression.

'Jock, for fuck's sake!' I feel I'm about to be sick.

However, it's so funny that I don't know what's worst – retching or laughing really hard. I find my composure after a minute or so, walk over and pat Jock on the shoulder. 'Jock, that's not the sort of behaviour I expect of my lads. But well done, that really *is* outstanding work, fella!'

CHAPTER 4

ALL THAT GLITTERS IS NOT GOLD

After the crew drop the guests off at the beach, we spend the rest of the day cleaning the boat top to bottom. The yacht is freshwater-washed and dried off with a leather rag. By late afternoon she is gleaming in the setting sun.

Mr Big and his hooker made it back in one piece – wet but uninjured. She looked like a drowned rat and I don't think she was all that happy with him. She'd probably spent an hour or so applying make up to her beautiful features and blow drying her jet black hair that morning, so you can imagine she wasn't best pleased.

The interior staff spend most of the day cleaning and polishing the lounges and cabins and hand-washing the guests' party clothes. All of us on the deck crew do feel for them sometimes. We get out in the sunshine and fresh air as part of our job. The interior staff, on the other hand, spend most of their days inside, apart from an hour or so at lunchtime. It's got to be tough for them seeing the same walls every day, when outside the weather is beautiful in the sunshine. They also have to deal with the guests when they come back drunk, and that isn't easy at the best of times.

The interior staff are all female and as you can imagine it can be a nightmare when they're menstruating together. Robbie calls it 'mad cow syndrome'.

Tom once asked him why he doesn't trust women.

'You should never trust a species that bleeds for one week of every month and doesn't die!' he once told me. Interesting point!

The deck crew get to do the boys stuff, such as taking the guests wakeboarding, jet skiing, diving and waterskiing, and this is always good fun. They also get to stand on security patrol on the quay in some of the classiest places on the planet, including the Bahamas, Caribbean, Amalfi coast, Greek islands and the Italian and French Rivieras. I must admit I would be telling lies if I said it doesn't feel fabulous when the yacht arrives at the quay to an audience of hundreds of spectators. You feel a bit like a film star. If the yacht is only in for a night, you can be sure that most of the deck crew will try and get the passerelle duty, so they can watch the world go by on the quayside. It's been known to be good for pulling the girls who can't fail to be impressed by all the bling and crisp, white uniforms.

* * * *

The crew get a call from the guests about eight o'clock, just as the sun is going down. The best time at the beaches around St Tropez is a couple of hours before sunset. The temperature cools down, the party atmosphere starts to heat up, and the beach bars blast out dance music. The beautiful people and the 'want to be seen' come out of the woodwork to party and dance. The booze flows, the music pounds and so does your head the following morning. Ginger Spice, Victoria Beckham and Robbie Williams have been seen here, among other star names. From what the crew hear, Robbie is a great guy and lots of fun. That is the kind of celebrity the crew like to entertain. They like people who are up for fun but not up their own arses with illusions of grandeur. Having money doesn't make them better people, it just means they've more in their bank accounts. Some celebrities believe their own bullshit, though, and they really are a pain in the arse.

I heard a story about a charter on another yacht where a very famous American pop singer came on and demanded that the freshwater tanks onboard were to be emptied and refilled with bottled Evian mineral water. That's tonnes and tonnes of water, for fuck's sake!

She also demanded the carpet leading to her stateroom be ripped up and replaced with red carpet. Apparently, she also wanted candles all the way from her stateroom, across the deck and onto the quay. The captain informed the owner of the yacht back at his home in Monaco, and he refused point blank. He told her to vacate his beautiful yacht immediately and never return.

Life is too short to entertain these divas, but many do, for the money. Many yachts can and will do anything the guests want, including ludicrous stuff. Never is this more apparent than at St Tropez during silly season or at Cannes during the Film Festival. One year we worked on a very well-known yacht in the charter business, moored up on the quay at Cannes. All the large and ludicrously big yachts were there, and the celebrities commuted back and forth between them.

Dozens of parties were held on the yachts and all the major players in the film world were there strutting their stuff.

One story that has done the rounds in the yachting world concerns a yacht owned by a beer company which held a party for the rich and famous stars in Cannes. Obviously the furnishings of these yachts are very expensive and plush, so the owners usually charter on the understanding that guests obey the house rules – such as not smoking inside.

This particular yacht had a 'no smoking' sign posted at its entrance on the quay. The staff also reminded all those boarding the yacht, including many of the Hollywood elite, of the rule. The story goes that a stewardess offered this very famous actor a glass of champagne and when he turned around he had a cigarette hanging out of his mouth with the ash about to fall onto the carpet. He looked high as a kite on something (allegedly). The stewardess very gently and tactfully reminded him that smoking wasn't allowed aboard the yacht. The actor, the story goes, looked her up and down before replying, in a sarcastic tone: 'Where am I supposed to go?'

'You can happily smoke at the entrance in the welcoming foyer, sir,' she replied.

Allegedly he then turned round and took a big drag of his cigarette and blew it slowly in her face, saying, 'Do you know what? I don't think I will,' before turning his back on her and carrying on his conversation as if she wasn't there.

Another story goes round about a famous model and her colourful tantrums. It's said that she was offered a glass of champagne and when she took a sip, spat it out and threw down the glass. She then furiously complained to the stewardess that the champagne wasn't the famous Cristal brand.

But for every diva and actor with a God complex, there are famous people who are seemingly lovely. Cuba Gooding Jr, Brad Pitt, Angelina Jolie, David Coulthard, Kevin Spacey and Cameron Diaz are but a few who are said to be delightful. From what the crew have seen and heard, they are really down to earth, respectful people who, for all their millions, have their feet planted firmly on the ground. I take my hat off to them.

If anyone asked us to name the most interesting person, we'd would most likely say Quentin Tarantino. We saw him at the Cannes Film Festival one year and were working in his vicinity when he was socialising at a party. There are many ways to describe the man but 'mad wizard' sums it up, and we don't mean that in a negative way at all. He's a fairly quiet guy on first appearances but get him to a party and give him a few drinks and he's a different person. He turns into this energy whirlwind full of fantastic ideas as if they were being fed to him from a higher source. It really is crazy to watch because you can experience this really creative mind explode in front of you. Jock says he'd love to hypnotise the guy and discover what makes him tick. There again, maybe the world isn't ready for that yet...

The other guys we find entertaining include Eddie Irvine, who used to drive Grand Prix cars for Ferrari, and the family of the Sultan of Brunei. Eddie was a legendary playboy. He must have been under an enormous amount of pressure from Ferrari to perform at the highest level. His yacht used to moor up right next to the circuit when the Monaco Grand Prix was on. There were much bigger and flashier yachts in the harbour, but the press and public would flock around this yacht like seagulls around a fishing trawler, hoping to get a glimpse of something tasty. He lived the dream of fast cars, beautiful women, tons of cash and outright fame. Let's face it, you have to give the guy respect for being under that kind of pressure and still finding time to live the lifestyle. It's doubtful if many people could have handled it!

As for the Sultan of Brunei, the story goes that either he or his brother had two yachts, aptly named *Tits 1* and *Tits 2*... and that's all that needs to be said about that.

When the average guy meets a celebrity of status, more often than not they become star-struck and fall to pieces. Sometimes this is highly entertaining. Jock once heard a story about a deckhand working on a yacht when the Duke of Edinburgh was a guest aboard. He was busy kneeling down polishing some brass work on deck when the Duke popped his head around the corner. This deckhand looked up to discover the formidable Duke standing before him.

'Good morning, young man. What are you up to there?' the Duke enquired.

Startled and completely in awe, the man leapt to his feet and hit his head on the heavy stainless steel bell above him. Apparently he did so with such force that the bell sounded loudly and he cut his head. He then completely lost the plot and gave the Duke a curtsy whilst holding his head, followed by a little tap dance, presumably because of the pain. When he saw the look of disbelief on the Duke's face, it dawned on him that only women curtsy. Trying to make amends, he gave the Duke a deep Japanese bow while apologising and referring to him, inaccurately, as 'your lordship'.

To add insult to injury he started shaking the Duke's hand vigorously with his bloodied right hand. Not a good day at the office. The Duke apparently gave him a look that said a million words and said something under his breath. For the rest of the cruise every time the Duke made eye contact with that particular deckhand he gave him a look of despair.

One common illusion about people who have lots of money is that whatever they say has to be correct just because they are rich. Another is that somehow they are more intelligent than the average person. This couldn't be further from the truth, if you ask me. I've lost count of the number of times crew members get asked the most outrageously stupid questions. I was once asked by a female guest if the stairs on the yacht go up or down. Another asked innocently, 'How long is the power cable from the mains on land to the boat to keep the lights on at night?' We were a few hundred miles out to sea at the time. She'd clearly not heard of onboard generators.

On one transatlantic voyage another barmy question was: 'Excuse me, what time does the helicopter come to the ship to take you all home at night?' This poor lady obviously didn't realise the crew slept and lived aboard for months at a time. One of the Australian crew played along with her and said that he had to bring an extra-large packed lunch to keep him fed there and back to Australia every night. Cheeky bugger!

Jock was once asked by an elderly lady about an island a few miles ahead of the yacht: 'Young man, how do you keep track of where all the islands are when they're floating around all the time?' The same lady dropped her expensive watch over the side and told him to dive down and get it. He politely pointed out that the water was several hundred feet deep. Undeterred, she demanded that he should dive down and get it immediately, informing him that a fit young man like him should be able to hold his breath. These people are not of this planet!

A guest once told the Captain that they didn't want to spend their planned three weeks aboard the yacht sailing from Monaco to St Tropez (France) to Marbella (southern Spain) to Croatia (the Adriatic) and back to Monaco.

'OK, madam, where *would* you like to go?' he said politely, even though he'd spent the best part of a week organising the trip.

'Oh, we still want to go to all of them but I want to do it all in four days and not three weeks,' came the reply.

This is of course impossible, as the total distance is a few thousand miles and the yacht's top speed is only 14 miles per hour.

I am frequently very, very surprised that some of the rich and famous can run a fucking bath, never mind their lives or a money-making business. I think it's completely crazy that society generally looks up and admires these people just because they are in films or on TV or have come into money. To be fair, most of the crew can see the point. Have we lost our bloody minds? There is a saying that familiarity breeds contempt and it is true sometimes. Maybe the crew have heard too many stories. They're not all like that, though, and many of our guests are intelligent and successful.

CHAPTER 5

MUDDY GEYSERS

It is seven o'clock in the morning and the yacht is moored up alongside the quay in St Tropez. The guests are still asleep in their cosy bunks. They had another late one last night but the decks are still beautifully clean, because as soon as the yacht was moored the guests went clubbing ashore and partied the night away, so they weren't on board making it untidy.

The crew are making their way to the crew room on the lower deck for breakfast, all except the watchman and the stewardess who had to stay up till the guests got back. Jock is on form and he's still trying to pummel his way into Zecky's affections.

'Morning sexy! You know what, Zecks, if I saw you naked, darling, I'd die happy,' he says with a cheeky grin.

Zecky gives him a look of pity. 'Well, if I saw you naked, Jock, I'd die laughing!'

'Easy sweetie, stop playing hard to get,' says Jock dryly.

'I don't want to shatter your illusions, sunshine, but if

you and that flea-bitten old mongrel on the quay were the last two living creatures on Earth, I'd be over there trying to shag Fido!'

'I love it when you talk dirty – it makes me want you even more, you saucy minx.'

'Want all you want sunshine, because you aren't getting it!' Zecky really was queen of the put-downs.

Jock starts to make his breakfast and cracks a couple of eggs into a sealed plastic container and pops it in the microwave. Two minutes later they explode, splattering everything inside.

'For fuck's sake! How many times have I told you to prick the yolks and then cook them on low power? I must have told you a million times already!' Zecky yells at him. She looks at me and raises her eyebrows. I can't help but chuckle at his culinary incompetence. I mean, how difficult can it be to cook a fucking egg?!

'Honestly, on average fifty million sperm are discharged at conception and I can't believe he was the quickest,' Zecky says, pointing at Jock.

Jock looks up and frowns. 'What's that supposed to mean?' he says, looking hurt.

'It means if your brains were dynamite you couldn't blow your fucking nose,' she says sharply. 'Now go over there and sit down.'

Jock doesn't argue and feeling suitably chastised, does as he's told. 'I was going to clear it up, you know,' he says under his breath.

'I've seen your tidying up and it'll be quicker if I do it.'

He winks at me over in the corner. 'She's a right feisty one, our Zecks.' He loves the ear-bashing he gets from her. I think it makes him feel wanted. The rest of the boys arrive to make some toast and to get their jobs for the morning. Tom and Robbie are arguing over which of the two hookers has the best tits and guessing who is the filthier in bed.

'It's no contest, Robbie. You can tell by the look in her eye and the way she walks that the blonde could suck a golf ball through 50 metres of hosepipe. That girl is just one hundred per cent sex! How does the dark girl beat that?'

Robbie puts his knife down and finishes chewing his toast. He then slowly leans forward and looks Tom deep in his eyes. 'Because, Tom my dear boy, once you try black you never go back!'

'What?'

'Black women are genetically blessed by the hands of God and it's as simple as that.'

'Explain,' says Tom.

Everyone is now listening intently to what Robbie is saying.

'All right, think about it. Take Naomi Campbell, for example. She is physically built for pleasure. Her ivory-white eyes contrast effortlessly with her dark ebony skin. She has those big full lips that you'll only ever see naturally on a black girl unless they are surgically enhanced. You can only imagine what they could be used for... '

'What? That's it?' Tom interrupts.

'I've not even started yet, Tom. Then there is the muscle tone and the high pert bums, not to mention the natural dancing rhythm that white girls can only dream about. All in all, it's just a much more attractive physical package, that's all I'm saying.' Robbie sits back, takes another bite of his toast and looks contented that he's proven his point.

'He paints quite a picture, doesn't he mate?' I say to Tom.

'Whatever!' he responds, feeling dejected.

I'm just about to go into detail about the morning jobs when Thrush walks in. There's no pleasantry from him and no light-hearted morning banter.

'My toilet is blocked so get your lads to sort it out for me as their first job,' he demands. The boys looked startled at his utter rudeness and they look at each other and roll their eyes.

'OK,' I say, forcing a smile.

I look up at Jock and give him a sly wink. 'Could you make the Captain a coffee, please Jock? Some of that new special brand you were telling me about?'

'Absolutely, no problem,' he says, jumping from his seat, before disappearing with a spring in his step.

'Would you like to sit down, Captain, and I'll take you through what I've got planned for the morning?' I ask him.

'After my toilet, of course,' Thrush responds sharply.

'Yes... after your toilet.'

Thrush sighs and looks at his watch like it's a real effort. 'Yes, all right, I suppose I can spare you five minutes.'

I'm pissed off about this but I don't show it. All Thrush is going to do all day is spend an hour on ship's business then watch TV or surf the net for the rest of the day. I start to explain the rota and work routine when a noise comes from down the alleyway where the 'special coffee' is being made. It sounds like the throaty sound that a coffee maker makes.

'When did we buy a coffee maker?' Tom says to Robbie.

'We didn't.'

'Then what...?'

'Shhhh,' Robbie says, kicking him under the table. He put

his finger over his mouth and signals for Tom to be quiet and eat his toast. The noise is getting louder and it sounds like someone clearing their throat. The boys can only imagine what Jock is doing. Then there is a short silence followed by the clanging of a toilet seat and then a flush.

I'm trying hard to keep my head on the work I'm telling Thrush about, but my mind keeps wandering to what Jock is doing to his coffee. 'So after that we'll be testing the fire alarms, Captain,' I tell him, trying to concentrate as best I can.

After a few more minutes Jock brings in the cup of coffee, looking a little flushed, and hands it to the Captain with a big smile. 'There you go, Captain, made you a special frothy coffee. It's a pretty unique flavour I think you'll find.'

The Captain just about manages a very quiet 'thank you' before taking a large gulp. Robbie, Tom and I look up at Jock who is stood behind him, and he's pointing to his crotch and signalling to them that he has just wanked into it. I think that's bad enough but then he points to his backside and makes a circular motion with his finger around his arsehole. To top it all, then he gets both hands and points to his mouth where there is a long thread of saliva hanging out like a shoe lace from a trainer. The Captain slowly looks up from the paper I'm showing him and Jock silently sucks the saliva back in without him noticing.

The boys watch the Captain take another drink and I can feel myself about to retch. I put my hand over my mouth and pretend that I'm coughing. Thrush puts the cup down and his top lip is covered in slimy, brown-coloured froth. I find it hard to hide the look of total disgust on my face and Thrush looks over at me.

'Are you all right? You don't look well,' he asks, peering at me over his glasses.

'Oh, I've got a bit of an upset stomach, Captain. It seems to be going round at the moment,' I say, trying my hardest not to look at his frothy lip.

'No doubt *I'll* be getting an upset stomach next, then.'

Jock, Tom and Robbie get up to leave the room.

'There's nothing surer!' says Jock as he leaves.

I finish up with the Thrush after about twenty minutes or so. Usually I would have been much quicker, but I wanted to make sure he finished every last drop of his coffee. Moral: never upset the people who make or serve your food and drink, because you never know what they do to it.

* * * *

I meet the boys up in Thrush's cabin to see what the problem is with his toilet. As I walk in to his en-suite bathroom Robbie is plunging away for all he's worth with a suction stick, but with little effect. Tom is holding the seat up with one hand and holding his nose with the other.

'Jesus, what has been coming out of his arse – fucking bricks?! It's well and truly blocked, mate,' Robbie tells Tom.

'Give it here, Rob. Let's get the job done and get the fuck out of here,' replies Tom impatiently.

Tom starts plunging at the U-bend with fresh intensity and after a couple of minutes a big gurgling noise suddenly comes from the pipe leading along the wall to the toilet. Tom and Robbie are stood directly over the toilet and they turn their heads and look at each other, their faces inches apart. The noise is moving towards the toilet quickly and whatever is coming along is headed their way. They know what's coming and so do I.

I make a quick turn and jump out of the bathroom and manage to escape its confines while Rob and Tom get their shoulders jammed in the narrow doorway as they try and follow me. They get stuck, turn to each other and then naturally look towards what is coming their way. As they do, the toilet belches out its contents with the pressure of the Yellowstone National Park geyser.

As I look back I'm lost for words, and both of them are stood there like scarecrows with looks of terror and total disbelief written over their faces. The walls, ceiling and both of them are covered in faeces, urine, used tampons, cotton wool, pubic hair and God knows what else. It's in their hair, on their clothes, on their faces and dripping off the end of their noses. They just stand there in silence. Tom looks at the state of Robbie with horror, wondering what he looks like himself. Robbie looks over at Tom with what appear to be tears in his terror-stricken eyes. 'KNOCK ME OUT!' he says between a clenched-teeth grimace.

'WHAT?' asks Tom.

'YOU... KNOCK... ME... OUT... NOW!' Robbie says loudly, slowly and deliberately.

He's speaking more from his throat than using his mouth and signalling a punching action with his hand.

'Why?' asks Tom, who is watching a dribble of dirty urine trickle down Robbie's nose.

'COS I THINK I'M GONNA LICK MY LIPS!'

I shouldn't have, but I laughed so hard I couldn't inhale for what seemed like a lifetime. They both spent the next hour in the shower scrubbing themselves with a wooden brush and strong antiseptic, calling Thrush all the names under the sun. They scrubbed so hard that by the time they turned up for the passerelle watch, all of their exposed skin was red raw.

I turn to Jock as they approach us and say, 'There's a funny smell round here.'

Jock starts sniffing the air. 'Yeah, can't seem to place it.'

'What do you reckon it is?'

'Don't know? Smells a bit fragrant to me... that's it, Eau de Toilet.'

'Fuck off, you two. I can barely move, my skin's that sore,' says Robbie.

Tom is obviously suffering as well but he's trying not to show it. He takes a swipe at Robbie to take the attention away from himself. 'I don't know Rob, you've no big-match temperament for the dirty jobs,' he tells him.

'I just don't like starting my day covered in a layer of shit,' Robbie says, losing his temper.

'All right boys, calm down. I've got some good news for you that might put a smile back on your faces.'

'What's that? You've won us both a skin graft?' asks Robbie.

'Well, the guests will be back for an hour or so today and then they'll be gone until tomorrow night. That means we can go for a few beers tonight, if you're up for it. The first few are on me, all right?'

The guests come back in the afternoon and quickly wash and change. They are picked up by a limo an hour or so later and taken to one of their associates' hillside villas overlooking St Tropez. That's it for the day, and the crew have a rare night off. It's time to party!

CHAPTER 6
GOLD DIGGERS

It's not very often the crew get time off in the middle of busy charter, so when we do we grasp it with both hands. Just having a night off is good news in itself, but to get a night off alongside in St Tropez on a Saturday night in summertime is the icing on the cake. The boys are looking forward to a few hours' quality time with each other. We all get on well, but yachting is hard work and the hours are long. We don't really get any privacy on board because we all share small cabins, so after a while the smallest things start to annoy us. Getting off the boat, out of uniform and sinking a few cold beers away from the arsehole of a Captain feels like Heaven. Everyone can blow off steam and let their hair down, at least for a few hours.

The boys meet in my cabin early in the evening and I open a bottle of tequila just to get them in the mood. We are in our 'going ashore gear' and Jock is wearing the most outrageously colourful green shirt. He calls it his 'falling down shirt' because he only ever wears it to get drunk in.

'Are you wearing that for a bet, Jock?' asks Tom cheekily.

Jock looks down at his shirt and starts stroking one of the sleeves.

'I'll have you know this cost me seventy quid, you cheeky bastard.'

'HOW MUCH?! Fucking hell, they saw you coming, mate. I wouldn't wipe my arse with that! You look like that green bird hand-puppet.'

Robbie looks up from fastening his shoelaces. 'What... Orville?' he laughs.

'Yeah, that's him... Orville!'

'You're only jealous, you bunch of fucking losers! Anyway, grab your tequilas boys!' Jock says, slapping Tom on the back.

All the boys take a drink to toast the evening. It's a bit of a tradition of ours before we go out on a mad one. We all raise our shot glasses and shout, 'Here's to you, and here's to me, the best of friends we'll always be, but if by chance we disagree, then fuck YOU and here's to ME!'

We knock back our tequila shots and Robbie quickly pours us all another. The next tradition is that each one of us states their aim for the night or tells the gang what the party tricks will be.

'Right, boys, your radical agendas for the night, please!' I shout.

Robbie starts and tells the group in the style of a loud US Marine Drill Sergeant: 'First I'm going stomp a few brain cells, followed by a howl at the moon session, followed by a game of hunt the cunt!'

'Excellent! Right, Tommo, what's yours?' I say, chinking his glass.

'To get my kicks before the whole shithouse goes up in flames!' he says in the style of Jim Morrison.

'OOOOOOOOORRRRRRRAAAAAAAAA!' everyone screams, while Jock starts howling like a wolf.

'All right, Fido, cool your jets for a second,' I tell Tom, laughing.

'Your turn, Jock!' Robbie says, pointing his shot glass at him.

He does his in the style of a news presenter, using a wall poster of a naked girl as his map. 'Intentions are to satisfy my primal instincts to the limit with my trusty comrades beside me create an absolute mayhem. I'm going to empty my bollocks into anything remotely female, and wet patches can be expected specifically in the areas here... here... and here,' says Jock, pointing to various areas of the female anatomy on the poster.

'Beautifully put, Jock. OK, boys, let's finish the bottle and put the cat amongst the pigeons.'

We leave the cabin with a tequila glow and on the way to the passerelle we pass Thrush holding his stomach.

'We're just going ashore for a few hours, Captain, so we'll see you in the morning,' I say as we walk.

'Well, don't be late. I may sleep in for an hour longer in the morning, so if you don't see me at eight you know why.'

We all stop momentarily before walking off the yacht. 'Something wrong?' I ask.

'I'm not feeling well at all, sickness and diarrhoea,' he says, holding his stomach.

'Drink plenty of fluids to replace the ones you've lost, Captain,' says Jock, who can't resist a little more piss-taking. 'I'll make you plenty of coffee in the morning.'

'Yes, OK,' Thrush replies wearily.

'We'll see you in the morning,' I say as we walk down the passerelle. We can't help but have a little snigger at Thrush's expense.

'Looks like your special coffee worked a little quicker than expected, mate,' Tom tells Jock.

'Oh, yeah, it's potent and it was lovingly prepared!' he says.

The quayside is bustling with tourists and locals admiring the yachts. It's a beautiful balmy night and the harbour front hums with chatter and music from the nearby bars and restaurants. As we walk off, people crowd round the passerelle to see if any of us are famous, and we notice a bunch of young, tanned girls looking over. They're all really pretty and obviously not local. I elbow Jock in the ribs. 'There you go, mate, there's your first target. Blonde, blue-eyed and five-feet five. Just your type.'

'Oh yeah... nice, very nice!'

'Now remember, Jock, softly, softly, catchee monkey. Put the gentle spadework in first and don't scare them off, like you did last time!'

'I didn't scare them off.'

'Yes, you fucking did! After a few beers you forget that you're not talking to the locals in Glasgow and you speak at a million miles an hour and your volume increases tenfold.'

'Shit! Really? I didn't know I was doing that,' he says, scratching his head.

I make eye contact with one of the girls and make beckoning signals. The girls talk among themselves for a few seconds before coming over.

'Hola!' says one of them and asks me something in Spanish.

Jock looks confused because he doesn't speak anything but English (or, rather, Scottish). 'Does she come with subtitles, mate?' he asks me, and I explain to her that we only speak English, a fact I'm deeply embarrassed about, and she quickly slips in to our native tongue.

'That is a very nice yacht,' she says in fairly good English.

'Thanks very much,' says Rob. 'We've just bought it between us a couple of days ago.'

We can see the dollar signs light up in their eyes. They lead us into the nearest bar and I order some drinks. The girl nearest Jock is wearing the tightest black leather trousers he's ever seen. They look like they have been sprayed on but she does look great in them.

'Bloody hell, how the hell do you get into those?' says Jock, to the point as ever.

'Well, you can start with a glass of champagne,' she responds with a wink. The words are barely out of her mouth before he's at the bar with a big grin on his face, ordering champagne. She sounds like she's from the north-east of England and from her thick accent we guess she's from the Newcastle area. She's very pretty but as rough as arseholes! We can all tell a mile off that they're a bunch of gold-diggers. They're easy to spot and we've developed an eye for them, particularly in the South of France where there is no shortage of money.

The girls are getting stuck into their drinks and it's becoming increasingly obvious that these particular gold-diggers are trying to get as much money spent on them as possible – the way they look, the way they act and the fact they repeatedly ask us lots of questions about how much money we have doesn't leave much to the imagination. After about twenty minutes the girls head off to the toilet to freshen up and discuss a plan to relieve us all of some hard-earned cash.

Jock and I follow them and listen in from round the corner.

'OK, let's get them to buy some more champagne,' says one.

'Yeah, we're on holiday and they can afford it,' says another. 'We'll have to find out what they do.'

Then the Geordie exclaims: 'Eh, fucking hell! All I want is a few inches and there is fucking *yards* of it out there! I'm definitely having that Scots lad's cock tonight!'

Jock and I look at each other and burst out laughing. 'She's a classy one, that Geordie girl,' I say to Jock sarcastically, as we go back to the boys.

'Just my type, mate. Don't think I'll need much spadework there. I think I'll nickname her Marg.'

'Marg? Why Marg?' I say, looking puzzled.

'Marg, as in margarine... because she'll spread easy!'

'I don't know where you get them from, mate. You're right, though. I reckon the only reason she wears knickers is to keep her ankles warm.'

Jock tells the boys what we've heard and his nickname for the Geordie girl, which Tom finds hilarious. At that moment we decide to turn the tables and play the first game of the night. We'll make up a story that we are rich businessmen in pharmaceuticals. We know they're after our cash, so we bet each other who can act the most unattractive in full view of everyone and still sleep with the girl at the end of the night. We are using the girls' perception that we are all millionaires to keep them interested and to test just how far they're willing to go for the sake of money and money alone. Time will tell.

The girls return after a few minutes, looking as thick as thieves. The first thing they ask for is a couple of bottles of champagne. We get them in and after a while the boys give me the wink to start the game off. I dream up a plan to be this really unattractive, cold-hearted businessman, a bit like Thrush but worse. This man has no respect for animal life and he has questionable hygiene habits. The Spanish girl takes a sip of her drink, looks up at me and starts questioning me about money.

'So what do you do to afford a yacht like that? You must be very rich!'

I immediately let out a loud belch followed by a little genital-scratching through my jeans. 'Well, I basically test beauty products on animals to see if they damage them before the products are fit for human use,' I say, keeping a straight face.

'Oh, erm… that must be interesting work,' she says, looking quite worried.

'Yeah, once you get used to the blood and the rancid warts caused by the products bursting on you, it's a breeze really.' Fart.

The girl now looks horrified.

'Doesn't that hurt the animals?'

Belch. 'Hurt… Who? The beagle puppies? Yeah, it's bloody agony for the barking little fuckers. Do you know that lipstick you're wearing?'

'Erm… yes,' she says, looking even more worried.

'That gave me a heap of trouble. I ended up burning the

faces off two dozen beagles before I got the mixture right on that one.'

'OH MY GOD... that's awful!' she winces, holding her hand over her mouth.

'Serves them right for shitting everywhere.' I look over at Tom, who's trying not to laugh.

Meanwhile Robbie is talking to one of the other girls. As he's talking to her, he suddenly develops a really bad nervous twitch while grabbing handfuls of peanuts and ramming them into his mouth. She notices a few peanuts have dropped into his beer and her look says it all. He just shrugs his shoulders and says he prefers them mushy because it's easier on his dentures. He then starts picking his nose and I think he's lost his index finger up one nostril, then slowly removes it with the contents of his nose in full view.

Tom is a bit slow off the mark, so to encourage him, Jock tells the girls what a fantastic dancer he is. This couldn't be further from the truth. Tom dances like old people fuck. I tell him to take his girl for a dance and he takes her by the hand to the small dancefloor. He starts his grooving and he's as out of sync as you possibly could be. There's lots of arm waving, crotch thrusting and leg shaking and then he starts body popping. He looks more like he's having a fit than busting some moves. All of the time he maintains this really serious expression like the one a chimpanzee makes when it's concentrating, and the girl's face is a picture of embarrassment. At the end of the number they head back to the bar and she downs her champagne in one, presumably to numb the embarrassment.

We order more drinks and after a couple of hours

everyone is wasted. After a while, when we are sure the girls think we are a bunch of fucking retards and are starting to lose interest, we start the game again, talking about how much cash we are all worth. Sure enough, they perk up and seem perfectly happy to put up with our awful habits.

'What a sick world we live in!' I whisper to Jock, not quite believing what I'm seeing. We have a few more drinks and decide to raise the stakes to see if we can push the envelope even further. We bet a hundred euros on who can make the first girl walk away, but without being offensive or rude to them in any way. Everyone starts pulling out all their tricks and Tom even launches into some spontaneous barking.

Jock decides to get his testicles out and grips his ball-sack between his thumb and index finger so it looks like a small brain, but somehow this seems to turn the Geordie girl on! She's laughing away and looking at him with 'come to bed' eyes, much to Jock's disappointment, so he rolls up a napkin and puts the end in the crack of his arse. I then set fire to it and he tries to run to the far wall and back before it burns his arse. We call it 'the dance of the flaming arseholes'. It's always handy to have some ice cubes standing by. I remember a few poor souls in the past who didn't make it back, and they were walking like John Wayne for a week afterwards.

After we all start to get a bit randy we give up on the games and tell the girls that, actually, we were playing a silly game and we are all really fairly normal – with the possible exception of Jock. Then we all head off to a club and have a great time dancing the night away and making out. Towards the end of the night the girls decide that we can come back to their hotel, and we figure that we aren't going there to play dominos.

The girls' rooms are right next door to each other and we all have a drink in Jock's room first, which is in the middle, so Rob and I are either side of him. In my room, I get undressed and I'm thinking about the fun I'm going to have with my sexy girl, who's in the shower. But the bedroom walls are paper thin and suddenly I hear loud giggling from next door and a thick Geordie voice shouting at Jock. She wouldn't be the first.

'Ehhhh tiger! Tits first, have you got no manners?' she yells.

Then there is a loud fumbling and noises of furniture falling over followed by even loader moans and shrieks. I think the bloody headboard's going to come through the wall at one point and it sounds like she's being murdered in there. My girl comes out of the shower and we try to get down to some fun but after about ten minutes I give it up as a bad job because of the noise next door. It's pretty damn hard to keep your concentration hearing those antics going on, so I get up and go and wait in the corridor where I find Robbie and his girl sitting down with their heads in their hands, laughing hysterically.

I point to the room I've just left and in between fits of giggles I tell them there was just no way I could carry on. Rob looks up with tears in his eyes and says he had the same problem. After a while we decide to head back to the yacht and leave Jock to rid himself of his sexual energies. Tom has also joined us by now and we kiss the girls goodbye, but about half way down the corridor I realise that I have left my wallet in Jock's room. After a bit of a discussion with the boys I decide I could probably open the door, reach in and grab it off the shelf right next to the door. There's still a hell of a din coming from the room, so I open the door quietly and then lean in to grab my wallet.

As I do so, I see Jock with his back to me and his jeans round his ankles. He's wearing her knickers on his head while shagging her from behind: she's bent forward over the back of an armchair and Jock's going at it like a man possessed.

As he's pummelling away she looks over her shoulder and gasps, 'No... no... not from behind, I want to see your face!'

The very drunk, panty-wearing Jock stops and thinks for a split second before pulling his picture ID card out of his shirt top pocket. He turns to put it in front of her face and carries on where he left off! I grab my wallet without them seeing and nearly fall out of the door laughing.

That is the beauty of Jock. His coltish behaviour and thought processes, especially when drunk, have to be seen to be believed, because there is no filter between his conscious and subconscious brain. What comes up – comes out.

CHAPTER 7

HEDONISTIC TENDENCIES

Next morning we meet on the bridge for a recap of the previous night's activities, and for me to issue the jobs for the day. The boys turn up bang on time. They're really good that way. They work hard and play hard and I have full respect for them all. We all kicked the arse out of partying last night and none of them moan about having to get up and do a day's graft on deck in the sweltering sun. They don't resemble the crew I worked with yesterday however. All of them look like living proof of life after death.

'Morning chaps!' I say, trying to sound bright and breezy. 'How are we all doing?'

'SHIT!' comes the unanimous reply.

'Well, you're not the only ones. I don't know if I'm Arthur or Martha today. I fancy a cigarette but I fear my breath is too volatile at the moment. These nights off are hard work, aren't they?'

I have to question Jock about his ID card moment last night. Only he could do that and think it perfectly reasonable.

'How do you know about that?' asks a puzzled Jock. 'I was alone.'

'Ha! You *thought* you were. Interesting headgear that, Jock, but I'd stick to the company baseball cap if you're on deck today. Very fetching though, mate!'

We tell him about the missing wallet and how he was caught going at it like a rabbit on amphetamine.

'What time did you get back?' I ask, fearing the worst.

'About an hour or so ago.'

'I bet you were sorry to leave, weren't you?'

'Quite the contrary. Bit embarrassing really, mate,' he says looking at the floor and going bright red.

'Why... what happened?' I ask, barely able to control my curiosity.

'Well, I woke up around six, still fairly pissed, and I figured out I'd better get my arse back here on time. Geordie's not in the room and all my clothes have gone, with my cash, bank cards and everything else I had in my pockets. I'm not thinking straight because of the drink and I'm in a bad mood because I'm already late. Then it dawned on me that she'd got up and left the hotel with all my gear.'

'You thought she'd robbed you?' asks Rob.

'Fucking right I did! I thought she'd checked out when I was asleep and fucked off with everything!'

'So what did you do?'

Jock starts to laugh nervously. 'Well, I just lost the plot. I'm thinking I'm going to have to walk back to the yacht naked, in broad daylight. I start swearing at the top of my voice and jumping up and down on the bed, calling her all the names under the sun, when I realise she's stood there in the doorway.'

'She came back to the room in the middle of your tantrums?' asks Tom, laughing.

'Yeah, she's stood there at the door with a cup of tea for me in one hand and a croissant in the other. She'd put the clothes in the wash.'

'You're fucking kidding me!' shouts Rob.

'No, I'm not! I felt like a complete wanker stood there naked in the middle of the bed with my morning glory hard-on, I can tell you.'

'So what did you say to explain?' I ask.

'What could I say? I'd just been calling her a fucking thieving gypsy cunt at the top of my voice! I just blushed, took my clothes and fucked off sharpish.'

'I take it you won't be seeing her again, then?'

'Errrr… no, mate.'

* * * *

I clap my hands to get their attention. 'Right boys, let's get back to business. We are expecting the guests back about 3pm and they've said they want to head over to the millionaires' playground, otherwise known as Porto Cervo.'

'Where's that?' asks Tom.

'It's over on the north end of Sardinia. It's a purpose-built resort and it has a very wealthy clientele. We'll motor over there tonight. We may or may not do a bit of scuba diving if time allows. It's a great little reef and there are loads of fish and things to see, so they should be happy.'

Tom puts his arms behind his head, smiles and leans back. 'I'm getting paid for this! It sure beats the hell out of watching ferrets shagging.'

'Yes indeed. Anyway, get the boat rubbed down and be in your uniforms by 1.30, all right?'

Just as the boys are getting up, Thrush walks on to the bridge. As usual there is no preamble. 'The guests have just called me and asked what the weather would be like for the crossing over to Sardinia. I had a look at the forecast and I told them it would be quite rough.'

'They're not going to like that,' I say. 'I suppose I'd better nip ashore and get some sea-sickness tablets.'

Thrush rolls his eyes and sighs as if I've just suggested the most stupid thing in the world. 'Well, if you'll let me finish I'll tell you why you shouldn't. They won't be coming with us. They'll stay at the villa tonight then fly over to Sardinia tomorrow or the day after and meet us there. They don't fancy rolling around for twelve hours being sick. Two of you will have to take some suitcases up to the villa as soon as they're ready. The girls are preparing them now.'

Jock rolls his eyes at me. 'I don't believe this lot. He's shelling out a fortune on chartering a yacht and he's hardly on it! Less work for us, I suppose.'

'That's one way to look at it.'

Before he leaves Thrush says, 'Can you come to my cabin, please?' pointing at me.

'Sure,' I reply, wondering what he wants me for. In his cabin Thrush tells me the limo will be here in half an hour. He then gives me some instructions.

'Right, the chauffeur knows where he's going but this is the guest's mobile number just in case.' Thrush then picks up a very large Jiffy bag full of used banknotes and hands it to me. I look inside and they are all $100 dollar bills. I guessed there was probably about $40,000 to $60,000 dollars in total. As he hands it over, he looks at me sternly.

'It's very important that you don't lose this. Keep it on you at all times and hand it over to the guest personally,' he says, in his condescending way. I just about manage to hold back a sarcastic, 'Oh really? I was just going to leave it on the dashboard, you fucking scrotum!' but think better of it.

* * * *

I take Robbie in the limo and within a few minutes we are headed for the villa with a few suitcases containing God knows what, and a Jiffy bag of hard cash. On the way, I quietly tell Rob what is in the bag.

'You know what, Rob? This is the edge. Did you ever think you'd be in this position when you were growing up?'

'Not ever, mate. You?'

'Nope. Do you know what? We could just vanish with the cash and never be seen again. What do you reckon?' I ask, joking.

Rob laughs before replying: 'I think I might decline. I don't really fancy waking up with a horse's head on my pillow or my own severed dick in my mouth, if you know what I mean.'

'You're not wrong, mate. I can't imagine our friend Mr Big would let us off with a slap on the wrist.'

Rob leans forward towards the cocktail bar in the back of the limo.

'Don't even think about it!' I say. 'You've only just got rid of the smell of booze from last night. You're on your best behaviour today.'

'I was just having a look,' he says.

'Likely story! I know what your "looks" end up as. I always know when you've been snooping around my cabin when I'm not there, you know.'

'How so?'

'Because the porn drawer is always left open, there's piss on my toilet seat and beer seems to go missing from my fridge. I've got your number, sunshine!'

Rob is quiet for a few seconds and then laughs: 'I thought I always got away with that.'

Eventually the limo draws up at the security gate at the front of the villa and a guy in a suit comes up to the window and looks in. The chauffeur explains that we've brought some of Mr Big's things from the yacht and he is expecting us. The suit steps back and radios the staff at the villa, talking in Russian. I can see a bulge around the side of his waist and I'm sure he's carrying a weapon. He presses a button on his remote control and the two huge, black and gold iron gates open to let us in. As we drive through the beautifully manicured gardens up the winding driveway we pass marble statues, peacocks and water fountains. The villa is on top of a hill and it has a large colonnade at the front.

'Fuck me! I bet this place cost him a bit,' Robbie splutters, looking around wide-eyed.

I'm equally awestruck. 'You're not kidding, especially in this neck of the woods. I reckon a good few million at least.'

We step out of the limo onto marble steps at the front door. Rob goes round to the boot and starts unpacking the cases. Mr Big's heavy mob come out and take the suitcases. I ask where Mr Big is so I can deliver the cash to him. One of the bodyguards nods his head in the direction of the door and says he's by the pool, in the garden. Robbie and I walk up the steps to the door and go in to the entrance hall, which is huge and elegant. We head through some side doors to the pool area and patio. It's like a cross between Hugh Hefner's Playboy mansion and the Garden of Eden.

A large pool is surrounded by palm trees, a sunken Jacuzzi, and a bamboo pool bar. Reggae music is playing and there are about twenty people – an equal number of men and women – around the pool. The women look like supermodels and are as sexy as hell. They're wearing bikinis which show off their toned, oiled-up bodies, and the men are all wearing shorts and shades. We have walked into a pool party in full flow and it's obviously centred on booze, coke and hired female company. We can feel the energy and the sexual tension. I notice that all of the men have the same tribal tattoo on their right shoulder and I wonder if this is a mark to signify membership of a gang.

Mr Big is on the other side of the pool and he signals me to come over. He's lying on a padded sunbed, attended by two beautiful girls. I wish him a good afternoon and then I hand him the Jiffy bag. He immediately opens it in full view of the girls. Their eyes light up when they see what's inside. He takes a few $100 dollar bills and gives them to Rob and I for our trouble, then he puts the bag under his sunbed. He doesn't even bother to count it. He looks over his sunglasses at me and his eyes are coked-up and bloodshot.

'I trust it's all there, gentlemen?' he says gravely, in a heavy Russian accent.

'Of course, sir. It's never left our side.'

'Because if it isn't… this is what you get.' He smiles and

runs the edge of his finger slowly across his throat, winking at us and laughing. Like sycophants, the girls follow suit.

I smile back at him, unsure what to do next. Mr Big then shouts to the bodyguard behind the bar to pour us a couple of drinks. After the throat-slicing display, Rob and I feel like we really need a drink right now. We thank him and make our way to the bar and sit down in the shade. One of the Japanese guys grabs one of the oily girls and jumps in the pool with her. This sparks off a riot and all the men start chasing after the girls and jump in the pool with them. The music volume goes up and soon the pool is a cauldron of bubbles, full of screaming, oily girls and gangsters.

The bodyguard hands us two large, ice-cold vodka shots. I mean shots in the loosest possible sense, because they don't resemble the small ones you get at home in the pub. These look like quadruples and are clearly made the way Russians like them.

'You have two of these and this will help your problem,' the bodyguard barman tells me.

'Problem?' I ask.

The bodyguard points to the near-naked girls in the pool, and then my crotch.

'The girls... they make you crazy down there.' He then points to the large vodka in front of me. 'And this stops your problem,' he laughs.

Rob grins and tells me the strong vodka might give me brewer's droop to prevent the trouser explosion that happened at the passerelle when the guests boarded the yacht. The bodyguard takes off his sunglasses and I recognise him as the guy who was carrying the briefcase. I wish the fucking ground would swallow me up again.

'Oh, right, thanks a lot,' I say, colouring up with embarrassment. I down the vodka, thank the bodyguard again and grab Rob's arm.

'Come on you, we're off.' As we start to walk towards the exit the bodyguard shouts something to the other guards. They all look over and give me the raised forearm 'boner' sign and burst out laughing. This certainly isn't your regular office job!

CHAPTER 8

KINDRED SPIRIT

Back on the yacht, heading out to sea for Sardinia, I bump into Zecky and tell her about the afternoon we've just had with Mr Big. 'My God, you see some sights!' she says. 'I've definitely chosen the wrong department to work in on a yacht. I just see the same walls every day.'

I know what she means. She must get sick of laundry, polishing, and serving food. 'Well, at least you don't get sunburnt, sweetheart. We wouldn't want that soft complexion of yours getting old and leathery, would we? Jock would no longer find you the sexual magnet that he thinks you are now.'

'If I thought that would work, I'd be on the sunbed 24-7 and turn into a prune, I can tell you that!' she laughs.

'You love it really… I know you have a soft spot for the boy.'

'Ha!' she grunts.

'Come on, Zecks – don't tell me you're not just a little bit curious?'

'I'm curious why men think it's funny to fart in their

girlfriend's face but, no, I'm not curious about Jock. Now bugger off! I've got the beds to make.'

I hear what she says, but I think there is some element of curiosity about Jock there. I go up to the wheelhouse to make sure that Tom is happy with the navigation plan for the voyage to Sardinia and that he doesn't have any problems. 'Hey, Tom, how's it going?'

'Hey, mate, had a good afternoon, have we?'

'You wouldn't believe me if I told you.'

'Why's that?' Tom asks, curious.

'Without going into too much detail at the moment, let's just say Mr Big is *some* boy.'

I'm just in the middle of explaining more, when someone approaches from behind. Tom quickly changes the subject to a work-related topic and starts waffling on about jet ski maintenance. 'So... after how many engine hours' running do you need to change the plugs?' he asks me with a knowing look.

I know the look and I automatically pick up from his question. It comes as second nature now because we've done it so many times before. I can feel Thrush approaching from behind me and I can smell his ridiculous aftershave that is only worn by teenagers who are trying to pull. As usual, he just barks what he wants.

'There has been yet another change of plan for the next couple of days,' he says with a weary voice. Thrush doesn't like surprises.

'What now, Captain? Have they decided to come with us after all?'

'No, but whatever they're doing at the villa they seem to

74

be enjoying it because they're not coming over to join us until at least Friday.'

'I'm not surprised. They all seemed to have smiles on their faces when we left,' Rob butts in.

'I guess that gives us a break for a couple of days then,' I say, half confidently.

'Unfortunately not, because Mr Thomas is in town and he'll be visiting Cannes tomorrow with a couple of friends. He's heard about the guests and wants to come aboard for drinks on the aft deck.'

'Who's Mr Thomas?' Rob asks me quietly.

'He's the owner the yacht and the guy who pays your salary.'

The Captain carries on his brief: 'Anyway, we're to go immediately to Cannes and prepare the yacht for them. We'll arrive first thing in the morning. If there's anything you need, let me know and I'll put an order in with the agent.' He then disappears as quickly as he arrived, presumably to play on the internet and pretend to work in his cabin.

'I'd like to order a new personality for him, boss,' says Tom.

'Urgently required, eh?' I add with a wink.

'And then some, mate... and then some!'

We arrive at the Cannes port limits just after sunrise on a beautifully calm summer's morning. We pass other luxury yachts at anchor in the bay, gleaming in the morning sunshine, including a mega-yacht owned by Roman Abramovich, the Russian billionaire owner of Chelsea FC.

The huge yacht – 377ft – is probably his finest. She's a state of the art motor yacht, but looks like a mini cruise ship. She has every conceivable luxury and allegedly it costs

$250,000 just to fill the fuel tank. She also has a missile tracking system just in case someone decides to assassinate the rich Russian – maybe an Arsenal fan. She cost $300 million, and she has a crew of forty-six. She's *not* your average sailing dinghy.

We reach our anchorage only a few hundred metres off the Promenade des Anglais. 'Let go the port anchor,' barks the Captain as he puts the engines astern. Jock releases the brake on the winch and the anchor chain rushes out with a clatter. The engines drag the chain out along the seabed and after a few minutes she is riding to the anchor nicely.

'That's the anchor brought up, Captain,' I report.

'OK, go about your business, then,' he tells us before turning his radio off without even a 'well done' or a 'thank you'. His rudeness becomes almost funny after a while.

'And a very good morning to you, Thrush!' says Jock, shaking his head. 'He's got all the warmth of a graveyard, that man.' We both look at each other and raise our eyebrows in disbelief.

'Maybe you should warm him up with some of your special coffee, eh?'

'Pleasure... consider it done.'

Jock and I walk back into the accommodation for a spot of breakfast before launching the yacht's guest tenders to refuel them ashore. As we walk down into the crew room, Tom and Robbie are talking about how much cash Roman Abramovich makes in interest alone, based on how much the newspapers say he is worth. 'Right, Tom, hand me the calculator,' says Robbie. 'If we take this figure he's reckoned to be worth, multiplied by this average percentage rate, divided by 365 we'll find out approximately how much cash he earns a day in interest.'

'Pass me the paper, I want to see,' says Jock. He takes a quick glance, puts the paper down and holds up his fingers and thumbs and starts counting.

'Christ, he'll be getting his toes out next,' laughs Zecky. 'What are you going to do when those run out?'

'Well, I've got one more appendage on me I could use in an emergency, but that one's gift-wrapped for you, sweetie,' he says.

'In your dreams, sunshine.'

'Anyway, that's about £90 million a year in interest or roughly 246,000 quid a day.' Jock announces, as if it's the most obvious thing in the world.

We all exchange glances, then Tom works it out on the calculator.

'Bloody hell! It works out £246,575 a day... Jock, you were nearly bang on!'

We all look at each other again in disbelief. Zecky, more than anyone, can't believe it. 'It must have been a fluke... surely?' she says, shrugging. 'So, what's £15 times 96, times 31, minus 395, smartarse?'

A bit of finger movement and a few seconds later Jock confidently tells her £44,245.

Zecky looks over at Tom for the answer on the calculator. 'Well... is it?'

Tom slams the calculator down. 'Fuck me Jock, you should be on *Countdown*!'

Zecky has her mouth wide open with shock. 'Is he right?'

'Bang on!' I say, leaning over to check the calculator. 'He'd give Carol Vorderman a run for her money.'

It's the first time the boys have ever seen Zecky genuinely impressed by Jock. It's as if she uncovered the equivalent of $E=mc^2$, and he knows it.

'I didn't think you took that much notice in the short period you went to school Jock,' I say, scratching my head in amazement. 'You must have got on well with the maths teacher, eh?'

'No, he wouldn't let me in his class for the last year.'

'How come?'

'I was trying to chat up the girl next to me and he lost his patience and threw the blackboard rubber at me.'

'So what did you do?'

'I threw it back and it hit him square between the eyes!'

'Is this the same teacher who suspended you for pissing in his petrol tank?'

'No, that was another one.'

'I blame the parents,' jokes Robbie.

Jock suddenly moves into philosophical mode. 'Well, you know what they say: for every action there's an equal and opposite reaction.'

'That's Newton's Third Law,' I tell him.

'That's right. Well it's just karma getting back at him for all the shit he gave me!'

'So come on then – how did you learn to do that so quickly?' asks Tom.

'My brother and I virtually lived in the bookies in our younger days and that's when I discovered a use for maths. We used to play a lot of darts for cash in the local afterwards if we won, so working out numbers kind of came natural after a while. The only other use of maths I found is geometry for snooker and pool, which we'd play for pints, so there was a bit of motivation there.'

'You're definitely a one-off, I'll give you that,' sighs Zecks.

The eggs that Jock put in the microwave a minute or two earlier suddenly detonate and everyone is startled for a second before they realise what it is. We look at each other and '*For fuck's sake*,' echoes around the room.

'You still can't microwave an egg, though, can you, sunshine?' I say, putting my arm around his shoulders.

'If I were you, I'd stick to cornflakes. It would save you a lot of time and effort in the long run,' Tom tells him.

'Just think of your cholesterol level as well,' Zecks says with fake concern. 'You don't want to be popping your clogs of a heart attack before your time, do you? Because you know that would break my heart.'

Jock shakes his head before answering. 'Ahhhh, it's a load of bollocks, that healthy eating lark. Take my granddad, for example. He was a miner from the age of 17 and he inhaled soot and dirt all his life. He smoked sixty Woodbine cigarettes a day, lived on bacon and polished off nearly a bottle of whisky a day. He died at 84. Health and fitness? Load of old bollocks!'

'What did he put his old age down to, then?' I ask. 'Positive thinking and other men's wives?'

'He always said thought creates form, and if you think you will achieve something for long enough it will happen. He said it was the law of cause and effect. He believed there are mysterious forces at work in the universe that conspire to give you the things that you want and all you have to do is want them enough. I for one believe in it.'

'So what did he put other men's wives down to then?'

'I don't know. I guess he liked to get his rocks off, but he did once give me some advice about marriage.'

'Oh yeah, what was that?' asks Zecks.

'He told me, don't be a fucking idiot. Why buy the chicken when you get the eggs for free? It's in a man's interest to delay marriage as long as possible and it's in a woman's interest to get married as soon as possible.'

'What did he mean by that?' says Zecky, looking a little confused.

'I guess he meant the eggs represent the sex, but I haven't really thought about the last bit.'

Tom suddenly jumps in. 'Maybe he's trying to say that men never really grow up, and they want to be kids for as long as possible. I guess men can father kids into their seventies and when they start getting older with a few wrinkles they just look windswept and interesting. So, maybe he's trying to say why should men rush into getting married, because it's not in their interest.'

'He's got a point,' says Robbie. 'After all, the only real reason a bloke gets married in the first place is because he wants his kids to have his name. If it fails, he loses half of everything he's worked hard for.'

'Bit unfair really, isn't it?' says Zecks.

'Well, yeah, it bloody well is!' says Tom.

'You should've been born a girl then, shouldn't you?' Zecky tells him.

'You're bloody kidding!' says Jock. 'You can keep your

menopause, childbirth, raging hormones, dieting, and periods. I'm quite happy being a bloke, thank you very much.'

'So what do you reckon he means by "a woman should get married as soon as possible"?' I ask.

'Goes without saying really,' answers Robbie. 'They get married as soon as possible because the clock's ticking and they want to have a family while they still can. That, and the fact that they're an altogether better proposition when they are young, wrinkle-free, firm and bendy!'

Jock stops cleaning the microwave for a second. 'Well, yeah, he's right. Nobody wants to look at an old granny with her tits down to her knees!'

'Honestly, you men are so bloody simple. All you think about is what you can put in your belly or on your dicks!' mutters Zecks, looking at the other stewardess for back-up.

Jock jumps in again. 'Well, at least we don't think shopping is a sport, eating the odd packet of crisps is over-eating, and the world revolves around diamonds. At least we *admit* we're simple creatures!'

'Tell me more about your grandfather,' I say to Jock. 'He sounds like a bit of local colour.'

'Tell him about the night out, Rob,' says Jock, starting to laugh.

Robbie sits up in his seat and remembers the story. 'Bloody hell, he was an original kindred spirit, that one. I did a safety course back in the UK a few years back and Jock and I took him for a quiet pint one night. Granddad has half a dozen Stellas, all with whisky chasers, and decides to paint the town red. He's matching us drink for drink and he's showing no signs of slowing down. In fact he seems to be speeding up.

'By closing time, Jock and I are wasted but the old boy gets the horn and takes us to the local pole-dancing club. We don't really want to go in but we think we'd better keep an eye on him and walk him back after the booze hits him. So we're in the club and Granddad's sat at a table with a Cuban cigar and yet another Stella and whisky chaser, getting a table dance from this hot little blonde minx. He's loving it and he has three lap dances with three different girls and then tries to borrow another thirty quid off me so he can see if she offers extras behind the curtains. Remember, he's in his eighties! We eventually get him to leave the club after much persuasion and promising him more whisky back at the house, so we take a wander over to the taxi rank.'

'This is where the fun begins,' interrupts Jock. 'We fancied a cigarette before we got in the taxi so I lit one up and we all had a chat about the night. Granddad turns to me, looks me up and down and asks if I have anything stronger than nicotine on me. I laughed my ass off. He then mutters about the "bloody youth of today" and starts unscrewing the top of his walking cane. He reaches down into a hollowed-out cavity and pulls out this fucking huge spliff made from his own plants!'

'You're kidding?!' exclaims Zecks, laughing out aloud in disbelief.

'No! We aren't... I'm telling you, he's some boy!'

'How old was he again?'

'About 81 or 82,' says Jock.

'Fucking hell! How the hell does he do it at that age?' asks Tom.

'I know! I used to nickname him "Duracell" because he just goes on and on.'

'Where did he get the weed from?' asks Zecky.

'He grows his own in his room at the old folk's home. The staff don't know what sort of plants they are but they're very pleased he isn't causing trouble any more. All they know is he's calmed down so they leave him alone, smoking in his room, and let him get on with his new hobby of botany. The manageress even brings him fertiliser for his plants. They put his good behaviour down to good care and attention, when in reality he's stoned off his tits most of the time!'

'That's brilliant! So what happened then?' asks Zecks.

'Well, we're all having a smoke of this lethal spliff and Granddad's talking about us all spending a weekend in Amsterdam for his next birthday, when he suddenly stops in mid-conversation.

'"I don't fucking believe it... the little toe rag," Granddad mutters, staring at the taxi at the front of the row. We ask him what's up and he explains that the driver is also a dodgy local electrician. Apparently, he'd been round his mate's house and done some shoddy work that caused something to short out and cause a fire.'

'So what did he do?' Tom asks.

Both Jock and Robbie start laughing hysterically and it takes them a minute or so to calm down enough for Jock to finish the story.

'Granddad walks to the taxi at the back of the queue, which is about ten cars in length. He leans in through the window of each taxi and he asks each one of the taxi drivers – all men – for a blow-job. Furious, all of them tell him to piss off, or words to that affect. When he gets to the front taxi, where this guy he's got a problem with is, he leans in and asks if he wouldn't mind taking a weary old man home. The driver agrees and Granddad jumps in the front seat. He shouts through the window at us to take our time finishing our smoke then he tells the driver he's dropped some coins on the floor by his feet. He asks him if he wouldn't mind leaning and picking them up, 'cos he's got arthritis in his spine. The taxi driver agrees and as soon as he bends his lap over to pick up the coins, all hell breaks loose in the taxis behind him.

'The other drivers are hooting their horns and calling the guy all the names under the sun. Rob and I haven't got a clue what's going on because we're now pissed and lethally stoned. After a couple of minutes, Granddad steps out of the taxi with a huge smile on his face pretending to do up his fly. He then walks over to us, takes a big drag of his spliff and asks us to get in. The taxi then heads off with the driver looking confused as to what all the fuss was about.

'After a couple of miles, Rob starts to feel a bit ill from the effects of the monster spliff. He winds down the back window and is sick into the road. A bit sticks on the outside of the door and there's a tiny bit of carrot where the window comes up inside the door. The taxi driver goes ape shit and pulls over. He locks us all in the car so we can't get out and calls Rob a dirty bastard. He then tries to get Rob to cough up a lot of cash for fouling his vehicle but 99% of it is outside of the cab, leaving the inside virtually as clean as a whistle.'

'So what did he do?' asks Zecky.

'Well, Rob does the decent thing, apologises and takes his shirt off to clean the door. He's trying to lean out of the window to get to it but he can't reach. Then a police officer walks up to the cab and the taxi driver tells him what happened. The policeman is no mug but he informs us that the law states that there is a cash fine for anybody who fouls a taxi, inside or out. We could all tell by the way he told us, and by the look on his face, that he knew the taxi driver was taking the piss.

'Suddenly, Granddad leans over to Rob and me tells us not to say a word and that he'll handle the situation. He politely asks the police officer if we can all get out of the vehicle to discuss the problem, and the officer agrees.'

'I still can't believe what Gramps did next,' says Robbie, with his head in his hands.

'What did he do then?' asks Zecks eagerly. 'Did you do a runner?'

'No, not at his age. He leans over to the copper and clarifies what the maximum fine is for fouling the inside of the vehicle and the copper tells him. "Right, no problem," says Granddad, who's as cool as a cucumber.

'Then he walks round to the driver's side of the taxi, opens the door, sticks his fingers down his throat and pukes all over the driver's seat, steering wheel and the dashboard. He calmly closes the door, walks back round to the policeman and hands him the cash. "I like to get value for money, officer, and that was worth every penny!" he announces, walking off into the moonlight and bidding us goodnight. He's a kindred spirit that one!'

CHAPTER 9

MAY THE FORCE
BE WITH YOU

Next day we finish our breakfast in the crew room and
go out on to the deck for the morning walk around.
'OK, lads,' I say, 'as you're all aware, the boss is flying down
to Cannes today and we've a new crew member joining.'

'Anyone we know?' asks Jock.

'No... he's only 19 and he's never worked on a yacht
before. He's fresh out of his college induction, so he'll be as
green as grass.'

'Ha! Fantastic!' declares Jock. 'A bit of fresh meat for us!'

'Jock, this is mainly directed at you – go easy on him. I've
heard the stories of the stunts you played on the cadet on your
last boat. Anyway, he'll be waiting on the quay by the steps at
two this afternoon. You go over there Jock and collect him
and bring him back to the boat, and Tom and I will take the
car to the helipad to pick up the boss. Before we get changed,
has anyone *not* met the boss before, apart from you Rob?'

'I've only seen him once on the quay about a year ago, so
fill me in on the details,' says Tom.

'No problem. He's a property tycoon, in his late fifties, usually wears Savile Row suits, bald headed, about five-eight, average build. He lives in a huge villa in Monte Carlo in the summer and St Lucia in the winter. He's a decent bloke from humble beginnings in London's East End, so he's a down-to-earth guy, but never forget who he is. His main interests while he's on the yacht are drinking whisky, having barbeques, and smoking cigars in the whirlpool spa on the sun deck. He likes his Jacuzzi at 33°C.'

'How much is he worth?' asks Tom, straight to the point.

'Thrush told me it was around 750 million at the last estimate, but it's probably more than that now.'

'What kind of car does he drive?'

'He doesn't drive any of them. He's a multi-millionaire so he gets someone else to drive him.'

'Ask a silly question, I suppose…'

'Yep! What kind of mood he's in and where he's travelling to will determine what car he wants us to drive.'

'Wants *us* to drive?' says Tom, perking up.

'Oh yeah. I usually pick him up and drive him to and from airports, but I also take him up to the country club in his guard's red Ferrari 360 Spider. He's also got a jet black Bentley convertible, a platinum Porsche Carrera 996 Turbo, and a Range Rover for when his back is sore and he doesn't feel like bending down. All brand new, of course.'

Tom is crazy about cars and I think the news that he may get to drive one of these machines is a bit too much to handle. He's got a grin like a Cheshire cat. 'We'll be picking him up in the Bentley today because he has quite a bit of luggage with him,' I tell him.

'Tell them about our race around Monaco,' says Jock.

'OK, but this goes no further. Jock and I once went to pick up the boss's son and his friend from Nice Airport but they decided not to come. We didn't get the message so we're hanging around the airport until midnight waiting for them. We finally get told they won't be coming, so we take the Ferrari and the Porsche back to Monte Carlo. We've driven both cars there because they wanted to drive them on from the airport to a mate's villa near St Tropez. It was past midnight and the roads were virtually empty and we decided to see what the cars were made of… so we had a bit of a race back along the motorway.'

'We were proper flying though!' Jock tells everyone proudly. 'We were side by side at 150mph on the long flat bit.'

'Fucking hell! What about the speed cameras?' asks Rob.

'Oh, it was OK,' I say, with a grin. 'We couldn't really see them long enough to worry at that speed, could we, Jock?'

'We come off the motorway and cruise down the hill into Monaco. Like he said, the roads are empty because it's around one in the morning, so we reckon since we're in two of the most prestigious cars in the world we'll have a race round the Grand Prix circuit whilst we're at it.'

'No way!' laughs Tom.

'Yeah, seriously. We think it would be something to tell the grandkids. Anyway, the Grand Prix track is basically a circular route on public roads, so it wasn't like we had to break in anywhere. We start racing at the roundabout next to the tunnel heading towards the marina and we do the circuit three times at speed!'

'Including the famous hairpin outside the Rascasse Bar,' adds Jock.

'It was pretty crowded at that time, and by the third lap a few people had lined the barriers and were applauding!'

'So that's our claim to fame, mate. We raced each other around the actual Monaco Grand Prix circuit and we were the only cars on it!' beams Jock.

'Ha! That's wicked. You'll have to take me next time,' adds an envious Tom.

'There won't be a next time, mate. That was definitely a one-off,' I tell him. 'Right, we'd better get our skates on then. Jock, go get changed and we'll get the show on the road. Just give me a ring on my mobile when you're on your way back, so Tom and I can make our way down to the boat and head over to the car.'

'No worries, mate,' says Jock.

An hour passes and Jock calls to say he'll be alongside the yacht in ten minutes.

'Have you picked up the new boy?' I ask.

'Yeah, he was waiting where he should have been.'

'What's he like?'

'You'll see, boss. I just hope his mum knows he's playing sailor boy, bless him.'

The guest tender approaches the yacht and the new arrival comes into view. He looks about 16 and five-feet-six tall. His freckly face hasn't a hint of facial hair and he still has remnants of puppy fat. He's dressed in a shirt, tie and blazer. Thrush joins me to help with the luggage – quite decent of him for a change. I hold out my hand and help him from the boat and onto the yacht. I hear him thanking Jock for helping him with his bag and he has quite a high-pitched, upper-class but nondescript English accent.

'Hello, are you the Chief Mate?' squeaks the new arrival.

'Why? Do I owe you money?' I say, trying to lighten the atmosphere and settle his nerves.

'Errrr... no... I don't think I have met you before,' he says innocently.

I look at Tom and he's trying not to laugh. 'You'll be happy to get here then?' I ask.

'Oh yes, but I must admit I've heard some bad things about the Captain. He's supposed to be, excuse my French, a bit of an arsehole!'

My welcoming smile vanishes as I grit my teeth and signal to him with my eyes that the gentleman stood two feet to his right *is* the Captain. I quickly bid him farewell and make a quick retreat to the boat with Tom.

'I'm off with Tom to pick up the owner, Mr Thomas, but Rob will settle you in,' I tell him as we leave.

As Tom and I look back on the way to the quay the Captain is staring at the new arrival like he's just stolen something from him. Not the best of starts for the new kid, and he's not going to last two minutes with any of the boys, especially Jock, the ultimate piss-taker.

Tom and I get a taxi to the garage to find the Bentley. 'We'll get the cleaning gear out of the boot and give her a rub down so she's spotless for the boss. I'm not sure if his wife will be coming along as well, but if she does, open and close the door for her and ask her if she has enough air in the back. She's a nice enough lady but she likes to be fussed over a bit, if you know what I mean. Give her a bit of special attention.'

'Anything else I should know?' asks Tom.

'He usually wants to know the latest football scores and

what his wife's movements are for the weekend. They aren't the best-matched couple, to say the least, and apparently she changed the instant he married her.'

'Did she turn into a professional nag or something?'

'They all do that, mate! My guess is that now he's in this predicament, he doesn't want to lose millions in a divorce settlement, so he tolerates her.'

Tom and I spend the best part of half an hour dusting down the Bentley and it's spotless by the time we see the helicopter coming over the horizon. It thunders in to the landing pad and the pilot helps the boss down the steps, but there's no sign of the wife. Two of the staff pull his two pieces of luggage from the hold and walk behind him to the car, where I greet him with a warm handshake.

'Good afternoon, sir. How was your flight?'

'Not bad. How's yourself?'

'I'm OK, thanks.'

'Haven't seen you in a while. I thought you might have buggered off to work for an Ibiza club owner by now and got rid of an old fucker like me,' he jokes in an unmistakable East End London accent.

'Ha! Maybe next year, sir, if you're lucky.'

I've worked for him for over a year now and we have developed a good rapport. He's a totally different person when his wife isn't around; he's always a grumpy old sod when she's with him. 'No wife today, sir?' I enquire.

'Thankfully not. I think she's doing something back in Monaco or she's going to watch an opera or something.'

Tom and I take him straight to his hotel where he's meeting a few friends for a reunion. They're in town for a couple of days playing golf, so he thought he'd catch up with them for a round or two and a game of poker. He must be pretty fond of them because he'd flown down from Bern to Nice in his private jet.

'This is Tom, sir, you've never met him. He works on your yacht with us. He's originally from Australia.'

'Good to meet you, sir,' Tom says, leaning round to shake his hand.

'G'day me old cobba,' the boss says, doing the worst Australian accent Tom has ever heard. They both laugh, because it's such a shit impersonation.

'I think you've misunderstood, sir. I'm from Australia not Pakistan,' says Tom with a smile. The boss finds this quite cheeky but funny.

'I see sarcasm is another service yacht crews are offering nowadays! Perhaps I'd better stick to making money instead of impressions.'

'I think that would be a wise move, sir,' I chuckle.

'I visited Australia a couple of years ago. I went down in a cage with the white sharks, and I ate kangaroo meat at a restaurant,' says the boss proudly.

'Oh yeah, how did you get along?' asks Tom.

'The sharks bloody terrified me! I tend to lose my sense of humour when I'm bottom of the food chain.'

We pull up at the front door of the hotel and the bellboy rushes out to take the bags. Tom jumps out just before the vehicle comes to rest so he can open the door for the boss.

'All the best then, sir, and have a nice time,' I tell him. He hands me 100 euros, but it's a pleasure to work for a guy like this, so I hand it back immediately.

'I'm very grateful, sir, but you pay me enough already… it's been a pleasure, really.' He looks genuinely touched and he holds my stare for a second. I'm thinking I might just have helped restore his faith in human nature a little bit.

As Tom and I jump back in the Bentley, a few of his friends meet him at the door. They all look like they're in a very jovial mood – or should I say half-cut. 'I think he's going to have a sore head tomorrow,' I tell Tom. 'They look like they're up for a party.'

'He certainly seems in good spirits. Is he always like that?'

'He is usually, when he's away from the wife! He calls her "the ball and chain".'

'So how did he make his money, then? I take it he's into dodgy dealings, eh?'

'I don't know all the details, but from what I heard he started out quite young, taking a lot of financial risks. He borrowed money on his house to put a deposit down on another one and he renovated it with his own hands. He sold that for a profit then bought two more and did the same on those. He kept on doing this for a few years until he had generated several hundred grand and then invested that on the stock market and online gambling. This kept making money, and as he carried on investing in many different concerns, he became a multi-millionaire after twenty years. He keeps his affairs private but apparently he has a lot of money in various football clubs. He's incredibly shrewd, but he's quite a relaxed, funny guy.'

I'm happy that everything has gone to plan so far and the boss has been picked up and delivered without a hitch, so before we head back I let Tom drive the Bentley along the coast road as a treat. I can tell he's been dying to get his hands behind the wheel from the moment he saw the Bentley. He's been asking me questions on how she drives and how easy the steering is, and how comfortable the driver's seat is.

'Cheers, you're a star! I've been itching for a drive of the beast.'

'Now remember, if you *bend* it you *mend* it. This car costs more than your average family detached house, so you'll be working your hands to the bone for the rest of your life if you damage it.'

He's only been driving for about ten minutes when a car full of young lads draws up parallel to us in the next lane. They're driving a customised sports car. It has a dodgy paint job, cheap body kit and one of those nasty spoilers on the back boot which looks like it has been stuck on as an afterthought. Tom and I look over at them and they start trying to bait us into racing them.

'Just ignore the little shits, Tom... Kids! eh?'

'I know, mate,' he says looking straight ahead not giving them any attention. A few minutes pass and they are becoming to get really irritating. Then a doughnut hits Tom's window, and they're leaning out of the car, giving us the one-fingered salute. Tom's got that look in his eye that just shouts 'LET ME!'

I hesitate for a second or two then tap him on the shoulder. 'Are you going to let them get away with that?' I ask.

'Do you know what, boss? I don't believe I am!' comes the reply from a now-smiling Tom, flipping the gearbox into sport mode and putting his foot to the floor. We charge off and even at 60mph we leave the other car standing like it wasn't moving at all.

'Fucking hell, what's that rumbling and shuddering?' I shout.

He looks at me, laughing. 'That's the rear wheels spinning.'

'But we're doing nearly 70mph!'

'I know! Fucking awesome, eh! Look out of the back window.'

There are two thick tyre marks along the road where we've just accelerated. Tom is still high on adrenaline as we motor down the last stretch of road heading back to the port and even though the car full of lads is no longer with us, he's going a little bit too fast for the speed limit. As we pass a fuel station a police patrol car parked in the slip lane zaps us with a radar gun. The laughing and joking stops abruptly as we both look in the rear view mirror to see if they are following us. Suddenly the patrol car pulls out and its roof light illuminates. 'Bollocks, he's after us, Tom.'

'How fast do you think we were doing?' he asks, looking worried.

'How fast do you *think* you were doing?'

'I don't know… 80 or 90!'

'Fuck! Well that's a whole lot faster than the speed limit, mate. My guess is we're in the shit, so you'd better pull over.'

Tom isn't the best person to be pulled over by a copper; he absolutely hates them and can't resist taking the piss. To make matters worse, he swerves the car across the road as he heads to the lay-by, because he's looking at the patrol car in the rear view mirror and not where he's going. The omens aren't good and I get the gut feeling things will go pear-shaped some time soon.

Tom winds down the window and the police officer strolls

up to the Bentley. He says something in French but we are both clueless. Tom looks up at the officer: 'Do you speak English?' The officer turns his head away and sighs, as if he's done this many times before. We're sure he has – there are probably more foreign drivers on the Cote d'Azur than French in the peak summer season. The officer is wearing dark shades. It gives him a menacing aura.

'Monsieur, your licence and registration,' he says in English but with a strong French accent.

'I don't have it on me, mate,' says Tom.

It might be fine calling an Aussie copper 'mate' because things are a lot more laid-back there, but it's not the kind of thing you do on the Cote d'Azur.

'Is zis your car, monsieur?' asks the officer, pointing at Tom.

'Nah, mate. We found it unlocked and thought we'd take her for a spin,' Tom says laughing.

I know what's coming but there's bugger all I can do except look the other way. The officer takes a few seconds to register the dialect and process what he's just been told. 'Soooo... you are zee driver of this vehicle... yes?'

'I know it's an automatic, mate, but I've still got to fucking be here.'

Silence.

'Do you know what gear you were in coming down zee hill?'

'Oh, you know... white shirt, black pants, and hush puppies!'

Silence again.

I nudge the piss-taking Tom on the arm. 'Mate, I don't

think you...' is all I get out before he pushes me away; I swear quietly under my breath.

'Sir, you were going 78 in a 60 limit,' he tells Tom, reaching for his ticket book.

'That's a bit disappointing. We reckoned we were doing at least 80 or 90. Can't you make it 100? I'm trying to sell the motor!'

I'm thinking we're in the shit, but I can't help but chuckle to myself at the bloody front Tom has sometimes. The officer puts pen to paper to write him a ticket.

'So.... what is your name, monsieur?'

'Walker.'

'Walker?'

'Yep, Walker...W-A-L-K-E-R...Walker.'

The officer writes it down.

'And what is your first name?'

'Luke... L-U-K-E... Luke.'

'And your middle name?

'Sky... S-K-Y.'

The officer writes it down and after a few seconds he realises what he's written. He rips up the piece of paper and opens the door.

'You two... step out of zee vehicle,' he says in a sharp tone.

I look at Tom and whisper to him: 'Shit! You've really done it now, you bloody comedian!'

After twenty scary minutes, a body search, a vehicle search, a fine and lots of sweet-talking, I explain to the officer that Tom gets nervous and that's where the jokes come from. Complete bullshit of course, because Tom just likes to take the piss. Eventually he believes me and sees the funny side. We are cautioned again and allowed to get on our way. We bid the officer farewell but Tom can't resist one more taunt before we leave.

'May the force be with you,' he tells the officer, as he waves his imaginary light sabre at him.

'The force was strong with that one,' I say as I accelerate up the road on the way back to the yacht.

CHAPTER 10

THE BIGGER THEY ARE THE HARDER THEY FALL

Tom and I drive straight back to the quay and we notice the yacht's tender moored up alongside the floating pontoon, but Jock is nowhere to be seen.

'Give Jock a shout and see where he is, mate,' I say to Tom, fearing the worst. Tom reaches into his pocket for his mobile. He thumbs in Jock's number. It rings six times then goes onto voicemail. Jock's voicemail informs us that unfortunately he's been called away on a matter of national security but we should leave a message and if he returns alive from his heroic adventures he'll call back.

'Just ask him where he is and tell him we're waiting by the boat,' I tell Tom. 'Ask him to call back as soon as he gets the message.' Tom leaves the message and then hangs up. We sit on the tender and smoke cigarettes for ten minutes, then Tom's crazy frog ringtone sounds.

'Mate, where are you? We're on the tender waiting for you,' says Tom.

'I'm at the bar on the main road. It's behind the quay.'

'You're in the bar?! Fuck's sake Jock!'

'I've only been here an hour. Take a walk over, I've just got a pint in.'

Tom hands me the phone and shakes his head.

'Jock! What the fuck are you doing! Don't move – we're coming over.'

'Aye OK, I'll get you both one in. By the way, you want to see the tits on the barmaid. It's like a photo finish in a zeppelin race!'

The phone then goes dead as Jock has hung up.

'Trust him to find the boozer at this time. Still, how much can one man drink in an hour?' asks Tom.

At the bar, Tom and I spot Jock, who is talking to a young guy I haven't seen before. I walk up to Jock and tap him on the shoulder.

'All right chaps!' he says cheerily, passing pints along the bar to us. 'This is Nick, my new mate from New Zealand. He's only 18 and he's just polished off four shots of tequila.'

'Oh yeah? What's the celebration?' I ask Nick.

Before he has a chance to answer, Jock puts his arm around his shoulder. 'Nick went out in St Tropez last night and had his first blow-job.'

'Oh... errrr, congratulations!' I tell Nick, sniggering as I shake his hand.

'Yeah, the poor fucker still can't get the taste out of his mouth, so he's trying a whisky this time!'

'Hey, piss off Jock – he's only kidding,' Nick retorts.

I turn Jock around and give him a bollocking for leaving the tender unattended. But there's no harm done, so we have a few laughs in Nick's company before we drag Jock away from the bar to a food table. I hope he orders something solid to soak up the four pints and whisky chasers he's downed, before we have to get back to the yacht.

'Bloody hell, Jock, are you on a mission to push your luck or something?' I ask him. 'If Thrush smells that on you he'll have your ass kicked into the middle of next fucking year.'

'Well, one beer led to a bit more, you know how it goes. Anyway, I'll order you all some grub to make amends,' he says, waving over to the waitress who is stood with an order book at the bar. She walks over to the table and smiles. Jock looks up at her with his alcohol-flushed face and proceeds to order in a very slow, very loud voice using lots of hand movement. He's clearly assuming she doesn't speak English.

'CAN I... (pointing to himself)... have ONE (holding his digit up in front of her face) EXTRA LARGE (now doing circular movements with his arms) TUNA (pointing to a fish ornament on the bar) PIZZA... and TWO (sticking his fingers inches from her face) MOOO... MOOO... BEEF (now holding two fingers up on his head like horns) PIZZAS... and THREE (again holding fingers up under her nose) GRANDE... GRANDE (holding his arms outstretched) BEERS (pointing to his glass).'

The waitress looks at Jock and repeats his order – in an unmistakable Essex accent. 'So you want three beers and three pizzas, one tuna and two beef, yeah?'

Jock looks at her open-mouthed. 'Errrr, yeah. Sorry darling... thought you were a foreigner.'

'Clearly, but why you thought I was stupid and deaf is more of a mystery.'

'Oh, right... I just looked over and you seemed that way.'

'What? Stupid and deaf?'

'No, foreign, for fuck's sake,' says Jock, holding his head. Can we start again? Where are you from?'

'Essex.'

'Essex girls, eh? I've heard about your reputations... Well, it's nice to see one upright and not lying on her back for a change.'

'Are you trying to be funny?'

'Ha! Yeah!' says Jock, slapping her on her arse.

'Well, I hope you find this funny!' she says, grabbing his wrist and inverting it painfully behind his back, then throwing her fist at Jock's nose. He falls back holding on to the seat of his chair: he's now sitting in exactly the same position but facing the ceiling and with a bloodied nose. The waitress screams at him to stay where he is before disappearing into the back room.

Tom sits facing me with arms folded and a big grin on his face. 'I told you these were good seats, didn't I, eh? We find a bar with the only psychotic Essex girl on the Cote d'Azur.'

Tom and I then lean down to have a word with the flattened Jock. 'I must admit, you've got *that* off to an art form,' I tell him.

'Uhhhh... uhhhh... what?' says Jock, still in the same position.

'Making a cunt of yourself! You should've opened your mouth a little wider, then you could have put the other foot in. How to win friends and influence people, Jock-style, eh?'

'Fucking hell, mate – she's got a punch like a steam hammer!' groans Jock.

'Just wait till I tell Rob you got bitch-slapped, mate. You haven't a snowball's chance of living this one down,' says Tom.

'Bit of an overreaction, I thought,' says Jock.

'Come on... We'd better get out of here, they're coming over.'

Jock gets up slowly with a helping hand from Tom and they start to walk towards the exit. The waitress stomps out of the door at the end of the bar to intercept them. She's accompanied by the chef – over six foot, with a shaven head and very muscular.

'Oh fuck! Here we go,' I say to Jock.

'Yeah, I see him,' replies Jock quietly.

'No prizes for guessing who he'd like a word with.'

'Hey you!' shouts the chef.

Jock stops in his tracks and turns round.

'My girlfriend says you touched her up when she came over to serve you.'

'That's not quite how it happened, I was just...'

'Nobody touches my girl. Now you're going get touched up, you fucking prick!'

I can't help intervening, because I have to back Jock up. 'Look, mate, he was just having a joke with her and she took it the wrong way and hit him. He shouldn't have touched her on the arse but it was innocent enough.'

I'm in the middle of explaining when he tells me to shut the fuck up.

'So, you did touch her, then?' says the chef, who is now getting angrier by the minute.

'Well, yeah... but everything has been taken out of context, mate.'

'I'm not your fucking mate, I'm your worst enemy. Now get your ass outside because I'm going to kick it off this fucking planet!'

Tom tries to calm things down but he's given the same treatment as me. Jock suddenly gives me a wink and holds his hands up in the air. 'OK, OK, you win. I'll come out into the back alley with you, but you're a big lad and I don't stand a chance so at least let me neck a tequila before we go.'

'You fucking what?!'

'To kill the pain.'

'Whatever!' the chef says snarling at him.

Jock walks over to the bar and orders a tequila from a very embarrassed French barmaid. The chef is standing inches away from him and he's spoiling for a fight.

'Tequila – make it a large one, darling,' says Jock. He picks up the shot glass in between him and the chef. The two are almost nose-to-nose and there's hardly enough room for Jock to bring the glass to his lips. 'OK, I'll just bolt this and then you can take me outside, but I don't want to fight you... as long as you know that,' Jock tells the chef.

'Well, you don't have much choice now, do you, dickhead?'

'OK, if that's what you want...' Jock slowly pours the tequila into his mouth, then blows it out into the chef's face and eyes. He does it with such strength that a cloud of fine mist can be seen in the air between the two.

The chef puts his hands over his eyes and stumbles back, blinded. 'MOTHERFUCKER!!!!' he screams at the top of his voice.

Jock then aims a very hard and accurate punch at the chef's unprotected balls and he bends over like he's been shot in the gut. His deep voice has changed to a high-pitched squeal and he's gripping his balls, blinded and in agony. As Tom and I look at each other in astonishment, we think that any minute the chef is going to recover and rip Jock a new arsehole. Fortunately, he's in too much pain and can't move, and Jock knows it.

Jock takes one step back, puts both arms in the air, stands on one leg and starts humming the theme to the *Karate Kid* film. He then does the Karate Kid's signature move and kicks the chef in the centre of his forehead, knocking him out cold. Jock, cool as a cucumber, winks as he walks past us towards the exit. 'The bigger they are, the harder they fall.'

'Well, let's just hope he stays fallen,' I say. 'Now let's get the fuck out of here.'

We don't waste time as we run back to the tender. We cover up the name on it in case we're spotted, get the throttle down and speed back to the yacht as fast as it can get us there.

'I'm kind of thinking Jock might have done that party trick a few times before,' Tom says quietly to me. 'It looked a little too well-practised to be spontaneous.'

'I think you're right,' I sigh. 'Crude, as only Jock can be, but very effective.'

CHAPTER 11

THE PANDA-EYED GOON

On the yacht, Robbie is giving the new cadet the mandatory safety tour. You can tell by the look on the lad's face that he's blown away by the beauty and class of the yacht. It's also easy to see that he's clueless, though. He's calling the bow the 'pointy end' and the wheelhouse the 'cockpit'. He's also bemused by the helm, or the 'steering wheel' as he calls it, which is a ten-inch-long, half-moon-shaped metal rig. In practice, navigation officers rarely use it because they usually alter course with the autopilot, unless they are in traffic or navigationally restricted waters. The cadet seems amazed at this – he was clearly expecting a huge, six-foot wooden wheel like you see in old pirate films.

Robbie enjoys showing the new arrival around the yacht. The boy's inexperience is very entertaining, and Rob is sure the crew are going to get hours of entertainment winding him up. I disappear down below decks for a quick coffee and I hear the stewardesses giggling away to each other. They're wondering if the new crew member will be 'fit', but they're in for a shock – he's barely out of nappies.

I go back on deck to see how Robbie is getting on and to check on the standard of work that's been done this morning. He's kneeling down polishing the stainless steel winch, listening to his iPod and singing away. I tap him on the shoulder to grab his attention.

'How's it going, Rob?'

'OK, mate.'

'Where's the kid?'

'Jock's got him into a job below decks. He took him away as soon as you went for a coffee.'

'Jesus, I wonder what he's up to now. I'd better go and try and save him from the crazy sod! What do you reckon he's got him doing?'

'God only knows… probably making him clean his cabin, I reckon.'

'He's been aboard less than half an hour, for fuck's sake! If he comes back up don't be too harsh on him just yet. Let him settle in for a few days first before we initiate him.'

'It's not me you have to worry about, is it, boss?' he says with a knowing look.

'You're not wrong there, mate. By the way, we're moving alongside the berth in three hours, and we'll be staying overnight until the boss leaves in the morning.'

'So he's definitely coming down, then?'

'Yep, and the crowd he's met up with look like they might be up for a boys' party, so it could be an eye-opener.'

'Well, we aren't exactly short of eye-openers this trip,

are we? I could've done with an early night tucked up in my wank chariot tonight instead of standing at the passerelle.'

'I know, mate, plus the weather will be shit for the crossing over to Porto Cervo tomorrow, so you won't get much kip then.'

'It's fucking typical, that! We hug the coast away from all the crap weather and seas for most of the summer, and the one time we've to make a crossing the weather turns shit. The hits just keep on coming!'

'That's sod's law for you. Anyway, I'll catch you later.'

I go back down below deck to see what mischief Jock is into. I'm not let down. Walking along the alleyway I hear a shrill, painful moaning from Jock's cabin. Jock has the kid in a headlock under his left arm and he's playfully knocking on the top of the kid's head with his knuckles.

'What do you mean, you've not brought any porn with you?' yells Jock.

'Sorry... I... didn't know... ouch!' gasps the kid.

'What about booze? You must have brought some booze with you!'

As I walk in the room Jock turns and sees me. 'You'll never guess what, boss...'

'I heard – and I think the rest of the yacht did as well. Let him go, for fuck's sake. He hasn't been aboard more than an hour! Go and help Rob finish up and then sort yourself out for moving the yacht to the berth.'

I hold out my hand and the cadet shakes it warily.

'Hi, mate! I didn't catch your name when we first met.'

'It's Tarquin, sir.'

'Fucking hell! How did you end up with that name? Mum and dad a bit rich and posh, are they?'

'Well, erm… yes, they are as a matter of fact. My mother is a merchant banker and Daddy is a maritime lawyer.'

'No shit! Don't tell me you've got a double-barrelled surname – that would really take the piss.'

'Er… well, actually my surname is Worthington-Smythe.'

'Oh for fuck's sake! Tarquin Worthington-Smythe, eh? Jock's going to rip you up for arse-paper. Anyway, Tarquin Worthington-Smythe, I'll call you 'Tar' for short. First things first: I'd better give you a few house rules. Unpack and settle in as soon as you can and don't take Jock too seriously. Treat everything he asks you to do with extreme caution. He'll take the piss and play all sorts of pranks on you, but accept it because we all go through it in one way or another when we first go to sea. Jock's a good 'un underneath but he's a rough old diamond. Just remember, it isn't the changes in life that are difficult, it's just the transitions. Remember that and everything will be cool, OK?'

'Right… OK.'

'Number two is, I run my department my way, and that way is a mish-mash between the right way, the wrong way, the book way and two decades of experience. If you do exactly what I say, when I say it, you'll be OK. The last thing I want is to be condescending, but you're still a young kid and there's a lot you don't know. And thirdly, don't call me "sir", because every time you call me that I think somebody important is stood behind me.'

'OK.'

'Oh, yeah – I nearly forgot: whatever happens between us

in our department stays between us. Don't mention anything, rumours or otherwise, to or in front of, Thrush.'

'Who's Thrush?'

'That's our nickname for the Captain. You know, he's the guy you insulted even before you stepped aboard.'

'Oh yes, I'm really, really sorry about that.'

'Sorry my arse, mate. We all hate the fucker and to be honest when I heard you say that I felt very close to you.'

'Why do you call him Thrush?'

'Because like thrush, he's an irritating cunt. He's only out for himself and he'll drop you like a sack of shit if you fuck up. Treat him like a mushroom.'

Tarquin looks up a bit lost. 'Erm... treat him like a mushroom?'

'Yeah, feed him shit and keep him in the dark. As for the lads, they're a good bunch. If you treat them fairly and you're loyal and truthful they'll eventually return the favour, once you gain their respect. Just remember they can be your best friends or your worst nightmare, so it's completely up to you. Are we clear, then?'

'Erm... yes, I think so.'

'Nice one. Right, sort out your shit and go and see Zecky the Chief Stewardess for some uniform and I'll see you in the wheelhouse a bit later for going into port. OK, mate?'

'Yes... thank you. Just one thing I'd like to ask.'

'Shoot.'

'Where is my cabin?'

'You're in it.'

'Oh, no – I think there's been a mistake. I was expecting a cabin to myself.'

'Well, you expected wrong then, didn't you? Everyone bunks up with a buddy, except the Captain, and you'll be taking the only bunk that's spare.'

'Who am I sharing with?'

'You're in the top bunk, in here with Jock.'

'But this place is the size of a cubby hole!'

'Well, what were you expecting, a master suite? You're crew, remember. Anyway, it may be small but it's clean and modern and the only time you'll be in here is when you're getting your head down for a few hours.'

'But how am I supposed to climb up to the bunk?'

'I must admit you are a bit of a short arse, aren't you, Tar? How tall are you? You look about five-feet-four?'

'I'm five-feet-five, actually.'

'Have you thought about being a burglar as a career move, Tar? You'd be fucking great at it.'

'A burglar? Why a burglar?'

'Because your arse would rub your footprints out and they'd never catch you.'

'Oh, right.'

'Come on Tar, smile, I'm only messing with you. You'll crack the fucking mirror with that face! Right, I'll call you to the wheelhouse when we go into port so you can see what it's all about and get the best view.'

'Oh yes, the best view of the port entrance and navigation light formations... I learnt about all that at college.'

'No, mate. Tits on the beach. They are far more interesting than lights. You'll get a real eyeful as we go in if you're lucky!' I say with a wink.

'Oh!'

'I'll see you in a bit.'

* * * *

I leave Tar rubbing his sore head and take a slow stroll up to the wheelhouse. As I walk in, I catch Thrush and his girlfriend on the sofa. She's stroking his hair like a lapdog and it turns my stomach to watch the pathetic pair. He spots me and breaks away from the caress like a schoolboy caught with his trousers down. He clears his throat and stands bolt upright. The bottom of his white shirt is sticking out of his fly. She quickly disappears off to the storeroom and I'm in two minds whether to say anything about his fly, but eventually decide not to. We can all have a few laughs out of this one and I just want to see how long he'll walk around like that before he notices.

Thrush decides to keep me in the loop for once and he gives me a work brief. 'OK, we'll be going to the berth shortly, so get on with the pre-sailing equipment checklist and I'll phone down the engine room and give them half an hour's notice for departure. Make sure the cadet is up here for when we sail, so he can see what we do.'

'He's already been told and he'll be up as soon as I call him.'

'You'd better call him shortly then, and by the way, I didn't appreciate his comment about me when he boarded. I don't like his attitude.'

'He's just wet behind the ears and lacks life experience, that's all. We'll all take him under our wing, but don't expect any miracles because he's got a lot to learn.'

'Well, you'd better make sure he learns quick or I'll hold you personally responsible.'

I don't say anything back because I just don't want to get into a slagging match, but I'm mentally calling him all the names under the sun.

I call Tar and he arrives on the bridge a few minutes later in his new uniform that is still creased from the packaging. He's sweating and it's obvious he's as nervous as hell. He looks bewildered at all the gadgetry and electronics, so I do my best to calm him down.

'You look very smart, Tar... the boss will be proud!'

'Thank you, sir.'

I scowl and make a show of looking behind me, as if to see whether there is someone important there.

'Oh sorry – you don't like to be called that.'

I give him a wink to put him at ease. 'That's all right, mate. Like I said, when you call me "sir" you make me nervous and besides, I actually *work* for a living. Right then, Tar, the first piece of equipment I'm going to show you is definitely the most important.'

'Oh, OK... is it the radar?'

'No, it's the kettle. Here's two cups and mine's a coffee. Milk with two sugars.'

'Oh, right.'

'You've got to start from square one and this is it... learning how to make a decent brew.' He asks if he should make one for the Captain, but I tell him Jock will make him a special one later. Then I take him through the pre-departure checklist. When we're at the radar he notices the Captain's shirt sticking out of his fly and he glances at me to see if he should say something. I quickly put my finger over his mouth.

'Don't say a thing, Tar,' I whisper. 'I know he makes you nervous, but this will make him seem more human to you. Every time he bollocks you or talks down to you from now on, just remember that shirt tail and what a twat he looks. It's a great leveller, don't you think?'

'You're right, he does make me nervous. I think I let myself down a bit when I first came aboard and made that comment about him.'

'Don't worry – what you said was bang on the money. It was just unlucky that he was stood next to you, that's all. What happened to you is nothing compared to what I did.'

'I can't imagine anything worse than what I did. What did you do?'

'Well, I'd been on a ship about a day and a half and we'd just departed the port at night. Nobody had told me you weren't allowed to smoke on the wheelhouse wing. It's technically an open air area outside on either side of the wheelhouse. I'm on watch on my own at night and I decided to have a crafty cigarette next to the doorway so the smoke wouldn't get inside and stink the place out. So I'm puffing away and I decide to flick the almost finished fag over the side of the ship. I stick it on my thumb and flick it with my middle finger but as it shoots out over the side, the wind catches it and blows it back on deck.'

'What happened then?'

'Well, I heard this loud "Aaaahhhh!!" The Captain was walking up the outside of the accommodation and it hit him on his right cheek, just underneath his eye. The bloody thing was going at a fair speed when it exploded on his face.'

'Crikey! What did he say to you?'

'Well, put it this way, he wasn't impressed. Anyway, we'll have even more fun in a minute.'

'Why?'

'Because that box next to Thrush contains his new binoculars. They only arrived this morning and I took them out of the box and smeared black boot polish around the eye pieces. He'll look even more of a clown than he does already after he uses them for the first time. He'll look like a fucking panda!'

'You'll never get away with it.'

'Won't have to, mate – I'll just blame you.'

'Oh no – you wouldn't, would you?' says Tar, looking terrified.

'No, of course not... well, at least not yet. I'll let you settle in first. Trust me, my nickname isn't Teflon for nothing.'

'Teflon... why Teflon?'

'Because nothing sticks!'

Eventually it sinks in and he smiles. I get the feeling he's not the sharpest knife in the drawer but I'll give him some latitude for now because he seems like a good kid. We work through the pre-departure checklist while Jock and Tom head up to the deck to pick up the anchor. Rob joins us on the bridge to take his position at the helm, because Thrush always goes to manual steering coming into port. The engineer calls up from the engine room and advises us that we've full use of the engines, then Thrush gives the order to Jock to heave up the anchor. The yacht becomes underway and slowly heads towards the marina. I give Tar a nudge. 'Any minute now, Tar, he'll pick up the binoculars to see if our place at the berth is clear.'

'I don't think we should be doing this, you know.' Tar says nervously, as Thrush moves over to the port side and picks up the binoculars.

Thrush speaks to the port authority on the VHF radio and confirms the berth, lifting the binoculars to his eyes for a better view. With a smirk, I whisper in Rob's ear that the eagle has landed. Rob is watching the instruments, so he hasn't had a chance to look at Thrush yet. Thrush puts the binoculars down and walks towards Rob to give the order for the next alteration of course. It has worked perfectly. It looks like he's just done ten rounds with Mike Tyson. Both eyes are circled with big, round black marks. I can't help feeling very proud of myself and I have a quiet chuckle.

Meantime, Thrush is giving helm orders. We have to acknowledge orders verbally by saying 'Roger'. The only problem is, Thrush mumbles and it's bloody hard to hear him. Rob and I have asked him a hundred times to speak up but he never does.

Thrush gives Rob a helm order of five degrees to starboard and Rob can just about hear him. Then Rob spots his panda eyes and nearly bursts out laughing but disguises it into a cough. Rob and I try not to make any eye contact, because that would really set us both off. Thrush is oblivious, and he walks out onto the bridge wing and gives another helm order but we can't hear what he says.

Eventually I lose my patience with the Thrush's almost inaudible orders and I'm thinking enough is enough. 'Fuck it! I've had an enough of this. Nobody acknowledge his orders until he does as we ask and speaks up so we can hear him properly.'

Rob is thinking along the same lines and nods his head. 'Right, sounds like a plan. It's not as if we haven't asked him before.'

Thrush mutters something inaudible and there is deliberately no response from Rob and I. A few seconds go by and again he mumbles something and again there is no response. After the third time he comes steaming back into the wheelhouse with an angry expression on his face.

'For God's sake, people,' he says furiously. 'Will somebody ROGER ME!!'

Rob and I look at each other and the sight of the human panda-eyed goon, with his fly open, screaming for somebody to 'roger' him is too much to bear. We immediately collapse into fits of hysterical laughter. After we just about manage to stop laughing, we explain again that we couldn't hear his orders. He finally takes the hint and speaks up and he berths the yacht without a hitch, but orders Rob and I to his cabin for another bollocking.

'I've got the sneakiest feeling we're in for a toasting again, mate,' says Rob.

'Yeah, I know, but it was worth it. Anyway, fuck him, we've asked him a million times but the prick doesn't listen. Just let me do the talking.'

Five minutes pass and Zecky comes to the bridge to tell us that Thrush wants us in his cabin – now.

'Come on then,' I tell Rob. 'Let's face the music.'

We walk into his cabin where he's sitting at his desk fuming with anger. His face is red with rage and his eyes are even redder from trying to rub the polish off.

'Close the door, NOW!' he shouts, stabbing the table with

his index finger. Rob and I step inside and do as we're told. 'WHO DID IT?!' Thrush shouts.

I decide to play the idiot and look confused. 'Who did what, Captain?'

'Don't take me for a bloody fool! You know what!'

'Sorry, Captain, I don't have a clue what you're talking about.'

'Who put black shoe polish on the binoculars?!'

'Shoe polish… around the binoculars?'

'YES! Shoe polish!'

'I've got no idea, Captain.'

'Don't lie to me. Just admit it. You did it, didn't you?!'

'I beg your pardon, but are you insinuating that *I'm* guilty? Based on what?'

'I want a full apology from you this instant or I'm on to the office about this and I guarantee you that you'll get a written warning.'

'On what grounds? Your opinion? I'm afraid you'll need to do better than that Captain. If you have any proof then I'd be glad to see it.'

He stands up and points his finger at me. 'In fact, forget the office – I'm giving you a warning right now.'

'Right, I've had enough of these accusations. I'm going to prove to you that it wasn't me.' I take the phone and dial a friend's number.

'What are you doing?' demands Thrush.

'Clearing my name.'

Even Rob has a confused look on his face. The phone rings a few times and I put it on loudspeaker so we can all hear. After a few moments my friend Zak answers.

'Hi Zak, it's me.'

'Now then, bitch… how's it going?'

'So-so, mate… sorry to bother you again.'

'You're OK, mate, I'm just on the crapper teasing out a monster turd. Feels like I'm trying to pass a brick!!'

Rob and I start to chuckle but we try our best to remain composed. 'That's delightful Zak, but listen. I haven't time to talk at the moment. I'm in a bit of a situation. Could you just tell me what you found on your new binoculars when they got delivered to your yacht last week?'

'Binoculars? Oh yeah, the eye pieces had boot polish on them. Some guy in the factory must have been a practical joker.'

'Thanks, mate. I've got to go now but I'll speak to you soon.'

'OK, mate, catch you later.'

'Cheers.'

I switch off the phone and go over to Thrush, looking him in the eye. 'I believe you owe me an apology, Captain,' I tell him with a very serious face.

'I'm not apologising for anything.'

'Right, I've had my lot of this. *I'm* calling the office now, and I'm going to tell them exactly what has happened and get them to make you apologise. I've even got a witness. If you want to go through that, then that's your choice.' I pick up the phone and start to dial the office.

Thrush grabs the phone furiously. He turns his back on me and mumbles, 'Oh, very well then… I apologise.'

'I'm sorry, what did you say?'

Again he mumbles his apology.

'Well, turn around and look me in the eye when you say it, so at least I know you mean it.' I know I'm pushing it, but I'm having too much fun. Thrush slowly turns around, makes eye contact with me for a split second and apologises again very quietly. It obviously kills him to say it.

'What about him?' I say, pointing at Rob.

'I didn't blame *him*!' says Thrush, sounding exasperated.

'No, but you would've done if I hadn't proved to you it wasn't us.'

'No, I wouldn't.'

'Yes, you would.'

'I wouldn't!'

'Well, why did you bring him in here then?'

Thrush is now going purple with frustration. 'OK... OK, I apologise to you as well Robert.'

'That's OK, Captain, everyone makes mistakes,' says Rob.

'Right then, we're all square,' I say, opening the door to leave. 'But I won't forget this in a hurry, Captain. Anyway, we've got work to do, so we had better get on.'

He's very frustrated now so he turns his back on us and looks out of the window to stew in his own embarrassment. 'Yes, OK... carry on.'

Rob and I walk out and close the door behind us. I look over my shoulder at Rob as we quickly walk down the alleyway and Rob's already looking at me with a big grin on his face. We don't say a word until we're out of earshot.

'What a *fucking* goon!' I whoop.

Rob starts to shake his head in disbelief. 'Fuck me, boss, you've got some front. They don't call you Teflon for nothing, do they? But who was the guy on the phone?'

'Just a mate who owed me a favour. I told him what I was going to do half an hour before. Although why he felt the need to tell me about his turd at that particular moment I'll never know!'

CHAPTER 12

PRIAPISM

The sun is just setting and the marina is starting to bustle with people and crew strolling along the quay. 'Have you seen the amount of booze up on the barbeque deck?' I say to Tom.

'Quite a bit is there?'

'I'm amazed the yacht's still floating, mate! The boss'll be down in about an hour. I've just been told he'll have about twelve to fifteen guests. Thrush says he sounds as if he's pissed.'

'If I wasn't so tired I'd look forward to it,' Tom says, rubbing his eyes.

'I wonder who's coming with him. When we dropped him off there was only about seven blokes.'

'I bet you he brings some chicks on board.'

'Nah, he wouldn't risk losing all his millions.'

'Yes, he would! He's pissed and we all know what he's like after a few. The wife's away out of town, I think. When the cat's away, and all that.'

Zecks walks on to the quay to have a word with us. 'Hey you two, how's it going?'

'Not too bad – how's your good self?'

'I've been rushing round like a blue-arsed fly trying to get everything sorted for his lordship tonight. Chef's sweating his knackers off in the galley, making his favourite nibbles. I think he'll be more interested in the bubbly though, to be honest.'

'That doesn't surprise me. He's been at it all afternoon in the clubhouse and hotel after his round of golf. I bet he's in a right state. Where do you want me to take them when they arrive?'

'Just bring them up to the barbeque deck where the food and booze is. Oh, and by the way, here are his epilepsy pills. Make sure he gets a couple down him, because he's prone to fits when he's pissed, as you well know.'

'Fucking hell, yeah I do. Remember last year when I got called out of bed by Jock? His written report was fantastic.'

'What happened?' asks Tom curiously.

'Last year we were cruising the Amalfi coast with the boss and we were anchored just offshore. The boss wanted a Jacuzzi underneath the stars, on his own, and it was getting into the early hours, so he told everyone to go to bed and he'd see them all in the morning. Anyway, Jock gives it an hour and hopes the boss has gone to bed so he can tidy the top deck and clean the area ready for his morning dip. As he walks up to the Jacuzzi he finds the boss lying down, half-naked and semi-conscious on the deck.'

'Was he pissed?'

'He'd had a few, but it was mainly due to a fit. He was OK

in the end because we got him off the yacht to the nearest hospital pretty quickly.'

'So what happened?'

'Well, I had to get Jock to write a full report on the incident for the office but as you know he's not the most educated bloke in the world and he doesn't really know about report etiquette. He's huffing and puffing about having to write it, so I just told him not to worry about it and not try to be clever. I told him to just put it in his own words and at the end put a "lessons learned" statement to help prevent the incident being repeated.'

'So what did he put?'

'I'll tell you exactly what he put. Because it was so funny, I memorised it so I could tell the boys. The really funny thing was, he wasn't *trying* to be funny. He just took what I told him literally. I'll try to do my best vocal impression of Jock, so this is what he wrote, and I quote:

"*I went for a lie down on my bed for an hour and watched* Sex in the City *whilst the boss was having a soak in the tub. I thought, when the boss buggers off to bed I'd clean the Jacuzzi area there and then 'cos I was a bit knackered and I fancied a good kip and a lie in. Anyway, I walk up to the top deck and I find the boss face down, arse up on the deck shaking and looking like a starfish. I thought he was taking the piss so I started to laugh a bit. After a minute or two I figured something was up and I bent over and saw his face. I saw foam coming out of his mouth. My initial impressions were fuck me... the cunt's got RABIES!! I then realised he wasn't arseing around so I went off to get my boss who was around Robbie's cabin having a livener. It turns out the silly sod was having a fit because he hadn't taken his epilepsy tablets. Lesson learned – make sure the boss takes his pills before he starts break dancing!"*

'That was his report before I doctored it. I emailed it to everyone I knew, because he'd taken my instructions so literally but with fantastic results. I don't like to remind him of it because he gets a bit embarrassed.'

Zecky jumps in: 'That's bloody hilarious! I can totally believe Jock did that. Do you remember that really posh dinner we had in Monaco last year? He made what I thought was a belching noise so I turned around and asked him if he had just burped.'

'Oh yeah, I remember.'

'He said of course he hadn't burped – he'd just lifted his leg to let out some gas! It didn't even register that farting is probably worse that belching. I tell you, the boy is a *savage*. Anyway, boys, I've got things to be getting on with so make sure he gets his pills and I'll see you later, OK?'

'No problem, Zecks, and if there is any of the good grub left, can you send some our way? A bit of fresh lobster would go down nicely.'

'Yeah, of course I will, sweetheart. There should be loads left because I've a feeling that they'll only be interested in booze tonight. By the way, where's Tarquin?'

'Oh, he's around somewhere.'

'Does his mummy and daddy know he's playing sailor?'

'I know he's a bit wet behind the gills but he seems a good kid. He's just got very limited life experience but all that's going to go after a few weeks living aboard here with us. His parents won't recognise him when he gets back. I know mine didn't. I take it you don't have any romantic intentions towards the young lad, then, Zecks?'

'I doubt if he even knows what it's for yet.'

An hour or so passes and the Captain receives a phone call telling him Mr Thomas and his guests are on the way. The hotel limo drops them off and it's a very merry bunch who get out. Jock and I are the first to meet and greet as we open the car doors for them.

'Hello Jock! How are you?' asks the boss, as he puts his arm around his shoulders.

'Never better sir. How was the golfing?'

'It was OK, but not as good as the drinks in the clubhouse afterwards. One of the girl caddies fell over and hurt herself on the green.'

'Really, where?' asks Jock.

'Between the first and second hole.'

'Well, that doesn't leave much room for a bandage, does it?'

The boss and his friends find this hilarious and they all slap him on the back.

Tom meets them at the top of the passerelle and invites them to follow him up to the barbeque deck where the food and drink is. They are only up there a matter of seconds when the boss puts on some lively music and they fire straight into the nosh and booze.

His friends are a good mixture of sorts. They're around his age and most of them are businessmen, dressed in slacks and shirts, apart from two in their late twenties who have obviously flown out with their fathers for the ride. They sit on the side of the yacht overlooking the quay, drinking cocktails and loving the attention they're receiving from gawpers on the quay. The boss seems to be enjoying himself with his mates and they're all swapping stories and quaffing champagne.

Then one of the boss's friends turns the music down so he can be heard to make a little speech. 'OK chaps, I just want to say a few words before we all get too ratted. I haven't seen you all for a good few years and it's been fantastic so far. It's great to see you all again and it takes me back to the time when we were kids and used to hang out together. Turning 60 makes you think about your life and what you've done with it, and you realise that you just have to take each day at a time and live every day as if it's your last. I think we're pretty much on the way to doing that tonight! I've had a great life so far and I think I've got a few more years on the clock, although I probably won't think that tomorrow morning. Anyway, I'm getting sick of my own voice now so all that's left to say is I thank you all from the bottom of my heart for turning up and taking the time out to meet up.'

Mr Thomas presents him with a gift-wrapped magnum of vintage champagne and a gold engraved personalised goblet. 'Bloody hell, cheers you big softy,' says the birthday boy. 'I wasn't expecting anything except your company.'

'Well, we've another surprise for you – well, I should say for all of us,' announces the boss. 'We have a group of fine young ladies arriving soon for a little bit of recreation while we're all away from home.'

'I take it what happens on tour stays on tour?' shouts one of the guests.

'Never was a truer word spoken,' says the boss, tapping the side of his nose. A big grin crosses his face and he thrusts his fist in the air before turning the music up and yelling, 'Let's 'av' it, then!'

'When the cat's away, the mice will play, eh?' Jock says to me.

'It looks like it. I had a feeling this was going to happen. But the boss is taking a big fucking risk because you never know who is walking along the quayside with a camera. I can't believe he wants to stay alongside. I'll go and have a quiet word with him.'

I take a walk over to the boss, who is by himself eating a big tiger prawn and smoked salmon, washing it down with champagne.

'All right?' he says. 'How are you doing?'

'I'm OK, sir. Are you having a good time?'

'Champion! Thanks for producing the goods tonight.'

'No problem. Just doing my job, you know that. I see you've got the hiccups there.'

'Yep, too much bubbly. Still, if you can't get pissed with your mates on a day like this, when can you, eh?'

'Exactly.'

'Try a bit of this, it's Loch Carnan smoked salmon – the best you can get, I reckon.'

He hands me a chunk of salmon on a plate and tells me to taste it. 'I get it sent over from the Hebrides once a month. Delicious, eh?'

I shouldn't really be eating on duty but he's offered it to me, so I'll play along. I squeeze lemon juice over the salmon and nod my approval. He winks and hands me a flute of Cristal champagne. The boss is great like that. It's the little things he does that make a big difference, and it only encourages the crew to do that little bit more for him. Last year we had a really busy season and made quite a lot of money for him. To show his appreciation he popped aboard and gave me $4000 in cash to take the crew 'for a drink' for a job well done. The crew really doesn't mind going that extra yard for somebody like that.

I wait for the right moment as the boss takes another bite of his salmon and then I drop the question as delicately as I can. 'Sorry to bother you like this, sir, but I couldn't help but overhear one of the guests say that we're expecting more guests.'

'Yep, that's right.'

He holds my eye contact for a few seconds, but as there is nothing forthcoming I have to prompt him. 'Do they have any, erm, special needs for the visit?'

'Not tonight, but one of them will need a padded seat for their arse tomorrow morning after I've had my wicked way,' he says with a twinkle in his eye. He's made it perfectly obvious now, so I get to the nitty-gritty.

'OK! I'll keep my voice down, sir,' I say, leaning in closer. 'I'm pretty sure I know what you mean.'

He slaps me on the side of his arm. 'Good man! I'm glad we understand each other.'

'How long will they be staying, do you think?'

'Just a few hours.'

I hate to ask him this, but I have to look after his best interests. I just can't imagine his wife will be too chuffed with him if he comes home and gives her a dose of something nasty.

'I take it you're OK for condoms sir? Safety first and all that.'

'Ah, yes... I've got a padded headboard at the ready so at least she won't get a headache.' I can't help but laugh at his attitude when he's clearly playing with fire. 'And don't worry about the condoms, my old mate. I've already got some stashed in my back pocket. Just make sure there is plenty of air freshener around in my room.'

'Air freshener? Why air freshener?'

'For the smell of burning rubber!' he laughs.

'Have we been on the Spanish Fly, sir?' I say, joking.

'No, but at my age you need all the help you can get. I tried some Viagra the other week and I haven't had a hard-on like that since I was in my twenties. You could have hung your coat on it!'

'Sir, just be careful not to take too much. Apparently it's not too good for your ticker and you don't want to end up having a situation like the one I found myself in.'

'Why, what happened?'

'Well, when Viagra first came out I was curious as to its effects, so I bought some. It was around the time when I was on leave from working at sea and most nights I was out on the town, drinking. After a while the booze takes its toll and sometimes I'd have the brewer's droop problem, if I was lucky enough to pull.'

'We've all been there at some time in our lives, mate.'

'I didn't want to miss out on a top night with the boys, either, but at the end of the night I wanted to be up to my nuts in guts. There was the dilemma – stay fairly sober and perform in the sack but not have a really funny evening, or get pissed up with the boys and have a corker of a night.'

'So which one did you choose?'

'I was a bit crazy in those days, sir, so I didn't choose one or the other – I chose both. I didn't want to miss out on a really funny night or a great shag, so I popped some Viagra twenty minutes before jumping into the sack.'

'Did it work?'

'Erm, yeah… a little too well. Even though I was hammered!'

'Why, what happened?'

'I was really sensitive to it and I got a boner like a totem pole. I must have taken too much, because I got priapism.'

'Priapism?'

'When you get an erection but it won't go down!'

'Well, that sounds fucking perfect! I can't imagine anything better that having a fucking great hard-on for an hour or two.'

'Try *nineteen* hours.'

The boss almost chokes on his tiger prawn. 'NINETEEN FUCKING HOURS? I bet she was sore afterwards!'

'Well, it certainly put a smile on her face and a grimace of pain on mine, sir.'

'How did you… you know… deflate it, then?'

'About half a dozen ejaculations, cold showers and a half bottle of Jack Daniels.'

'Fuck me, mate – that's priceless! I always knew there was some reason I hired you!'

'That wasn't the worst of it, though, sir. It was bad enough having a dick that looked like it had been through a mincing machine but I almost lost my job because of it.'

'Your job? Why?'

'Because I was supposed to go to work in the morning but I didn't make it out the house because my stiffy wouldn't go down. I couldn't very well turn up at work doing a wigwam impression, now could I?'

'That's one of the funniest things I've heard, mate. I can't imagine what your boss thought when you told him. What did he say?'

'He almost sacked me! He said I sounded pissed and I told him I was, and why I was, but he found it hard to believe the story, as you can imagine.'

'So how did you prove it too him – or shouldn't I ask?'

'Well, all I could think of at the time was to produce photographic evidence, so I sent him three photos on my phone. One was of the naked girl in bed, one of the packet of Viagra, and one of my stiffy.'

The boss is now laughing so hard it looks like he might choke at any second. 'Did he believe you, then?'

'Well, he said he wasn't a hundred per cent convinced, but he thought it was such an original story he'd let me off. So remember, sir, take it easy on them tonight.'

Mr Thomas finally catches his breath while wiping tears from his eyes. 'I'll bear that in mind. Right, I'm off to join the party. I'll catch you later, Bonk-on Billy!'

'OK, sir, and by the way here are your epilepsy pills. Don't forget to take them, because we don't want you to have another fit and start break-dancing again, do we?'

CHAPTER 13

ESCORT THE ESCORTS

'What was the boss laughing about just then?' Jock asks me.

'I was telling him the story of my Viagra experience. Told him to take it easy on them because of what happened to me.'

'Everyone seems to be enjoying themselves, by the look of things.'

'Yeah, it won't be long before the old boy starts busting some moves before disappearing somewhere quiet for a knee trembler.'

'Are we going to have a bet on the length of time it takes him to go for it, then?'

I jump at the chance of taking a bet with Jock because his past record of unsuccessful bets are exceeded only by the number of verbal warnings and work reprimands he's been given. 'Yeah, OK, you're on, sunshine!'

'Fifty euros says he'll disappear with her within the hour. Let's make it interesting – we should make it at least a hundred.'

'It's your money you're throwing away, Jock, but if you want to make it a hundred, so be it. It's all the more beer vouchers for me. So you reckon an hour do you?'

'Yep.'

'No way, mate,' I say, shaking my head. 'He's got guests here. He'll want to make sure they feel welcome and he'll want to enjoy himself with them,'

'Yeah, I know, but they've been brought here for a reason, and since it's his yacht and he's entertaining, my guess is he'll lead by example and start up the proceedings, so to speak.' Jock is watching the boss intently to try and get some idea of what's going through his mind.

'I still reckon he'll have a laugh for a couple of hours first before releasing the meat,' I say confidently.

'OK, whatever, but just make sure that you don't go spending your money, because my pocket will be bulging tonight, my old china.'

'Bollocks, I can feel it in my bones. I reckon I'm on a winner here. Let's face it, your past history of wins is pretty shoddy, isn't it?'

'That's all going to change tonight, matey.'

'All right, let's make it interesting. You know that hot chilli sauce on the table in the mess room?'

'Yeah, I fucking love it.'

'Up your nose?'

'Eh?'

'Whoever loses has to snort a half capful of that up each nostril.'

Jock's smiling face is a little more serious now. 'Are you serious?' he asks nervously.

'Yeah.'

'That stuff really hurts. When I went to sea on a ship and passed over the Equator for the first time, the crew had a crossing-the-line ceremony for the first-timers. I was only a kid and they got me shit-faced, tied me face down on top of the bar table, covered me with oil and stuck chicken feathers all over me. Then the rotten bastards poured a whole bottle of chilli sauce down the crack of my arse.'

'I bet that hurt, didn't it?' I ask, grimacing.

'I screamed the fucking house down. There's a photo around somewhere of this young, naked, screaming kid running up the alleyway looking like a plucked chicken.'

'So, Jock, the question you have to ask yourself is, are you a man or a mouse?' I'm deliberately teasing him because Jock will never back away from a bet, especially if it's worth a hundred euros.

'Nah, I'll do it, because it isn't me who's going to be sniffing it, pal.'

'All right then, bud. It's a bet! Now back to business.'

We take a look over at one of the boss's guests trying ever harder to worm his way into one of the girl's knickers, and it's obvious she's having none of it. He's boring as hell and he keeps readjusting his tie and pulling his sports jacket over his sweaty shirt in a bid to cover the rolls of fat hanging over his belt.

The girl looks over at us and you can tell she wants Jock and I to do something to help. I give her a wink and tell Jock to get her away from the sofa and into the party crowd when he sees me drop the tray. I take a food tray with some nibbles on it and walk over to offer the bloke some, then dump the tray and its contents on his lap, making it look like an accident.

'Jesus Christ!' he shouts. 'What the hell are you doing?'

'I'm very sorry, sir. The tray just slipped out of my hand.'

'You shouldn't be so bloody clumsy.'

'All I can do is apologise, sir. Let me escort you to the men's room and we'll get you cleaned off. There's a hand drier in there and your shirt should dry in a few minutes.'

He makes his apologies to the long-suffering girl and follows me to the men's room. Jock then goes straight over and rescues her. 'We saw you were in trouble so we thought we'd help you out,' he tells her. 'Hope you don't mind.'

'Mind? You both deserve a medal.'

'I'll take you over to speak to another group, so it looks like you're mingling.'

'Thanks for that. I owe you one.'

'No problem.' Jock takes her over to the dancefloor and she starts to dance with a few of her 'associates'. All of the guys watch as they dance and whisper to each other. The girls are as thick as thieves but doing the job. She's obviously formulating a plan to rid herself of 'Mr Blobby' and making arrangements for back up should he or some other boring arsehole bother her again. A few of the pissed-up guests down their drinks and make their way to the centre of the floor where the girls go to work and start grinding on them and buffering their egos. It's pretty funny to watch.

The boss gets unsteadily out of his seat and eagerly jumps in to the party, busting his moves – there's leg-strutting and arm-pointing all over the place. He's grinning from ear to ear as a couple of girls join him and he's got his pissed-up eyes locked on to the ample cleavage of the girl in front of him.

Jock and I share a smile as Mr Blobby comes back out and notices that his girl is no longer there. He spots her on the floor and shuffles on and starts dancing within her group. I say 'dancing' in the loosest possible way. By the way he's going, he could be having a seizure. He's invented a new dance that is somewhere between body-popping and punk-pogo.

I look at my watch and there's around ten minutes to go until Jock's hour is up and he loses the bet. I point over at him to get his attention. I point to my watch and then to my throat, making a cutting gesture before pointing back to him. Jock understands straight away what I mean and he starts to look fidgety, looking over at the boss. Another ten minutes and he has lost the bet!

After about twenty minutes, the guests – apart from the energetic younger lads – start to filter off the dance floor and flop down on the sofas. More drinks are quaffed and a few of the guests are starting to look pretty cosy with some of the girls. One is sat opposite where Jock is standing and she's wearing a very, very short skirt. He leans over to me and cups his hand to block out the music.

'If there are three types of mini skirt, one being mini, two being micro, and the third being "don't bend over", then that's definitely the third,' he jokes.

'I know, mate, but don't be so bloody obvious. You're not the most subtle guy.'

'I can't help it. With all this skirt around I feel like a dog with two dicks.'

'Jock you *always* feel like a dog with two dicks. You want

to calm it down, my old son. You'll wear yourself out, the way you live the fast life.'

'Live fast, die young and leave a good-looking corpse. Anyway, you can talk.'

'Well you certainly walk the walk, Jock, I'll give you that. I don't know how you stay in shape. You live on bar snacks, smoke like a chimney and drink like a fish. You must have internal organs as tough as tyres.'

'Genetically gifted, me, boss,' he boasts, flexing his arm.

* * * *

After about half an hour, the flirting between the guests and the escorts gets carried to another level. The two young lads are smooching with girls on the dancefloor and their hands are straying all over their bodies. A few of the old boys have taken this as the green light, and all over the back end of the yacht couples are having fun. The boss is sat with his mate whose birthday it is, and two of the girls are dancing and laughing in front of them. The men's facial expressions have gone from cheeky grins and smiles to concentrated carnal lust. The birthday boy leans over to the boss and says something to him and the boss nods in agreement. Moments later, he and the boss take the girls by the hand and head towards the boss's cabin on the next deck. That's probably why Mr Thomas chose the sofa nearest the door to the lounge, so as not to draw attention when they succumbed to their desires.

All is well so far, so Jock and I leave Zecks and her crew to attend to the other guests. We tell Zecks who's gone where, who's with whom, and who's drinking what, then Jock and I join Rob and Tom in the crew room for some supper. Zecky's come up trumps tonight – she's laid on lobster, champagne, tiger prawns and duck cooked rare that the crew love, not to mention cake, so everyone's happy.

'How's it all going up there boys?' Tom asks as we sit down at the feast.

'Everything you'd expect, mate. There'll be a few sore heads tomorrow.'

Jock joins us at the dinner table. 'Not to mention a few sore cocks if they keep heading the way they're going.'

All is quiet in the mess room as we all take a well-earned break, tucking in to the food and catching up on a bit of TV, until the ship's mobile suddenly starts ringing loudly.

'Who the hell is that at this hour?' I think to myself. I wave over to Rob who's at the end of the table. 'Get the phone, mate.'

'Hello… Rob speaking.'

The voice at the other end is quite difficult to hear because of the reception within the confines of the steel yacht, but Rob can just about discern a quiet, well-spoken female voice at the other end.

'Hello Robert, this is Mrs Thomas speaking.' Rob's face drops like someone's just told him he's got an hour to live. He stops chewing his food, looks over at me with terror in his eyes and mouths: 'IT'S THE BOSS'S MISSUS!!'

Jock and I look at each other in disbelief.

'WHAT?'

We can hear the voice on the phone repeating: 'Hello? Hello? Robert, are you there?'

'Stall her, for fuck's sake!' Jock whispers urgently.

'Errrr… hello Mrs Thomas, how can I help?' He jabs his finger at the crew room door, indicating to Jock to close it so the sound of the music is muffled.

'Yes, this is Mrs Thomas. I've just been to see a show with some friends and we aren't far from the port, so rather than going back to the hotel I thought it would be easier to stay the night aboard.'

Rob takes a big gulp and rubs his hand through his hair wildly before responding. 'You're coming down, tonight?!'

'Yes, me and a friend. We'll be going straight to bed, so no need to wake Zecky.'

'Do you need picking up, Mrs Thomas?'

'No, no… we are only about twenty minutes away. I'm just calling up to find out what berth you're on, so the driver can pull up to the passerelle.'

'We're at Berth 13, Mrs Thomas.'

'OK… I'll see you in or around twenty minutes then, Robert.' Before Rob has a chance to say anything, Mrs Thomas hangs up.

Rob looks over at Jock and me, his face as white as a sheet. 'She's coming down.'

'When?' we respond in tandem.

'NOW!'

'NOW! You're fucking shitting me!' I say, leaping to my feet.

'RIGHT NOW?' cries Jock.

Rob is now looking exasperated. 'Yes, Jock – right fucking now! I think we established that in Act One!'

'How long have we got and who else is coming?' I ask.

'Twenty minutes – her and a friend.'

'Right, everybody calm down and do exactly as I say, because I need all of your very best to get the boss out of this one. Do you know what will happen if she comes aboard and she finds all these escorts here?'

Jock is now rocking from side to side and blinking manically. 'OH FUCK! THIS IS REEEALLY BAD!'

'No shit, Sherlock. Right, Jock, this is where your direct personality will, for once, pay dividends. I don't care how you do it, but get the escorts to the forward deck, quick sharp. And by quick sharp I mean like YESTERDAY! I'll turn off the lights to the forward deck so it will be in near darkness.

'The plan is to get the girls away by lowering them down in the boat into the harbour. Then you can drop them off at another pier around the corner. We can't afford to have them being seen coming off the yacht onto an illuminated quay and then walking all the way up to the gate. If Mrs Thomas bumps into them she'll put two and two together and then we're all royally up shit creek without a paddle. It wouldn't surprise me if she's deliberately checking up. Jock, you go and get it sorted. Tell them we've had a bomb threat and we need to get them off then leave it at that.'

'Don't worry boss, I'll have them up on the forward deck ready faster than you can say fuck me sideways,' says Jock.

* * * *

Tom and Rob start the forward boat crane and slew the boat out ready for Jock and the girls. I radio Zecky and tell her what's happening and brief her to quickly organise her crew to put new bedsheets down in the rooms that have been used and to tell her crew that, should they be asked, nobody except the boss's male friends were on board tonight. She's then to stand by the passerelle and keep a look-out up the quay for the car bringing Mrs Thomas. As soon as she see's it, she's to radio me.

'Every second counts, Zecks, so your girls are going to have to move like there's no tomorrow.'

'I think you're right. I'm on it!'

'Good. By the way, Zecks, when you get to the passerelle use the remote control and lift it clear of the quay so she won't be able to board the yacht. I'll send an engineer down to the stern to make it look like there's a problem and he's fixing it. It may give us a few valuable minutes. When the boat is clear I'll do a couple of whistles down the radio. When you hear this give the engineer the wink and he'll lower it so she can get aboard.'

'Cool.'

'Ha! Cool isn't the word I'd use, Zecks, more like pressure cooker meltdown hot, but I know what you mean. Right, I'm going to have to burst my way into the boss's room and get him and his mate. They were last seen going in there with two of the escorts.'

'Rather you than me, matey!'

I'm not relishing what I'm going to have to do next. God only knows what I'm going to see when I open the door. However, it may not be as bad as Jock's little hotel escapade a few nights ago. That one would take definitely take some beating.

As I run down the alleyway to the room, I see Jock running up from the other end, holding onto the arms of two girls who are looking very nervous. Jock on the other hand is grinning and smiling and clearly loving the drama of it all.

'I was BORN for this!' he shouts as he runs past.

The door to the boss's room is right ahead of me and as I approach it I can hear music coming from within. I stop for a moment with my hand on the door handle, catch my breath and gather my thoughts. Then I knock rapidly and enter the room – I'm not expecting the boss and his mate to be playing Scrabble.

The room is gently lit with candles and a dim corner lamp: just enough light to keep the ambience cosy. The music is loud and ballsy. The boss and his mate are sat in comfy armchairs, drinking Scotch and getting lap dances from the girls, who are down to black lace stockings and suspenders, which they're starting to peel away to the music. I really don't want to interrupt them but I've got to. As I open the door the bright light from the alleyway shines through and they all look towards me, squinting as their eyes adjust.

'Sir, I need a word,' I shout over to the boss.

'What? Now!?' he says, looking at me in astonishment. 'I'm kind of in the middle of something here.'

'Afraid so, sir. It's kind of important.'

'Oh, I'm sure it can wait till the morning. Close the door on the way out, mate.'

In the past I've never pushed the boundaries with the boss, and I would never dare, but tonight there is no other option. There's just no time, and so much is on the line. I stride purposefully up to him, pushing my way past the two girls. I stand over him, and tell him the bad news.

'Sir, we've a bit of a crisis on our hands. Your wife is expected in the next ten to fifteen minutes, or maybe even sooner. I've got a plan, but there's no time to explain. We need to move all the girls to the front deck, right this second.'

His face drops in terror and his eyes widen so much I

think his eyeballs will drop on to the floor. He's already starting to breathe faster with panic as he leaps out of his chair and runs over to the volume control of the sound system. He quickly turns it right down and switches the overhead halogen lights on.

'GET THE FUCK OUT, NOW!!' he shouts, pointing the girls towards the door. I tell them to pick up their clothes and then I grab their arms and push them through the door.

Jock is running back down the alleyway towards me as the radio in his pocket crackles. 'A car is at the gate at the end of the wharf. If it's her, she'll be here in a few minutes,' Zecky reports breathlessly.

'Calm down, Zecky, just stick to the game plan and keep the passerelle up so she can't board. I think we'll only need another three or four minutes. Tom, are you there? How are you getting on up forward with the boat?'

'There are two more girls to get in and then I think we're good to launch.'

'Cool. The boss's wife will be at the passerelle any minute, so when the boat is in the water don't use much engine power so she can't hear it. She won't be able to see the forward end of the yacht where you launch from because of the other yachts rafted up alongside us. As long as she can't get up the passerelle we'll be home free.'

'Gotcha!'

Jock ushers the two half-naked girls up the alleyway, but as he's running with them he's looking over his shoulder and watching their tits bounce instead of watching where he's going. After a few moments he disappears off the top of a flight of stairs at the end of the alleyway and there is loud crash as he plummets into the fire door at the bottom. Within seconds he's back up to the top of the stairs, giggling, and carries on where he left off. I make a mad dash to the lounge area and give the place a quick inspection. I pick up a stray handbag and a lipstick on the table and pass them to the stewardess to throw them in the boat. All of the boss's mates are next to the bar wondering what the hell is going on, so I quickly brief them and ask them to sit down and act normally.

I radio to Rob: 'Are you missing any girls?'

'The last one is just getting in, boss.'

'OK. When she's in, lower the boat to the water and quickly take them round the corner to the quay. Drop them off and tell them to wait in the bar across the road. I'll send a taxi to pick them up and take them wherever they need to go.'

'Cool.'

Moments later I hear the boat being launched and I head back to calm the boss. 'Right sir, the girls are off, your mates have been briefed and there's no evidence left lying around. Your wife will be none the wiser, but she'll suspect something if you're acting weird and you're flustered. Now, take your shirt off and give it to me.'

'Shirt... why?'

'Lipstick on the collar, and you smell like a perfume factory.'

'Oh, right! Shit!'

'The main things are taken care of. We just have to sort the details, because it's the details that will sink the ship, so to speak. Jump in the shower and scrub yourself from head to toe, and if she asks where you are I'll tell her you're freshening up from playing golf. As far as she's concerned all you've done today is play golf then come back here for some drinks with the boys, OK? Right, I'll see you on the aft deck in ten minutes. I've delayed things long enough, I'll have to let her on.'

'Christ, if you must,' he says, still looking flustered.

'By the way, I'd make that a cold shower if I were you, sir – looks like you need a bit of cooling down.'

I leave the room and dispose of his shirt in the crew waste bin. I give a couple of whistles down the radio and walk aft to meet Mrs Thomas.

Jock meets me half way along and we walk down together. 'What a tangled web we weave, hey boss?' he grins.

'It's not over yet, mate. Hope for the best but plan for the worst.'

As we arrive at the back of the yacht, Mrs Thomas is just stepping aboard with her friend. Zecky stalls her for a few minutes, handing the women cooling lemon flannels fresh from the refrigerator, then keeps her chatting about the opera. Every time she looks like she's going to walk into the accommodation, Zecky asks another question, playing for time. Ten minutes pass and suddenly the boss walks down the stairway looking as cool as a cucumber.

'Hello, dear! I wasn't expecting you.'

'The opera was closer to here than driving back home, so I thought we'd stay here tonight,' she tells him. 'How was your evening?'

'Oh, quiet. Just quiet drinks with a few friends after a game of golf,' he says, leading her away to the lounge.

CHAPTER 14

INITIATION BY FIRE

It's 11am the following day and all the tidying is done from the night before. The guests have been fed and watered and sent on their way, happy enough. A good time was had by all, even when *she* turned up. She only hung around with her friend for half an hour then went to bed, leaving the boss and the boys to get drunk and re-live old times. It's the most excitement they've had in years!

Mr Thomas and his wife are up early and all seems to be well. They're in the Jacuzzi, soaking up the morning sun and they both seem happy. The boss is looking a little shabby but he's sipping one of Zecky's miracle-working Bloody Marys with an aspirin, so all will be well shortly. Rob's on the quay polishing the Bentley, and the chauffeur is having a fried breakfast in the crew room before taking Mr Thomas and the wife back to Monaco, leaving in about an hour.

'Bloody hell! That was a close one last night,' Tom says, shaking his head.

'Yeah, I know, mate, but it's over with. Part and parcel of

the job, I'm afraid. I'm glad Tar was tucked up safe and sound in his stinker though. I can't imagine he'd have been able to handle the pressure all that well, being a first-timer and all.'

'He'd have probably shit his pants, eh?' chuckles Jock.

'Well, who could blame him? We almost did, and we've been doing the job for years.'

'You're not wrong there. The adrenaline was surging and I couldn't stop giggling,' says Jock.

'I noticed, mate. What was all that about? I take it that was nervous laughter?'

'I don't know, really. Every time I get nervous I just seem to giggle. I guess it's my fucked-up way of dealing with pressure. It's dropped me in the shit a million times.'

'How so?'

'See this scar on the back of my head?'

'Yep.'

'That was my old man. He came back one night after the pub and his dinner wasn't cooked and waiting for him. One thing led to another, as it usually did when he was pissed, and he started to batter Mum. He hated people laughing at him, so all I could think of to get him away from her was to giggle at his drunken attempt to knock her head off. I was hurting inside every time he hit her, but he was a big guy and I was only a nipper, so I'd no chance on a one-to-one physical with him.'

'Bloody hell, Jock ! You've never told me this.'

'Yeah, well… anyway, I started laughing at him and he'd turn his attention to me and not Mum.'

'So you got a pounding?'

'Yeah, one of many, but the pain was nothing compared to Mum getting punched.'

I can't help but give the big guy a hug and a punch on the shoulder. 'So many people take you the wrong way, mate. If only they knew what makes you tick rather than the public image. There aren't many people who would do that, especially at that age. I know you fuck up and give me some headaches with your antics but you're a good egg inside. People just need to look a little deeper where you're concerned.'

'I don't care, mate. The people that matter don't mind and the people that mind don't matter.'

'Wise words and you're right.'

I've always known Jock was a good 'un. When I look him deep in his eyes I see no hidden agenda whatsoever, just pureness. That's very rare in this world. There's an ancient pearl of wisdom that says that 'the nail that stands out gets battered' and that's Jock, in both meanings of the word! He does stand out because he's different. If you'd had the life he's had, wouldn't you? Basic he is, but he has a pure heart and an endearing, coltish nature.

* * * *

I go down to the crew room for some breakfast and I brief the Captain on what happened last night. He hadn't been around because he was in bed when it all kicked off and I didn't have time to wake him. He'd have been half-asleep and clueless anyway. That's one of the things that annoys everyone about this goon. He gets uptight and annoyed about tiny insignificant things, then goes to bed when the boss comes aboard. If he was half the Captain he thinks he is he'd be on deck with his crew getting stuck in. To be fair, though, the crew are glad he isn't. If I or any of the crew have to speak to him twice a day it's twice too many.

The quickest way to make an absolute fortune would be to buy Thrush for what he's worth and sell him for what he *thinks* he's worth. His inability to think outside the box is pretty entertaining. If it isn't written down in the rule book he's fucked. God help us if he had to think on his feet and make a spur of the moment decision. The job would go to rat shit.

After the boss has had his Jacuzzi and he's feeling human again, he seeks me out. 'Hey, mate! I've got to thank you for saving my bacon last night,' he says, putting his arm around my shoulders. 'That was quick thinking and you earned every dollar of that huge salary I pay you.'

'It's not nearly big enough, boss,' I tell him jokingly. 'I felt every day of my 35 years in last night's little escape and evasion exercise.'

'Oh, come on now. A young lad like you can handle it.'

'It's not the age – it's the mileage, boss, and last night you put another fifty thousand miles on my clock!' I say, gasping for effect.

'I must admit I was shitting bricks myself there for a minute. I honestly thought I was done for. My arse was twitching more than a rabbit when a ferret gets put down its warren.'

'Well, that makes two of us, sir. All I kept thinking was half of your millions going up in smoke in the divorce court. You'd need a lawyer that not only knew the law inside out but also knew the *judge*. That could've been the most expensive shag in history!'

'All's well that ends well, thanks to you and your crew, so here's a little something to say thank you.' The boss hands me a big envelope full of cash. 'I trust you'll spread the wealth, mate. Make sure everyone gets their fair share and make bloody sure they don't mention anything to anyone else about last night.'

'Our lips are sealed – guaranteed. You don't have to do this though,' I say, holding out the envelope.

'No really... fill your boots. You all deserve it.'

'Second thoughts – yes, we fucking do. I think we deserve a pint or ten. Based on the fact that we probably saved you millions in the divorce court, I don't feel too bad about accepting a little extra this time. I'll need the extra cash for a new ticker if you keep this up!'

The boss laughs and I can see he is happy to make the bonus payment. 'Another thing I'd like to do for you all is to let you have the use of the Wally power for the weekend when you aren't chartering. Just bring it back in one piece, that's all I ask.'

I can barely believe my ears. Personal use of a Wally yacht! Now that *is* a gift. He uses it as a weekend boat sometimes because it's more compact and great for getting into the smaller berths and jetties. In my eyes she's without a doubt one of the sexiest modern power yachts you can lay your hands on. His is 118 feet long and made of reflective metal from bow to stern. She's got all the comforts of home in the interior but also has some serious grunt. Three main engines kick out 5600hp each. She's the ultimate as far as I'm concerned and if I had the money, no question, this is the yacht I'd buy. With a futuristic design she's like something out of *Star Wars*. Having a free weekend in one of these is on a par with a go-kart driver being let loose with a Formula 1 car.

An hour later I gather all the crew to the after deck to see the boss and his wife off. Jock takes the luggage to the Bentley, then opens the door and gently helps Mrs Thomas in. She likes the fuss but the boss is the opposite. He can't be doing with 'all that bollocks'. We wave them off and as soon as they're gone we start the yacht's main engines and let go from the quay. Once we're out of the harbour we make a south-easterly course for Porto Cervo in Sardinia to meet up again with the Russian guests.

It's about 150 miles to the Bonifacio Strait, the stretch of water between Corsica and Sardinia. It will take the yacht around fourteen hours to get there at cruising speed. We could make it more quickly if we went at full speed, but for every extra knot or two of speed, you burn an extra third in fuel. For that, it's hardly worth the expense.

Tar is on duty in the wheelhouse for the crossing. It's getting a bit bumpy out there on the ocean and the yacht is pitching and rolling in the swell. Tar had arrived at the wheelhouse ten minutes before the watch, ready for Tom to hand over to us. Jock also turns up, holding a sandwich the size of a proverbial doorstep.

'Right then, Tar,' I say, 'first things first – make us all a coffee. I'm still half-asleep.'

'OK, how do you take it?'

'Up the arse,' shouts Jock from the other side of the bridge.

'Very funny, wiseguy. Sharp as a razor. Tar, I like mine NATO standard, mate.'

'Erm... I'm not sure what that means exactly.'

'Milk and two sugars. Jock likes his coffee like he likes his women – hot, black, wet and sweet.'

'You know it makes sense,' says Jock.

Tom begins handing over the watch – including the course and speed and traffic situation – and Tar is listening intently. There's usually a handover sheet with about twenty different checks to make and pass on to the relieving officer. However, Tom's handover usually consists of the latest joke he's heard, what stupid fucking questions Thrush has been asking him, and what the latest football scores are. Today's handover from Tom consists of the following:

1) Who has the best tits – Carmen Electra or Lucy Pinder? (two minutes)

2) Why is belly button fluff always blue? (thirty seconds)

3) What is Tarquin's punishment to be if he doesn't memorise certain collision regulation rules? (three minutes)

4) How easy it would be to hijack a private yacht and nick the cash from the safe whilst at sea (ten minutes)

5) What's the point of eating sweetcorn if it comes out the same way as it goes in? (thirty seconds)

After discussing these five relevant and important issues, Tom decides to leave us all in peace. Jock, Tar and I are alone and we discuss what Tar's punishment will be if he doesn't remember his test of the collision regulations.

'It's like this, Tar,' we tell him. 'If you're going up for your oral examination soon, you're going to have to learn the collision regulations thoroughly, as well as a million other things. Some regulations you'll have to learn verbatim. One thing is guaranteed, mate: if you fuck up on the collision regulations or buoyage in front of the Marine and Coastguard Agency examiner, your ass is grass. Some things you can screw up and he'll let you get away with it, but those two are critical because you can run the ship aground if you don't know them.'

'How many rules are there, then?' asks Tar.

'There are thirty-eight rules and four annexes, so there's a lot to learn. You've not only got to know what they actually say, but also *how* to use them. There's no time like the present, so since you're up here as look-out, you might as well learn Rule 6. That's the look-out rule. It's probably the shortest rule of the lot, but it's an important one. You've got twenty minutes to memorise it or you'll be punished by Jock here.'

'Punished?'

'Of course. When I first went to sea we lost privileges if we couldn't remember rules come question time. That usually meant stopping our beer allowance for a few days. I'm not going to do that to you because you look like you need a beer to loosen up a bit. However, Jock and I had a curry earlier, so I think farting on your head would be sufficient for a fuck-up.'

'What do you reckon, Jock?'

'Couldn't agree more but it has to be bare arse cheeks to face,' says Jock.

'Well, that goes without saying – is there any other way?'

'That's agreed then.'

'What about if he fucks up on a really important rule? I reckon he gets the metre-long wooden ruler across his arse.'

'I concur. That's sorted then. Right, Tar, Rule 6, verbatim, twenty minutes, and the clock starts now.'

Jock and I go out on the bridge wing for a cigarette and have a giggle at Tar trying to memorise the words to the rule. 'Initiation by fire, eh, Jock?' I say. 'To be fair though, if he can keep his head and remember everything with the thought of what we're going to do to him, he'll breeze the exam. It's better than stopping the beer tap, because you need one after a hard day's work.'

'You're right not stopping his beer, boss – that's a bit too cruel.'

'I wouldn't dream of it. Anyway, if I was going to stop anyone's it would be yours, sunshine. That way I might get some peace and quiet.'

After twenty minutes or so Jock stands in front of Tar and starts loosening his trousers with a big grin on his face.

'What time are we on, Jock?' I shout from the bridge wing.

Jock is humming the *Countdown* clock tune as he's unzipping himself: 'Doooo doo da do, doooo doo da do, da da da... do do do do DO DO DO DOOOOO!!!!'

'Times up, Tar. Let's have it,' I say, clapping my hands as Tar looks on nervously.

'Oh, come on – this isn't fair. How do you expect me to learn it under this sort of pressure?'

'This is nothing to what you'll feel in the exam room. Now let's have it: what part of the collision regulations is it and what section?'

'Erm... Part B, the Steering and Sailing rules.'

'Good start! What section is it?'

'Erm... Section 1.'

'So far, so good, mate. You might have to zip yourself up again, Jock. Right – crunch time... and I want the rule verbatim. Any fuck-ups and I let Jock's performing rectum loose on you!'

'Oh, bloody hell! Errrr, right... *"Every vessel shall at all times maintain a lookout by sight and hearing as well as all available means appropriate to the prevailing circumstances and conditions, so as to make a full... a full... appraisal... erm... so... so as to make a full appraisal of... a full appraisal."* Oh shit!'

Jock starts laughing loudly and drops his trouser to his ankles.

'Oh, look, there's no need for this,' says Tar quickly moving away from Jock.

Jock shuffles after him in hot pursuit. 'You can run but you can't hide, Tar. The rusty tea towel holder is puckered and ready.'

Jock manages to manoeuvre him into the corner of the wheelhouse in between the radar and the radio station. He backs in to him, arse first, and then grabs the back of his head before shoving it tight up against his hairy cheeks. 'I believe the ending you were looking for, Tarquin Worthington-Smythe, was *"and a full appraisal of the situation and of the risk of collision"*,' he says loudly, before letting go an almighty fart in Tar's face. Even from several metres away it sounds loud.

A long groan comes from Tar just as Thrush comes round the corner to check on everything. 'WHAT THE HELL'S GOING ON HERE?!' he bawls, palms outstretched.

'Just training the cadet, Captain,' Jock explains, without missing a beat.

The Captain takes another look at Tar with his face next to Jock's hairy arse. He doesn't really know how to deal with this, so he rolls his eyes and walks back out. Jock's face goes crimson with the straining then he lets rip with another almighty fart. As he does, his face changes from smiley to serious, as if he's just been caught off guard. He thinks for a moment, then nods his head and goes for number three.

'What were you thinking just then, Jock?' I ask.

'Thought I'd followed through there for a second,' he says laughing.

'Well, be careful because he doesn't need any more freckles, mate.'

'Noooo, I don't!' snuffles Tar.

'All right, Jock, let him go. That's the first lesson out the way.'

Jock releases Tar while sniffing the air. 'Fuck me, that was a ripe one!'

'Judging from Tar's watery eyes he doesn't doubt it, mate. Not to worry, Tar – you'll get your own back soon enough. Jock lost a bet last night and he has to inhale some chilli after the watch.'

The navigation watch passes fairly quickly and I send Tar down to the engine room for some false errands such as 'rubber nails', 'glass hammers', 'golden nuggets' and 'long stands', much to everyone's amusement.

It also comes on foggy for an hour or two and we can't see more than twenty metres ahead. I start a close watch on the radars, slow down and complete all the usual wheelhouse checks for doing a blind pilotage in thick fog. This is important because you can't see any other ships around so there is a greater risk of collision. The safe navigation of the vessel has to be done on radar, which acts as your eyes. We don't tell this to Tar though, because there's far too much fun to be had.

We send him up to the bow of the yacht, which is as far forward as you can get. He's equipped with a VHF radio, a catapult and a bucket full of pebbles, and he's told to fire each pebble in front of the yacht at regular intervals. If he hears a clang, or anything that sounds like a pebble hitting a ship, he should run like hell and radio them immediately so they can quickly alter course. It's an absolute joy to watch as he fires each pebble out into the thick fog with his catapult. Every so often his mind plays tricks on him and he's seen leaping to his feet then sprinting as fast as his little legs can carry him down the deck with a look of terror on his face!

CHAPTER 15

HE SPEAKS THE LANGUAGE LIKE A NATIVE

It's been a long, painful few hours for Tar in the fairly rough weather of the crossing to Sardinia. The movement of the ship, as well as Jock's farts and the fear of crashing into a ship in fog, have really got to him. In at the deep end, I think it's called.

'You all right, bollocks? You're looking shit,' says Jock, offering his own personal empathy to Tar in a way only he knows how.

'No! I'm not feeling too well,' murmurs Tar.

'You'll be right, buddy. Just stay in the fresh air and look at the horizon.'

'How's that going to help?'

'I don't know… it just does. Try and eat something as well. Buttery toast works.'

'You're just saying that because you want me to be sick.'

'For once, little mate, I don't, because I'm fucked if I'm going to clear it up!'

'Nothing to do with not wanting to see me in discomfort then?'

'Fuck no – that would be hilarious!'

'Errrr… I actually think I might feel better if I *was* sick,' he says, holding his stomach. 'My dinner seems to be lying in my stomach like a lead weight. I can't seem to make my self sick, though.'

'Fair enough, matey. Wait there and I'll be back in a minute.'

Jock then disappears and comes back up to the wheelhouse with a jar of cockles in vinegar, warmed up in the microwave. He doesn't show Tar until he's out on deck. 'Right then Tar, hold your head back and empty this into your mouth. It's nothing that will hurt you.'

Tar is feeling so shit he does as he's told. He empties the small jar and its warm vinegary contents into his mouth. The yacht pitches and rolls in the waves. Jock waits for a second but there's not much of a reaction. Tar chews and swallows the first lot without much effort.

'Are these cockles?' he asks.

'Yeah.'

'I don't see how's they're going to make me sick, because I actually like cockles.'

'Trust me, they will, mate.'

Tar holds his head back and empties the rest of the warm contents into his mouth then hands the jar to Jock. There's one left, so Jock picks it out with his finger and thumb and holds it up close to the boy, who's still chewing.

'Cockles, eh? Looks and tastes like a skanky old whore's clitoris, doesn't it?'

Tar stops chewing and looks at the wobbling, warm

cockle between Jock's finger and thumb and then instantly retches over the side of the yacht.

'Too easy!' Jock says, as he does an about turn and comes back inside, giggling.

'Oh Christ, Jock! What have you done now?'

'Chill, mate, it was for his own good. He said he'd feel better if he puked. He gave me the green light to do my worst.'

'Well, *you'll* be cleaning it off the side of the yacht if we get into port and it's dried on, so be warned. How's he doing anyway?'

'I've seen him look better.'

'I think he's had enough for one day, so we'll send him for a lie down.'

Jock goes outside and tells Tar to get to bed for a few hours, for which he seems very grateful. As the yacht heads out of the fog and into open water and sunshine, Thrush joins us in the wheelhouse. I don't really think he ever knows what to expect when he walks into a room that Jock is in. Fortunately, this time Jock is being professional and watching the radar. He's also keeping an eye on other vessels with the binoculars and reporting them to me, like he is supposed to. Thrush joins him, but not before checking the eyepieces of the binoculars for boot polish. After about five minutes of silence he obviously can't find anything to moan about, then mutters something.

'I'd like you to slow down next to that fishing boat ahead of us and ask the skipper if we can buy some fresh fish off him,' he says.

'OK, what fish are you after?'

'Some mackerel, octopus or tuna would be nice. We may have a barbeque over the next couple of days.'

Jock and I can't believe our ears. He's actually thinking about the crew for once!

'OK, I'll ask him when I get up closer.'

After ten minutes the yacht is stopped in the water 100 metres off the fishing boat. I try to contact them on the VHF radio. 'Fishing vessel *Porcupine*, fishing vessel *Porcupine*, this is the yacht off your starboard bow on Channel 16. Over.'

After a minute or so there's a response, but in Spanish. I try to communicate in my very poor Spanish but it's no good. I try in English but they can't understand me.

'I don't suppose you speak Spanish, do you Captain?'

'Unfortunately not. I only speak French.'

'Neither do I, so I guess that's that, then.'

'Why did you learn French over Spanish?' asks Jock.

'I thought it sounded smoother than Spanish.'

After a moment's contemplation, Jock puts his binoculars down on the table. 'I'll speak to them for you,' he says.

The Captain turns towards him. '*You* speak Spanish?' he asks in the most condescending way possible.

'Yeah, no problem,' says Jock. 'Me, I speak Spanish like a native.'

There is a brief pause then Thrush asks Jock to speak to the person who picked up the VHF on the fishing vessel. 'Tell him that your captain would like to speak to his captain because we would like to purchase some fresh fish. I'll turn up the speaker volume on deck so it will be loud enough for them to hear you over the machinery.'

Jock takes the radio handset, clears his throat and lifts the microphone to his mouth. I'm already waiting in anticipation of what will come out of his mouth. I don't have to wait long. '*HELLOA HELLOA!! MY CAPITANO WANTA SPEAKY TO YOUR CAPITANO... PRONTO... PRONTO... FOR FRESH FISHY... OKAYYYY!!!!?*'

'Oh, for God's sake,' groans Thrush, putting his hand over his eyes.

'Errrr, Jock, when you said you spoke Spanish like a native, did you mean a Native American?' I ask.

The Spanish fishermen look very confused. I call Zecky to the wheelhouse and explain what we want to say; she speaks through the handset and gets an instant response. She seems to be arguing about the price of fresh tuna and true to form she won't be ripped off. She can haggle with the best of them, even salty old fishermen. After a few moments she leaves the wheelhouse and goes on to the foredeck outside. She haggles some more and shouts something over to the fishermen. They all applaud and start cheering. Next she calls the wheelhouse.

'Are you there?' she says through the radio.

'Yeah – what is it, Zecks?' I answer.

'Do me a favour and put the music CD on. Choose track six and plug it through to the loudspeakers for me.'

'Why?'

'Just trust me. To get a bit you've got to give a bit. The dirty old sods will give us two big tuna and some swordfish steaks for a pole dance.'

'A fucking pole dance?! Which dirty old bugger wants that?'

'The old guy with the grey beard mending the net on deck. They've probably been at sea a while by the looks of it, bless 'em!'

'Are you sure, Zecks? You don't have to, mate. We only want some fish.'

'Do you know how much that would cost on the market? It's a good deal, believe me. Anyway, I'm going to tease Jock and I want some sushi tonight, so it's as much for me as anyone else!'

All the crew of the fishing boat are now gathered on the foredeck in the blazing sun. The music starts and Zecks climbs up and holds on to the foremast, bumping and grinding up and down it. The fishermen are going nuts and the wolf whistles nearly block out the sound of the music. She starts peeling off her clothes and the roars become louder.

Jock looks astounded at Zecky's performance. 'Bloody hell! Makes me love her even more,' he mutters.

After a few minutes the music stops and she puts her T-shirt back on. A minute or so later one of the fishermen throws over a couple of large plastic bags full of fresh tuna and swordfish.

'Looks like we'll have a feast tonight, boys,' she tells us through the handset.

Zecky's great to go ashore with when you're in foreign ports and you fancy a beer, or you want to buy things in the market. Last time we were in Turkey I saw a black leather jacket I fancied but at a price I didn't. Zecky told me to wait in the bar opposite the stall and get some beers in. She went up to the stallholder looking gorgeous, with freshly applied make-up, hair brushed and cleavage showing a little lower than usual. After around ten minutes of flirting she got the price down from $230 to $130. The guy thought he was going to take her out for a drink that night, but we sailed a couple of hours later.

Zecky once had a good money-making routine. Every time the yacht berthed at a Turkish port and a big cruise ship was in, she'd circulate around the passengers coming off the ship. Some of these ships carry thousands of passengers all wanting to buy niff naff and trivia. If they stopped at Egypt they would want wooden camels or pharaoh ornaments. If it was Greece they would want Greek god statues, and if it was Turkey they would want Turkish rugs. Some of these rugs cost a fortune. Zecky's cut would be ten to twenty per cent of the price it was sold at.

She'd walk up to the American tourists, as bold as brass, and ask them if they wanted a rug. If they contemplated the idea for a second she'd hand them the business card of one of the many shops and stalls on the front, with her name on it. At the end of a day she'd make hundreds of dollars in commission. She also used to buy navigation charts of the Mediterranean and work out where the cruise ship sailed from and its itinerary for the voyage. Then she put lines on the chart showing the voyage, leg by leg, with distances and fancy marks on them. Then she'd roll them up, tie a ribbon round them and sell them to the punters. You have to hand it to her for her savvy; she's a smart entrepreneur. She could sell sand to the Arabs – as well as fleece some expensive fresh fish off some salty old fishermen by wiggling her arse.

CHAPTER 16

ALL YOU NEED IS A GOOD ASHTRAY

As we wave goodbye to the cheering Spanish fishermen, Zecky looks up to the wheelhouse, licks her finger and makes a downward motion with it in the air to signify that she has one up on Jock. These two seem to have an unwritten scorecard of who can acquire things that benefit the crew without paying for them. At the moment it's evens and both seem to be equally matched, but it's just for fun.

Jock's last freebie was some free fuel when he was refuelling the yacht's tenders which were used for towing the guests for waterskiing. He pissed in a sample of fuel and took it back to the fuelling station demanding that the boats be refilled for free.

The vendor didn't argue because Thrush refills the yacht there every so often and he's on a nice little scam. Thrush gets a receipt for a full tank of diesel, however the vendor doesn't fill the tank but still charges the full amount. On a big motor yacht with big engines this can be substantial. For argument's sake, let's say it cost £10,000, although it could be a whole lot more. But with only £7,000 of fuel actually supplied to the yacht, Thrush and the vendor share the £3,000 difference between them. The crew don't see any of this, of course. It all goes to keeping 'Puppy' and Olga in Gucci.

As a result the crew have to dream up their own methods to top up their wages. It's hardly a crime – it's just the way it works out in the charter world. Everyone has a scam; it's just the amounts that differ.

Zecky will only use certain suppliers for food and beverage – ones that offer a 'kick-back' of around five per cent, but it can be a lot more. I will only use suppliers for the deck equipment who do the same. Sometimes a yacht pulls into a port where they need to drop the anchors. The ports get very busy in the Mediterranean and there isn't much space on the quay. Because of this yachts and powerboats save space by not berthing lengthways alongside a quay, because this takes up more of the premium space. Instead they reverse into the berth, so only the back of the yacht is against the quay.

To make sure the yacht is stable, ropes are put out from the back of the yacht to secure the stern and the anchors are dropped into the water at the forward end to secure the front of the yacht. The only problem is that when you get lots of yachts which all have their anchors out ahead of them in a small area, the chains lay on top of each other. This can cause difficulties when one of the yachts wants to leave, because if he pulls his anchor up he'll drag the other yachts' chains and anchors with it.

Because of this, divers have to come to the yacht just before departure. They'll dive down to the seabed with bags which they attach to the anchor chain and then pump full of air. This makes the chain rise up off the bottom and then the other anchors can be manoeuvred around it. This way it doesn't matter if the yacht berths before or after the others because she can leave at any time – provided she has divers available. The availability of the divers can change dramatically. The quickest and best service goes to the yacht which gives the biggest tip.

The crew will tell the Captain they had to tip fifty euros, but in fact they only tipped thirty, ensuring they pocket twenty. It's the same whenever they arrive or depart a port. The port staff handle the ropes as we throw them ashore. On paper they got tipped the same fifty euros but sometimes they won't get tipped at all if they are the slightest bit late. Fifty euros in your back pocket. One thing is for sure though, they are never late again, so it works both ways.

* * * *

I hand over the navigation watch to my relief and then go down below decks to freshen up and get some dinner. I'm half way though my shower when I hear paper rustling and then a cheeky fart. I pull the shower curtain back to find Jock sat down on the toilet. He's got his trousers around his ankles, with a chicken leg in one hand and my *FHM* magazine in the other.

'All right, matey?' says Jock taking a bite of his chicken and turning a page.

'Jock! What the fuck are you doing taking a crap on my toilet?!'

'It was a bit touch and go, mate, and Tar's locked the door of our cabin.'

'Christ, couldn't you wait five minutes?'

'Not really, mate. The tortoise head was running for daylight, so to speak.'

'I'll see you in the crew room for some dinner, you bloody reprobate,' I shout, as I towel off, get changed and leave the cabin.

'Yeah, all right mate. Make me a brew while you're in there, would you?'

I walk down the alleyway shaking my head. First he takes a crap in my cabin and now he wants *me* to make *him* a brew. Unbelievable!

As I walk in to the crew room the table is laid with a heap of food and wine. Chef has cooked up some great food, as well as preparing some of Zecky's fresh fish. There's nothing quite like eating fish that has been swimming around in the ocean only an hour or so ago. Fish you buy at the shops at home can be days or even weeks old.

The chef, Mr Kerr, isn't a bad cook but he's so full of shit. He learned his trade at the restaurants on the Cote d'Azur so he knows his stuff, but he's a bloody pompous pain in the arse who looks down his nose at people just because they don't know about fine food and wine. He's a small, dumpy little man, very well spoken and looking like a cross between Colonel Sanders and Chief Wiggum from *The Simpsons*.

Jock nicknamed him 'Wan' because of his surname and for some reason he liked it. One of the crew once told him it stood for 'Nourishment With Attitude' rearranged to 'WAN' so he thought it was a compliment. In reality Jock just meant 'WAN-KER'. It isn't rocket science, but Mr Kerr just never saw it. Thrush and he get on well, as you'd imagine. They both try and polish each other's egos and it's laughable to listen to.

Chef is also one of those really irritating people who asks himself questions, then answers them himself for everyone to hear. Tom once asked him if he was going to make some homemade burgers for the barbeque. Typically the chef stopped his work and arched his back while stroking his chin to answer him.

'Will I be making burgers for the barbeque? Let's see now. Am I a classically trained chef? YES I AM! Have I learned my trade in the best French hotels and restaurants? MOST CERTAINLY! Will I be insulting my culinary talents by making burgers? NOT A CHANCE!'

Tom decided to answer him back in the same style, just to take the piss. 'Am I going to tell Jock on his birthday that he can't have a simple burger? I DON'T THINK SO! Will there be a forfeit if you don't make burgers? YES THERE WILL! Am I carrying a fire extinguisher? YES I AM! Will I be inserting the flexible pipe up your big fat arse and pulling the trigger if you don't? OF COURSE I WILL!'

Jock takes no prisoners as far as Chef is concerned. When Mr Kerr joined the yacht from working ashore he wanted to convince the crew that he was a master wine connoisseur. He went on about this grape and that grape for what seemed like an eternity until Jock decided enough was enough. At the next mealtime Jock got him talking about wine after he'd brought out a really good bottle of Bordeaux. It was an expensive one but the contents had been drunk the night before at a party. Jock had taken it out of the waste, filled it with cheap cooking wine and stuck it in front of him to see how much he actually *did* know about wine.

Chef picked up the bottle and took a sip. 'Ah, yes... a classic red Bordeaux. I can taste blackcurrant and plum. Fruity but classically metallic with a round full finish. I can see this is not a cheap wine.'

'How much would you say that cost, then?' enquired Jock

'Oh... this brand is rather expensive and you can taste the quality.'

'You can tell good wine from a bad one, can you?'

'Of course – it's as easy as one, two, three.'

'Well, that's your cooking wine, you bullshit merchant!'

* * * *

The yacht alters course so the swell waves are astern of us. This makes the yacht's movement settle and it's a bit more comfortable. Tar and Jock join me in the crew room and the boy is looking a little better, bless him.

'You feeling stronger then, Tar?' I ask.

'A little, yes.'

'Well, you've got a bit of colour back in your face now, mate. Anyway, you can get your own back on Jock shortly because if you remember he's still got to snort the chilli sauce because of the bet he lost.'

Tar raises a smile and takes a seat. Zecky makes him a coffee and gives him a hug. He's obviously brought out her maternal side. 'Don't you worry, Tar, you'll soon get used to it. Your body just thinks it's normal after a while and you won't even notice the yacht's movement.'

'That feels like a million miles away at the moment,' Tar

says. 'I'm going to stock up with all sorts of drugs when I get into port. If anyone needs anything, just let me know.'

At that point, Jock walks in and catches the end of the conversation. He sits down next to me and stares at Tar, not believing what he's just heard. After a few moments of staring he shrugs his shoulders then reaches into his pocket and slams down fifty euros.

'Fuck me, Tar, I wouldn't have thought you were the type but I admire your honesty. Get me as many bags of weed as you can get with that, and none of that weak shit either. If I'm going to get high I want to be in fucking ORBIT, know what I mean?'

Tar looks confused. 'Weed… no, I think you've… I can't get you any weed.'

'We'll just get us some E's, then… Mitsubishi's, if you can get them.'

'I think you've caught the tail-end of the conversation, Jock. I wasn't offering to buy drugs.'

'I just bloody well heard you!'

'Not weed or E's! I meant sea-sickness tablets, for God's sake!'

'Sea-sickness tablets? Why? Do you chop coke up with them or something? I fucking hate it when dealers do that. Oh, hang on a minute – do you stick them up your arse like a suppository? I've heard about this.'

'No, no, you've got it all wrong.'

'Have you tried sniffing vodka, Tar? That's a bit rushy but a lot of fun!'

Zecky has to explain to Jock that Tar had been talking about getting some tablets for his sea sickness.

'Oh for fuck's sake, Tar, forget all that shit. All you need is a good ashtray and a full packet of Marlboro.'

'Honestly, Jock, you're certifiable,' says Zecky, shaking her head.

'Oh, thanks very much.'

'That means you're a nutter, mate,' I tell him, bursting his bubble.

Jock shrugs his shoulders like he's heard it a million times already.

'I blame the parents,' says Zecky with a mock sigh.

'Come on then, Jock, you owe me a forfeit, my old mate,' I say. 'Chilli sauce, remember?'

'Oh, I don't know, mate… it's pretty hot.'

'You should have thought about that before you made the bet, then, buddy. Anyway, if you can snort vodka, as you've so delicately told us, then this should be a breeze for you.'

'Yeah, come on, Jock. You've given Tar enough shit already, so it's payback time for him… and he gets to choose the chilli sauce.'

Tar can't help but raise a faint smile. You can see he'd enjoy getting his own back on Jock, but he's wondering if there will be repercussions.

'What do you reckon then, Tar? The sweet but sticky chilli sauce or the Tabasco?'

'Well, that's a tricky one. The sticky one would be harder to get down and would leave more residues, so he'd be coughing it up for a while. The Tabasco on the other hand is a lot hotter, so that would be more painful.'

'You're between a rock and a hard place, really, aren't you?' I say, slapping Jock on his back.

'Fuckers,' says Jock, holding the two sauces out in front of him and inspecting them.

'You see, mate, every time you think of betting you'll remember this pain,' I tell him. 'Neuro Linguistic Programming I think it's called. When you snort it we're all going to shout "DO NOT BET!" and hopefully it will be etched into your subconscious for ever.'

'Which sauce then, Tar?'

'The Tabasco, I think.'

'Tabasco it is then. Right – on the count of three. One... two... THREE!'

As we anticipate, Jock doesn't back down from a challenge and he holds the bottle to his right nostril whilst pinching the other. Then he tips his head back and inhales sharply.

'DOOOOOOOO NOT BET!' we all shout at him.

He puts the bottle down on the table and maintains his composure for a few seconds. Then the pain hits him and no doubt it feels like he's just shoved molten metal up his nose. His face turns bright red and his eyes bulge. Suddenly he jumps to his feet and lets out an almighty scream before leaping over the table to the cold water tap.

'AAAAHHHH!! FUCKING HELL – I'm on FIRE!!' yells Jock, jumping up and down on the spot and throwing water in his face.

I grab Tar's hand and shake it while gesturing over at Jock. 'And that's how we learn, Tar – that's how we learn!'

I don't know if Jock *will* learn, though. I know of three fairly nasty cases of gonorrhea Jock has had, but it doesn't stop him screwing around. My guess is that this will be no different.

After ten minutes of torture Jock gradually recovers and Rob, sitting in the corner with Sally the stewardess, is pondering Jock's state of mind. 'That boy is troubled,' he mutters, pouring himself a large Jack Daniels and Coke. He pours Sally one and asks if anyone else is indulging. Everybody is, and I know what's happening here – they are all having a few stiff drinks to make sure they sleep long enough in the uncomfortable sea conditions. If they don't get any sleep they will feel like zombies the next day and be in no state to look after the guests.

Tar takes a sip of the Jack Daniels but it's clear he doesn't usually drink. He nearly chokes and some of it comes back up out of his nose.

'My God – that tastes horrible!' he says, holding his nose.

'You see, and *you* think I'm *enjoying* myself every time I drink a bottle of it,' Rob jokes. 'The first gulp is always the hardest, buddy. Besides, you'll sleep like a baby after a couple of these.'

'I think after a couple of these I won't ever wake up,' Tar replies, looking at the glass.

'Rob's measures *are* a bit on the liberal side,' I tell him.

'A *bit* on the liberal side? You could fuel a jet car with it,' adds Sally, who is also struggling to get it down.

'Like I said, Tar, have a few of these and push your lifejacket under one side of your mattress, then sleep in the "V" between it and the bulkhead,' says Rob, making a V shape with his hands. 'It will stop you rolling around when the yacht rolls and pitches.'

'What's a bulkhead?'

'It's nautical talk for a wall. Bulkhead is the wall, deck is the floor and deck head is the ceiling.'

'And dickhead lives between them all in the Captain's cabin, right?'

'You're catching on, Tar, I'll give you that,' Zecky grins.

'There's millions of jargon phrases and words in the nautical world, Tar,' adds Rob reassuringly, 'so don't worry – you won't learn them all at once.'

'There can't be that many, can there?' asks Tar, naively.

'You're kidding aren't you, mate? If you think about it, hundreds of everyday phrases have come from working at sea. It's one of the earliest industries.'

'Like what?'

'Well, you name it,' I say. 'Let's put it this way, I'll pour us all a drink for every slang word or phrase that comes up in our immediate conversation around this table.'

'All right, but it has to be in context.'

'No problem. Let's see… Jock's just been for a shit, right?'

'Yeah.'

'Admittedly in *my* bloody toilet,' I add, shaking my head at him.

'I was just keeping it warm for you, boss,' Jock grins.

'Well, the word shit comes from the sea… and I shit you not.'

'Really? How?'

'Years ago almost all goods had to be transported by ship, and it was also before commercial fertilisers were invented. Shipments of manure were common. It was shipped dry because in dry form it weighed a lot less than when it was wet. Once seawater hit it, it not only became heavier but a process of fermentation began. A by-product of that is methane gas. Methane gas is explosive.

'As the stuff was stored below decks in bundles you can see what happened. Methane began to build up and the first time someone came below at night with a naked light... BANG! Ships blew up like this loads of times before some one asked the question, what the fuck is going on? After that, the bundles of manure were always stamped with the instruction "Ship High In Transit" stamped on them, which meant for the sailors to stow it high enough off the lower decks so that any water that came into the hold would not touch its cargo and start the production of methane. Thus evolved the term "S.H.I.T."'

'I wish we could stow your bowels high in transit,' says Tar to Jock.

'I know. It's like a rat's crawled up you arse and died sometimes,' adds Sally.

'I must admit they can be fairly fragrant,' says Jock, knocking back his drink.

We have a few more drinks and everyone's volunteering phrases and words.

'Wanker?' suggests Jock.

'Don't know that one but I bet it is slang for Thrush,' says Tar.

Now that Tar's had a few drinks he's become quite funny. '*Down the hatch*, then Tar,' I say, filling everyone's glasses. 'That's a drinking expression that originates from sea-going procedures. The cargoes were lowered into the hatch.'

'Neck it and pour another then, Tar,' says Jock.

'Oh... I don't know if I can drink this all in one just yet,' he says wearily.

'Honestly, Tar, you'd better *toe the line* with this drinking game... There's another.'

'What?'

'"Toe the line" – meaning to conform to rules. It originates from a time when a ship's company was lined up to be given pay. Each sailor stepped forward to a line marked on the deck and gave his name.'

'This is too easy. We'll be as pissed as rats at this rate.'

'What do you mean *will* be?' says Tar, who's feeling the effects already.

'Now, now, Tar – you can't wimp out of this now or you'll show the boys your *true colours*,' says Rob.

Tar looks at Jock in anticipation. Jock smiles and nods his head slowly. 'I'm afraid so buddy. "True colours" relates to naval etiquette. While allowing false colours or flags to be displayed when approaching an enemy ship, it insists that true colours are flown once battle begins and they start firing at each other.'

Less than an hour later everyone around the table is pissed, but especially Tar. He's hugging Zecky and she's hugging him back in a motherly, protective way. He's got the side of his head planted firmly on the side of her left breast. 'You feeling better now, Tar?' she asks.

'Never bloody better,' he burbles.

Jock is staring over at the pair of them and you can see by his look of concentration that his mind is working overtime. He taps me on the leg under the table to attract my attention then whispers quietly in my ear, 'Do you reckon if I act all vulnerable she'll let me rest *my* head on her tits?!'

CHAPTER 17

DON'T YOU JUST LOVE THE SMELL OF PUPPIES?

The next morning Thrush makes a loudspeaker announcement through the yacht, half an hour before we arrive at the port limits. There's a few groggy people assembling on deck, having seen the painful side of three bottles of Jack Daniels last night. Tar's sat on the open deck next to Jock and he looks a little worse for wear. Jock on the other hand is as fresh as a daisy. He's done the decent thing this morning, getting Tar some Alka-Seltzer, a strong coffee (of the non-special kind) and some toast.

The girls are on deck helping the boys get out the rubber fenders and the ropes, ready for going into port. The fenders are the big, inflatable rubber type covered in a towelling material to prevent scratches and bumps as the yacht backs in to a slot on the berth. The quay is packed with yachts, and at first glance it looks like we'll need a shoehorn to fit the yacht into the space allocated to us. There should just be enough room for the width of the yacht and the fenders to back into. Although Thrush is a dickhead of the highest order, he's adept at manoeuvring the yacht. It's a shame he doesn't have the same skills in man-management.

After breakfast and a couple of cigarettes the crew start to feel human again. Some are down in the water, cleaning the tidemark of algae growth on the hull. They are usually helped by the resident grey mullet or 'shit-gobblers' – the fish known as the dustbins of the sea. Some people catch them and eat them – in the Black Sea and Caspian Sea among other places – but the very thought of eating something that's just been sucking on shit kind of puts you off.

A ship I once worked on in Croatia was moored alongside a berth in a harbour for several months, and because it didn't move the algae built up on the hull, caused by a sewage overflow a short distance away. Every day at 10am and 4pm the overflow used to release waste and debris and the grey mullet would wade in, all guns blazing! There were hundreds of them in the dirty water, swimming in between prophylactics and sanitary towels, chomping on floating turds. Then a small boat used to come along with a couple fishermen aboard wearing long, thick rubber gloves. They would throw a net and scoop up the fish and sell them at the local fish market.

I reckon those fish are grey for a reason: *you* would look grey and pale if you ate the shit that they do. Nobody ever eats grey mullet on the yacht any more.

* * * *

Zecky is on the aft deck helping Jock with the fenders, and they're having a banter about the differing benefits of being female and male. Zecky gets into full flow when Jock asks her to name some reasons why it's better to be female.

'Well, Jock, if this yacht sinks when we're out at sea, us girls would get off first, for a start,' she says, ticking off her reasons with her fingers. 'We can pretend to cry to get off speeding fines; we don't look like a frog in a blender when dancing; we can hug our friends without people thinking we're gay; and if we shag someone and don't call the next day, we're not the Devil.'

'Is that all?' says Jock, raising his eyebrows. 'I thought you were going to convince me.'

'I've only just started, sunshine. Free dinners, free drinks...'

'I can get free drinks.'

'Only when you know the barman. What else? Taxis stop for us, men die earlier, gay waiters don't make us feel uncomfortable, we never regret piercing our ears, we get an excuse to be a total bitch once a month, and we're more cultured.'

'I'm cultured.'

'You're cultured? Are you bollocks! The first time we visited Venice you told me that you didn't reckon much to it and we should come back when it wasn't flooded, for Christ's sake!'

'No fucker told me most of it was supposed to be under water!'

'If you *were* cultured, my boy, you wouldn't need to be told. And what about that time after the last charter when we all ate out at that French restaurant?'

'What about it?'

'We all ordered that wonderful chicken dish... *supreme de volaille a l'estragon*. When you were asked why you weren't ordering it, you said you didn't like that foreign *Mexican* crap.'

'Well, how did I know it wasn't Mexican? I don't speak the lingo!'

'Didn't the French music, the French décor, the French wine, the menu written in French, not to mention the restaurant's name – Café de Paris – give you any indication?'

'Must have had an off day.'

'To top it off, once you were informed it was a French restaurant, you asked the waiter if he had frog's legs.'

'They serve frogs legs in France!'

'Yes, I'm well aware of that, Jock, but when he said he *did* have frogs legs you asked him to hop into the kitchen and get you a burger and chips.'

'Yeah… well, it was a joke, wasn't it?'

'Ha! Well, maybe the frog's legs thing was, but you still ordered burger and chips in a top quality French restaurant. I bet the Michelin star chef was pulling his fucking hair out! Anyway, why is it better to be a man, then?'

'Loads of reasons.'

'Go on then, convince me,' she says, smiling.

'We can go to water parks and wear white T shirts, and chocolate is *not* the meaning of existence to us.'

'Well, it isn't to me.'

'Yeah, right! I'm amazed you don't piss around your chocolate drawer to mark your territory!'

'Go on then, name some more.'

'Hairdressers don't rob us blind, two pairs of shoes is enough, underwear cost less than ten quid for a three-pack, and we don't have to stop and think for a few minutes before tightening a bolt! Oh, and by the way, Zecks, my new nickname for you is *spanner* because you make *my* nuts tighten.'

'Anything else?'

'Fucking loads – our telephone calls are over in thirty seconds, we can open jars, we can do our nails with a pocket knife, Christmas shopping for ten relatives begins on 24 December and lasts forty-five minutes... and we know stuff about engines.'

'Finished?'

'Nope. We can easily pee in public, which infuriates every woman because secretly you'd like a cock.'

'Secretly we'd like a cock?!'

'Of course you would. '

'For what reason?'

'For that reason.'

'Admittedly it would be easier to pee in public, but that's it. As for *needing* a cock, we can buy a vibrator at Ann Summers that will out-perform most of your gender.'

'Well, feel free to put me to the test, my darling.'

'Nice try, sunshine.'

'Anyway, that vibrator comment was below the belt – that's every man's fear.'

'We *know*! That's why whenever we buy one it has to be just the right size. Not too big to upset your fragile egos and God help us if we bought a black one. You'd be thinking we have a thing for coloured men.'

'Well, it's a touchy subject. How would you feel if we went out and bought a synthetic pussy? Could you imagine us disappearing off to the toilet during a boring meeting to go service ourselves with a plastic girl?'

'Ha, not really, no.'

'Anyway, a vibrator can't mow the lawn and get a round of drinks in, can it?'

'Well, if it could, you'd be extinct. OK, we both have some valid points but back to your point about us secretly wanting a cock.'

'Yeah, what about it?'

Zecky slowly walks over to Jock, lifts the top of her shorts, puts her hand on the back of his head and points his head down. 'I have one of these, and because I have one of these I can have as many cocks as I wish.' She then gently slaps his cheek and struts off to the other side of the boat to man the fender as we start to back into the berth.

* * * *

Thrush berths us successfully and we get ready to pick up the guests again. They've been staying at one of the top hotels in Porto Cervo on Sardinia's exclusive Smeralda Coast and they've asked to be collected at noon. They want to go waterskiing and perhaps take in a little diving before partying at the Billionaire Nightclub, a haunt of the rich and famous, tycoons and celebrities.

The Smeralda, or Emerald, Coast is one of Sardinia's main claims to fame. An idyllic resort on the north-east of the island, it has secluded little bays and coves lapped by a crystal-clear, emerald-green sea. Prince Karim Aga Khan IV visited it in the 1950s and established a resort. However, it's not a resort in the usual sense of the word; its natural beauty is fully protected and there are no high-rise buildings.

As well as the main harbour in Porto Cervo the larger bays are full of beautiful mega-yachts, and it's entertaining to watch the yachts battling for an anchorage and all the owners vying to impress. The helicopters get polished on the flight decks and everything is pristine. It's a case of who has the biggest dick with their floating penis extensions. If someone orders a new yacht to out-size the largest yacht in the world, you can guarantee that someone else will have an order in as soon as a bigger one is launched. It's a case of you've got an nine-inch dick, but I've got a ten-inch.

* * * * *

Noon approaches faster than we anticipate and we are a little behind with the cleaning and polishing. Because of this, and the fact that Rob is still hung over, I just leave him and Tom to work in the fresh air. Jock and I will escort the chauffeurs and drive out to the Hotel Cala Di Volpe to pick up the guests. Silvio is the chauffeur in my limo. He's a really good Italian guy whose family has lived in Sardinia for centuries. He likes to drive at this time of year in case he meets someone famous. He has photos and autographs of many of the rich and famous and the car glovebox is full of them. If you need anything in Sardinia, Silvio is your man. He knows people everywhere on the island. As I get in the limo I'm welcomed with a friendly shoulder-punch.

'Well, fuck me if it isn't the Italian stallion,' I say, greeting him with a reciprocal punch.

'Eh, mate, ya' big clown. You not Captain yet, ya' waster?!'

'Working on it mate, working on it,' I respond, in equally jovial fashion. 'Hope you're going to keep your eyes on the fucking road this time, buggerlugs.'

I'm very fond of Silvio and vice versa but I hate driving with him while we are having a conversation. Silvio is typically Italian and he likes to get up close and personal when he's talking to you. He likes to hold eye contact with you and he's very intense and demonstrative with his hands and arms to fully underline the point he's trying to make. However, this isn't always the best thing to do when you're trying to negotiate the busy, winding roads of Sardinia in the height of summer. If you take your eyes off the road for a second you're asking for trouble. There is a very apt joke that does the rounds: *How do you stop an Italian man from talking to you? You tie his hands behind his back.* If you have ever worked with Italians you'll know that this is very true. You've got to love them, though. They are passionate people. Just look at the cars they build and their architecture and clothing.

Silvio has just come from Bosa on the west side of the island, a little beauty spot next to the River Temo, famous for its Malvasia wine, and he hands me a bottle because he knows I love it so much. He also gives me another bottle from the island's Sella e Mosca vineyard. The Sardinian red wines made from local grapes are fantastic. Pleasantries aside, we set off to the hotel and Silvio starts his usual non-stop barrage of questions. I'm trying my hardest not to engage him or get eye contact but it's not much good. The more he talks, the more animated Silvio becomes. I figure the only way to get us both to the hotel safely is for *me* to talk non-stop to make sure that Silvio doesn't have a chance to get in to his full stride. I carry on talking until we arrive at the hotel safely, followed by Jock in the second limo.

The Hotel Cala di Volpe sits on a great stretch of coastline lined with some pretty strange rock formations that make the area really beautiful, and you can smell the fragrance of oleander, laurel and juniper carried on the ocean breeze. The coast has loads of inlets of clear, warm water – perfect for swimming, snorkelling and scuba diving. It was built in the 1960s by the renowned architect Jacques Couelle, an honorary member of the prestigious Académie des Beaux-Arts of the Institut de France. Its exterior was conceived to look like a typical white stucco Mediterranean fishing village, with interconnecting terracotta rooftops, turrets and terraces. Inside, archways and columns support beamed wooden ceilings, with locally crafted woven textiles, woodcarving and tile-work. It all adds up to one of most glamorous resort destinations for celebrities, royalty and the international social elite.

Jock and I walk up to reception and are met by the concierge. If this guy can't get you what you want, nobody can. He has to deal with top-end guests all day long. I ask him to let Mr Big know we are here and as we wait for him to phone the room we stand in the hall and observe the guests. There are no football shirts in this hotel; everyone is dressed stylishly and immaculately. After a minute or so the concierge tells us that the guests are out waterskiing. We thank him and walk through the gardens to the jetty on the hotel's private beach, but Mr Big is out on the water with the other guests.

'That's good, mate,' says Jock. 'I'm dying for a piss so I'll just go drain the main vein while you wait for them.'

'OK, but don't be long in case they come back early.'

'Sorted.' Jock disappears and I look around for some-where to sit out of the sun. I notice a large table in the shade where an elegant, middle-aged and quite attractive woman is sitting. She is adorned with a wide-brimmed hat, designer sunglasses, a sarong and a bikini top. I walk up and politely ask her if I may sit down.

'Certainly,' she says. 'It's much cooler here in the shade.'

'Sure is, it must be over ninety degrees in the sun today.'

'I'm Sarah.'

'Pleased to meet you, Sarah. Are you having a nice holiday?'

'Wonderful, thank you. This hotel and island is beautiful. I'll definitely be here again.'

'It's very nice indeed, isn't it? Are you here alone?'

'Oh no, I'm here with my two girls.'

'I see. Do you mean your daughters?'

'In a funny kind of way they are, yes?'

'Where are they today?'

'Underneath the table next to your feet.'

I lean down and lift up the tablecloth to find two small dachshund puppies. 'Their legs are a bit short,' I say, jokingly.

'They reach the ground, don't they?' she laughs.

'Good point. I love them when they're this age. Don't you just love that puppy smell?'

'Yes, it is adorable, isn't it?'

'Can I have a sniff? It's been years and it would take me back to when I got my own puppy all those years ago.'

'Of course, go ahead.'

'They don't bite, do they?'

'They will probably lick you to death but that's about it.'

I scoop up the tiny puppies, one in each hand, and lift them to my nose. 'Ahhhh, I'd never get sick of that puppy smell,' I laugh, placing them back under the table.

Sarah and I carry on talking for a few minutes when Jock returns and sits down. 'This is Sarah, Jock. I've just smelled her puppies.'

Jock stares at Sarah, looking quite astonished. 'Really?!'

'Yeah, it was great.'

Sarah starts to get up. 'Feel free to smell them yourself. Many people have; they're irresistible.'

Jock shrugs his shoulders, with a slightly bewildered look. 'Oh, what the hell,' he grins, leaning over the table and cupping both of her ample breasts in his hands before burying his face between them and inhaling deeply.

Sarah and I look on, flabbergasted and speechless.

'Not bad, not bad at all,' he says, nodding at her and juggling each breast before sitting back down.

CHAPTER 18

CRUEL TO BE KIND... OR SO HE THINKS!

Although she is initially shocked and quite taken aback at Jock sniffing her boobs, Sarah eventually sees the funny side of it. I'm sure it isn't every day that she has her fun bags manhandled and sniffed by a complete stranger. Still, that's Jock for you I suppose: two plus two equals five. Jock and I eventually leave Sarah and her cute puppies (both sets) in peace to go for a smoke.

'Fuck's sake, Jock, what were you thinking?' I ask, unable to control my laughter.

'You told me *you'd* just sniffed her puppies,' says Jock.

'Well, that's true but didn't your brain compute the fact that I might have meant actual puppies rather than her tits?'

'I didn't see them until she jumped up and they came running out from underneath the table.'

'OK, fair enough. I'm just going to nip to the toilet, mate, then we'll go back to reception and find out what the score is with the guests. Where are they?'

'What?'

'The toilets. You've just come back, right?'

'Er… yeah, but you don't want to go in there yet.'

'Why not?'

'It's was a bit fragrant in there when I left.'

'Upset stomach have we, mate?'

'Yeah, something like that.'

'It's been a few minutes so I'm sure it's fine now. Anyway, I'm bursting to go, so where is it?'

Jock shakes his head and grudgingly walks me over to the toilets. As we approach, a man walks out with a disgusted look on his face. 'Right, wait here Jock. I'm just going to drop my load then we'll get on.'

'Er… yeah, all right.'

I walk in to one of the cubicles and I'm met with a sight to behold. The toilet bowl looks like a mud bomb has blown up inside it and the stench makes me gasp for breath. 'Ohhhh for fuck's sake!'

'Sorry, mate,' says Jock.

'I take it this was your cubicle then, you dirty bastard?'

'Yep, I'm afraid so.'

'Don't you ever flush? That's fucking horrible!'

'I tried but the water wouldn't wash away the bits on the side of the pan.'

'I'm amazed any went in the water at all! It looks like you've stuck a stick of dynamite up your arse and it's exploded when you sat down! Bloody hell, some of it isn't even inside the toilet bowl,' I say, jabbing my finger at the porcelain.

'Well, I got caught short there. It was on the way, if you know what I mean.'

'Caught short? What the hell have you been eating – hand grenades?!'

'No, I've been on the salts for the upset stomach.'

'Salts! You've been doing fucking somersaults in there by the look of it.'

'Well, I was hovering a bit. I don't really like to sit down on public toilets... germs and all that.'

'Jock, I've seen you pick up polystyrene food containers with half-eaten cheeseburgers out of the bin outside of a kebab shop before now!'

'When?'

'Last time we were in the UK. We were on the piss in Newcastle, remember?'

'Oh yeah, but I saw the girl buy it fresh and only take a mouthful out of it then throw it in the bin. Waste not, want not.'

'That's hardly the point really, mate, and for fuck's sake, what's with the colour?'

'The colour?'

'Yeah, the colour. Are you a bloody amphibian or something?'

'What are you on about?' says Jock, looking really confused.

'Your shit... I'm talking about the colour of your shit!'

Jock holds his hands out, looking even more confused. He puts his head back in the toilet cubicle, looks down into the porcelain then turns back to me.

'I can't see anything wrong with the colour,' he says, shaking his head.

'Are you seriously telling me you think that colour is normal?'

'Yeah, looks all right to me.'

'It's fucking GREEEEN!'

Jock looks back down into the porcelain and muffles his thoughts under his breath. 'I thought everyone's shit was green.'

'No, mate, it's usually brown or sometimes tan-coloured but never green. I'd go see a doctor if I were you. Anyway, sort it while I go in another, because you can't leave it like that. It's enough to turn anybody's stomach.'

* * * *

Back at reception the concierge tells us that Mr Big and his guests will be down for their limos in fifteen minutes. When they arrive, the guests are accompanied by bell-boys running around after them carrying their luggage, like seagulls circling a trawler in hope of a tasty morsel. Silvio is running a cloth over the limo paintwork as we approach. The limos are already immaculately clean but it gives the impression of perfection and pride in our work.

Mr Big sits in the back with the blonde and the brunette and I am in the front with Silvio. The others go in the other limo. We head back to the yacht and the journey is fairly uneventful, except for the fact that Silvio can't stop looking in the rear view mirror to get an eyeful of the ladies. At least it keeps him quiet while he's driving but he still has his eyes on anything but the road.

The girls are dressed in shorts and bikini tops that don't leave a great deal to the imagination. They are professionals and no doubt they have cost Mr Big a hefty fee for their services. He's obviously interested in cosmetic image rather than emotional content. The girls are just doing a job – boosting his ego.

In the quietness of the drive back to the yacht I have a rare moment of clarity. I'm looking at the two girls in the back via the mirror, and I'm thinking to myself how I long for an honest, pure relationship again. I remember back to my younger, wilder days of promiscuity and to the times when I was in loving relationships. I think about how people change and grow as a person as they get older and mature. The things that I wanted as a late teenager and man in his twenties no longer matter to me now.

I remember the superficial relationships with different girls I had back then, and how none of them made me truly happy, even though they were fun at the time. I look out at a field and I see dozens of shallow holes in the ground but only one deep water well. In my present state of mind I see this as an omen. You can drill a hundred shallow dry holes and not spend enough time digging, or you can persevere and dig one deep well to discover sparkling, life-preserving water. I look back on my past relationships and I realise that being in a committed, monogamous relationship gave me more freedom and rewards than any of the other, shallow relationships I'd experienced. From that moment on, whenever I saw Mr Big and his escorts I looked on him not with envy but a little pity.

Five minutes away from the yacht I telephone Zecky and let her know that we'll be there shortly. As the limos pull up, Rob and Tom are stood by the passerelle ready to help the guests aboard and take their luggage. Zecky is also waiting with her ice-cold, lemon-scented face towels.

As the guests are welcomed aboard, Mr Big and his bouncers head up to the top deck overlooking the quay for a cold beer and no doubt a line of coke. The two girls disappear below, no doubt to take a shower and apply their warpaint.

As the girls strut along the teak deck towards the aft accommodation door, Rob turns to Tom. 'It must be a nice job being a pro. All you have to worry about is keeping your body in shape and your make-up fresh. Think I might become one because it looks a piece of cake to me,' he jokes.

'Not with your ever-growing beer belly, sunshine,' says Tom. 'I know what you mean though. I bet they get paid a bloody fortune, as well!'

'All they have to do is suck up to the client, then lie on their backs and suck on something else. It's bloody easy money! What do you reckon, Tom? Shall we become ladies of disrepute?'

'You wouldn't catch me sucking someone's dick for all the tea in China.'

'Well, you wouldn't have to, you clown. You'd be a *male* pro.'

'I fucking am anyway, with the shit I have to do for the guests to get a tip!'

'I don't think that spending an extra couple of hours taking the guests waterskiing is on a par with taking a shafting up the shitter, mate.'

'Well, you've got a point there, I suppose.'

'Hang on a minute. What would happen if you're hired by a big, old, six-foot, eighteen-stone lush with loads of money? Let's just say she wanted you to ravish her but she has a body like a sack of potatoes?'

'You'd have to ravish her in segments. Big flabby segments.'

'Ha! Seriously though, you're a professional so you have

a job to do. How would you get the job done to her satisfaction?'

'I suppose you'd think of the cash, close your eyes and pretend it was Pamela Anderson.'

'That would take a lot of imagination! You're humping away on an eighteen-stone mass of blubber. It would be like shagging a walrus. With all the will in the world, you'd have a difficult job pretending it was Pamela Anderson.'

'I don't think *you'd* be able to shag a six-foot, eighteen-stone woman, Tom. You're only ten stone and five-feet-seven. You'd disappear in a fat fold somewhere. She'd envelope you like a Venus fly trap.'

'Death by lard, eh? What a way to go. Imagine that on your tombstone. *Here lies Thomas. Loved by all, except for the lard ass that shagged and smothered him to death.*'

'How would your parents tell your mates? They would have to lie to save face.'

'They'd have to say that you died whilst rescuing a drowning child or something.'

'Anything but *Here lies blah blah blah. Died whilst shagging a porker.*'

'What position do you reckon fat birds fuck in, then?'

Rob and Tom are quiet for a second as they ponder the question. Then Rob comes up with an answer. 'Well, if she was shagging you, ya' little short arse, there's no way she could squirm around on top, with her weighing eighteen stone.

'Imagine the view I'd get from underneath. I'd have her arse cheeks covering my legs and her belly rolls on my chest.'

'At least it would keep you warm, mate. Like the way a penguin covers its egg in the Antarctic.'

'Her big flabby tits would be bouncing like basket balls on top of her belly and because she's looking down at me she'd have more chins than a Chinese telephone directory.'

'All right then, we'd have to count out the "her on top" position. The weight would probably cut off the circulation to your cock, which would mean a serious case of Mr Floppy. That's no good, when she's just paid a small fortune to hire you.'

'What about her underneath and me on top then?'

'There's two problems there, mate.'

'What's that?'

'You'd have to be hung like the proverbial rutting rhino to get anywhere near her fanny, because you'd be lying on a blubber mountain. You have to shag her off the horizontal with her lying on a table and you stood up, holding her massive thighs in the air.'

'Plus, if I was on top I'd end up burning my bare ass on the light bulb, eh?'

'Christ, this is a real dilemma.'

'Doggy is it, then?'

'It would have to be, wouldn't it?'

'You'd just have to part the huge arse cheeks before going for gold.'

'It'd be a bit like parting the Red Sea.'

'Do you reckon if I slapped her arse hard enough, the pressure wave would travel up her fat and clout her on the back of the head?'

'I don't know, mate, but it's theoretically possible.'

'I wonder... I wonder how much fat birds can shit.'

'Ahhhh, for fuck's sake let's not get on to that, mate!'

'Loads, I reckon. They must eat their fair share of pies to put on the poundage.'

'Well, they don't get that size by eating salads, do they?'

'I used to know a fat chick once. She blamed her size on big bones.'

'Ah, that old chestnut. Did she also blame incredibly heavy shoes whenever she stepped on the scales?'

'Yeah, and the scales always read heavier due to them being partially broken.'

'Or the other old chestnut that "I'm this size because I have a hormone problem."'

'A hormone problem that makes her a greedy fucker.'

'I'll have a family bucket of fried chicken and fries, a chocolate milkshake, and let's see... better throw in a chicken wrap...'

'Because she obviously missed breakfast!'

'A large popcorn chicken... and a DIET COKE!!'

'I know, mate. You feel like shouting at them, don't you? "THE DIET COKE IS NOT GOING TO STOP YOU POUNDING THE 10,000 CALORIES YOU'VE JUST STUFFED DOWN YOUR CAKEHOLE FROM SETTLING ON YOUR ASS!!"'

'Ha! I can't even think about how much they would shit after that. Imagine someone of that size trying to squeeze out the last twenty-four hours' worth of fry-ups and desserts? How would they get their ass on the seat?'

'I guess they would throw one flabby arse cheek one side of the toilet then throw the other cheek over the other side.'

'I wonder if some big girls ever cover up the air gaps between the toilet seat. It would be a nightmare if that happened and they pulled the chain on an aeroplane with a big vacuum suction.'

'Oh shit, yeah – it would cause an air seal, then a vacuum in the toilet bowl and suck them inside out.'

'At least they'd be thinner when they got off.'

'You would be if your bowels and intestines were sucked out and flushed around the U-bend.'

'Euuuurrrr!!!! That's it, mate – time out, time out! You deserve a red card for that one.'

'Right, come on, let's stop this conversation right here. It's turning my bloody stomach. Let's get the luggage down to the ladies.'

'Where are they again?'

'Master bedroom.'

'What, both of them with Mr Big again?'

'Yeah.'

'Dirty bastard.'

Tom and Rob fetch the guests' bags from the limo and take them down to the master bedroom. Rob knocks on the door and waits for an answer before entering. A voice calls out 'Come in!' and Tom and Rob shuffle in, carrying the heavy bags. One of the girls is lying on the bed watching TV and the other is rubbing oil into her superbly toned, bikini-clad body, ready for sunbathing.

The oiled-up brunette smiles and asks them to put the suitcases on the bed so she can sort out the clothes that need washing. The boys stand back a metre from the bed as she stands in front of them. She bends over and takes out the clothes, telling them which clothes need hand washing and which can be machine washed and at what temperature.

However, when an oiled-up, bikini-clad, high-class hooker with the body of a supermodel is bent over a metre in front of you, it's pretty difficult to take in anything she is talking about. After a minute or so she turns around and hands each of the boys a set of clothes.

'Thank you, boys, and we'll see you later,' she says with a wink.

The blonde on the bed is giggling, clearly amused at the boys' inability to multitask. Tom and Rob say thank you, walk out of the room and close the door behind them.

'Did you remember anything she just said to us in there?' says Rob to Tom.

'Not a fucking word, mate. My brain seemed to be on other things.'

'You're not alone. I think we'll have to start carrying a Dictaphone with us every time we talk to those two, so we can play it back afterwards.'

They drop the clothes off with Zecky at the laundry and explain the situation. She laughs and tells them she'll handle it and they head back up to the outside deck to talk to me and Jock.

'I take it the pick-up was uneventful, then?' says Rob.

'Depends which way you look at it,' I say, pointing at Jock.

Both Tom and Rob start to laugh, expecting another Jock story. They aren't let down when I tell them about the toilet and breast-sniffing incidents.

'They're strange dogs, dachshunds, aren't they, Jock? I guess they're small and easy to miss,' says Rob trying to make Jock feel a little better.

'Weird-shaped little fuckers, aren't they?' agrees Jock.

'Yeah, they are,' says Rob. 'I think it's a bit cruel that the owners and breeders make them that way. They must suffer from back problems when they get older because they have such long backs. I bet their dicks get dirty because they're so close to the ground. They must get all sorts of infections.'

'Sounds a bit like me. I wish I had a ten-inch cock instead of this fucking massive thing,' says Jock, grinning.

'Ha! You should have a licence for that, mate,' says Rob.

'You wouldn't be the first to say that. Anyway, I think it's bloody cruel what they do to dachshunds to make them longer. If I could get my hands on the bastards I'd grab them by *their* necks and ankles and stretch *them* like they do their puppies. How long do you reckon they have to pull them until they're at the right length?'

'Eh?'

'Pull them – the puppies – to make them longer... how long?'

'Ha! Nice one... you almost got me there, mate.'

I then turn to Jock who is looking at me with another confused expression on his face. 'Oh for fuck's sake, Jock!' I say, holding my head in my hands.

'What?'

'They don't hold them by their necks and ankles and pull them! They breed from the ones with longer backs over many years to create the breed's look.'

'Oh, right. Well, I'm glad about that because I don't like to see animals in suffering,' says Jock.

'Good on you, Jock, because neither do I. Whenever I run over something on the road I have to stop and make sure it's dead, or I have to put it out of its misery.'

'Me as well, mate. I remember this couple moved in next door to me about a week before I moved out of my pad back in Glasgow. They had this poor, skinny dog.'

'How skinny was it?'

'Skinny, mate. It had big long legs, a tiny stomach and a long slender head. They had two other little dogs that looked like little terriers. They used to take them all out in the field behind us every day and come back with rabbits.'

'Sounds like the guy was a poacher.'

'Anyway, I used to shout at him out of my window that he should bloody well feed the skinny one up, but it never got any fatter. On the night I moved out of the house I went into his yard and put the poor little sod out of its misery.'

'You *killed* his dog?!'

'Yeah, well, more like put it out of its misery. I couldn't bear to see it looking so skinny; it obviously never got fed. I could get my hands around its waist, for God's sake! I'd see the poor little bugger running after rabbits in the field so it was obviously bloody starving. It was the best thing to do for it, I reckon.'

'How did you put it out of its misery – so to speak?'

'Shovel on the back of its head. It didn't feel a thing.'

'Jock, do you know what breed of dog it was?'

'Er, yeah... I remember its owner got mad at me and shouted back it was a whuffet or something and that they were supposed to be skinny. Lying bastard. I reckon he just couldn't be arsed to feed it.'

'Jock, are you sure he didn't say *whippet*, mate?'

Jock snaps his fingers in front of my face. 'Yep that's it...

whippet. I remember the poor little fucker could run like lightning as well.'

Rob, Tom and I all cup our heads in our hands and let out a long groan. 'Jock, I hate to have to tell you this, mate, but you slaughtered a perfectly healthy hound. A whippet is like a miniature greyhound and they're used for dog racing on the track or chasing hares and rabbits in fields. They are *meant* to be lean, you nobber!'

'So you're saying I...'

'I'm afraid so, mate.'

'Fuck!'

CHAPTER 19

SWINE RODEO

Poor old Jock disappeared below decks to the crew room with his tail in between his legs, you might say, after I pointed out the error of his canine execution.

'His heart was in the right place I guess and it's a mistake any of us could make,' says Rob.

'Er... no, it isn't!' laughs Tom.

'No, I guess you're right, mate. There aren't many people that would make that mistake and go to such drastic measures.'

'Jock wouldn't hurt a fly intentionally, though. He obviously thought he was doing the best thing, in the big scheme of things.'

'I'm sure Hitler thought the same back in Germany during the war,' says Zecky, walking up the deck behind the boys.

'How's tricks, Zecks?' I say.

'Could be better. I've just been babysitting Jock down below. He's coming to terms with his canine slaughter. And I've just noticed that there are jizz stains on two of the girls' garments you gave me. It looks like my afternoon will be taken up with a pair of Marigolds, some stain remover and a bowl of hot water.'

'Errrr!!! Russian jizz, eh? I bet that's a bastard to get off. Does it smell of vodka and pelmeni?'

'Firstly, I'm not going to sniff this jizz in a million years and secondly what the hell is pelmeni?'

'It's a national dish of Russia – meat covered in dough.'

'Or in this case clothes covered in *man* dough,' says Rob, laughing.

'Whatever's in his jizz, it's going to be a bloody nightmare to get out.'

Tom suddenly puts on his finest and deepest Russian accent to mimic Mr Big. *'Ahhhh, Miss Zecky... I was wondering if you 'av ridded my lover's clothes of my crusty Russian jizzzz?'*

'That was quite a decent accent for you, Tom,' I tell him. 'Your portrayal of foreign languages is usually on a par with Jock's timekeeping – shit!'

'I bet you never thought in a thousand years when you applied for this job that one day you'd be in Porto Cervo, surrounded by mega-yachts, removing a dodgy millionaire's jizz off a dress,' Rob says to Zecky.

'You're not wrong, and by the way it's *two* dresses, each owned by a different girl. He's a naughty boy, is Mr Big. Maybe I should give the job to Tar,' she giggles.

'Oh, don't you worry, Zecks, he's going to have enough on his plate for the rest of the trip without him cleaning off jizz. Anyway, Jock has come up with a plan to rid him of some of his. Jock reckons what Tar needs to loosen him up is a few nights on the beer and a dirty shag,' I tell Zecky, laughing.

'What?!'

'Jock has come to the conclusion that Tar needs to lose his cherry and get laid for the first time,' says Rob.

'Has he now? Who's the lucky girl going to be, or shouldn't I ask?'

'We don't know yet but it's in the pipeline, so to speak.'

'Don't you think you should let it happen naturally?'

All of us look at each other and shake our heads with a look on our faces that insinuates that what Zecky has just suggested is a ploy to kill our fun. 'Naahh!' comes the unanimous reply.

'Well, be nice and make it special for him because he'll remember it for the rest of his life.'

Jock is clearly over his extermination sadness as he bounds up behind Zecky to join in the conversation. 'I don't remember my first time, so that's a load of bollocks,' he says, giving her a friendly swipe on her bottom with the back of his hand.

'Hey you! Don't touch what you can't afford,' she says.

'You don't remember what you had for breakfast a few *hours* ago, Jock. There again, that's what decades of alcohol abuse does to your memory,' I tell him.

'There is definitely a price to pay for such frivolities,' he laughs.

'Jock, I'm fucking amazed you can walk and talk at the same time, based on what he's just said,' says Rob.

'Cheeky bastard! It's true though, my short-term memory is fucked. I can't remember anything.'

'How long have you had this problem?'

'What problem?' jokes Jock.

Tom has a puzzled look on his face. 'I'm a bit surprised, though, even for you. How the hell don't you remember the very first time you had sex? You don't just forget that. I remember my first time like it was yesterday.'

'Go on then. Where were you?' says Jock.

'It was a full moon party in Thailand.'

'How old were you?'

'Seventeen.'

'What was her name?'

'Fuck knows.'

Everyone bursts out laughing. 'You see, even you don't remember, so I'm not on my own,' laughs Jock.

'Hang on a minute. The salient point here is I was in the moonlight on a beach in Thailand stoned off my lord. I was seventeen and she was around twenty-one. She was from France and she was around five-feet-six with shoulder-length curly hair and great tits. We did it lying on the sand and she was on top. I got sand down the crack of my arse and lasted about two minutes with all the excitement of the first time. The fact that I don't remember her name doesn't really count for anything. It's the vibe, the surroundings and the cosmetics that you mainly remember.'

'All right, fair point, mate,' Jock concedes.

'What about you, Rob?' asks Tom.

'It was a small goat at a farm in Wales. Her name was Flopsy and we shared a wonderful moment together.'

Zecky splutters over her coffee.

'It was idyllic,' Rob goes on. 'It was by the river when

our eyes met. I coyly took a wander over and asked her if she'd like to have a drink with me at the trough. She said yes, then after a wonderful afternoon I asked her for dinner in the next field where we dined on a hedge... it was just magical!'

'I always knew you were part Welsh. Really, do you remember everything, though?' asks Jock.

'Sure! Just imagine trying to find lingerie that would fit her woolly behind properly.'

'Ha! Come on mate, seriously, your first girl I mean.'

'Yeah, I do actually. My parents were away on a night out. I was fifteen and I got abused by the babysitter who was called Claudia. She kind of violated me, really.'

Zecky puts her arm around Rob to comfort him. 'Oh Rob, that's awful. Poor you, that must have been horrible.'

'Horrible my arse! It was fucking brilliant. For months afterwards I used to tell my folks I was scared to be left alone in the house when they went out. They took pity on me and they'd get Claudia round to baby-sit. I was milking them of sympathy while the babysitter was milking me... literally. It was the best time of my fucking life!'

Zecky has a good laugh before offering her perception on the differences between the sexes. 'What are you like? This is the difference between men and women, you see. We want romance and a connection and you lot just want a wet hole and a beer.'

'Well, yeah, but not necessarily in that order,' adds Tom, joking.

'Listen, Zecks,' says Jock with a serious face. 'Tom doesn't speak for all of us. Sometimes we like a cuddle and a bit of tender loving care as much as women do. Sometimes I like to lie down and talk for a while to connect, then lay her down on a bed covered in fresh rose petals with some gentle soothing music in the background.'

There is a long pause before Rob breaks the silence. 'That's actually a load of crap really, isn't it, Jock?'

'Yep, it's all about a good deep dicking for me!'

'Thought so.'

'Got any more jokes, have we, Jock?' asks Zecky, looking fairly underwhelmed.

'I know a great joke about women.'

'No Jock. Not that one – it's a bit offensive,' I warn him.

'No, go on, Jock. I'm a big girl – I can take it.'

'All right, what's the function of a woman?'

'Go on.'

'To be a life support system for a pussy.'

Even Zecky finds this funny. She can't very well tell him off, considering she told him earlier that men would be extinct if vibrators could get a round of drinks in.

'That's charming, Jock,' says Zecky, 'but I still can't believe that you truly can't remember who you first had sex with, out of all the girls you've been with.'

'Look, if you eat a tin of beans you don't know which one makes you fart, do you?'

Everyone has a good laugh at this before I steer the conversation back to the job and matters in hand: 'Anyway, Zecks, what do the guests want to do today?'

'The girls are being taken into Porto Cervo so they can to get some clothes for the Billionaire Nightclub tonight.'

'That'll cost him,' I say, raising my eyebrows.

'You're telling me!! It's all designer labels over there. You'll have to pop up to the Captain and get some money out of the safe. Mr Big told me on the phone this morning that he wants another thirty thousand in cash.'

'How the other half live, eh?'

'It's small change to him.'

'Let's hope he tips as much as he spends. If he does, it's going to be one hell of an end-of-charter-party.'

'What does he want to do himself?'

'Are you ready for this?'

'Go on then.'

'He wants to go horse-riding, and two of you are to go with him because his bodyguards will be with the girls. To be fair, I think he's sick of the sight of the guards and he wants a bit of freedom and a couple of fresh faces.'

'That's a tricky one. Can anyone ride a horse?' I ask, looking around at the boys.

At that point Tar joins us and catches the tail-end of the conversation. 'Did you say can anyone ride a horse?'

'Yeah.'

'Well, I can.'

'That figures. Well-off family living in the country – he's bound to have owned a horse or two at some point,' sniggers Rob.

'What was he or she called, then?'

'She was a black thoroughbred called Ebony and I had her for about five years until she was stolen.'

'I take it you didn't get her back, then?'

'No. She's probably in a barn somewhere being used for breeding.'

'All right then, Tar, you can go, since you can ride. Who else has ridden?'

I look at Rob and Tom but they shake their heads.

'I've ridden a horse a few times,' says Jock.

'I'm not talking about those festering old donkeys you see on the beaches at British seaside resorts, mate.'

'Yeah, I know.'

'When have *you* ever rode a horse?'

'Well, it was a while ago but it was back home.'

'Jock, you're not having me on, are you? If I'm going to send you with Tar you'd better know what the score is, because no doubt the client will be hiring some decent nags and trotting through countryside.'

'Yeah, no problem.'

'I don't know if I believe you, Jock, but you've never lied to me yet, so if you shake my hand on it I'll let you go.'

Jock shrugs and puts his hand out for me to shake.

'All right, mate, I've not got a particularly good feeling about this but you've shaken on it, so that's that.'

'What time do you want them ready, Zecks?' I ask her.

'Three pm at the passerelle.'

'Right then, that's sorted. I'm going to go see Thrush and get some money out of the safe for the girls to waste in town, all right? You two had better crack on with cleaning the boat, and give the jet skis a good look over,' I tell Rob and Tom.

Rob, Zecky, Tom and I move off the deck to carry on with our chores, leaving Tar and Jock. As Tar starts to walk away Jock holds his arm to stop him and quietly asks him to wait until they're on their own.

'Right, Tar, you're going have to give me a few pointers on how to drive a horse, mate.'

'What? You've just told everyone that you've ridden before.'

'Well, my knowledge of riding a horse stems about as far as going backwards and forwards on a rocking horse at my granddad's house as a kid. That and jumping on the backs of big pigs at my mate's farm.'

'Rocking horses? Pigs?!'

'Yeah. When I was a kid my mate used to run into the pig-pen on a farm with his capgun to scare the pigs. They used to shit themselves and run out of the pen towards the door and I used to hang on to a wooden beam over the exit. When they passed under me I'd let go and fall onto their backs then hold onto their ears.'

'You rode pigs and used their ears as reins?!'

'Yeah, but only the big strong ones.'

'You're kidding?'

'No, mate, my record back then was twenty-five seconds before it flipped me off!'

'I very much doubt they enjoyed the experience.'

'Big Samson didn't. You'd have to run like hell and jump over the fence before he caught up with you. He was a big boy!'

'I'm not surprised. I think I'd want revenge if someone jumped on my back and held onto my ears. So your total riding experience to date basically consists of a metal rocking horse…'

'It was a wooden one actually.'

'Sorry, a wooden rocking horse and a few pissed-off porkers?'

'Basically, yeah... that's about it.'

'You'll bloody *kill* yourself on a real horse, especially if it gallops. It will probably be a twitchy thoroughbred so you'll need your wits about you.'

'My granddad said never work with kids and never trust anything that's bigger and dumber than yourself. I'll be doing both of those this afternoon, so you're going to have to give me the basics if you don't want me to kill myself.'

Tar looks more than a little flustered and nervous at the task ahead of him. 'Jock, riding a horse is not the same as riding a bike. It's complex, and each horse is different. It can take ages to get the basics but to get proficient at it can take years. And we're bloody leaving in an hour!'

'You'd better get cracking then, matey.'

'Oh Jesus... where do I start?'

'Look, all you need to tell me is how you start it?'

'Start it? It's not an engine, Jock.'

'You know what I mean: start, stop, turn. The rest I'll figure out as I go along. If it doesn't do as I tell it, I'll give it a bollocking.'

'A bollocking... oh Jeeeesus!' says Tar, rubbing his forehead and looking worried.

'Relax, little man – everything will be cool.'

'Jock, you shook hands on it to say you've ridden before.'

'Well, he didn't specify what type of horse, so technically I didn't lie. I've always wanted to have a go on a real one. Anyway, how hard can it be?'

CHAPTER 20

LIVE FAST, DIE YOUNG AND LEAVE A GOOD-LOOKING

Jock and Tar get changed into something suitable for horse-riding, and Jock seems to be getting into the spirit of things. He's put on his tight jeans and has 'borrowed' Rob's leather cowboy boots and Zecky's kangaroo-skin cowboy hat that she uses at the beach. It's even funnier because he's not taking the piss: he's finally getting to live his dream of becoming a cowboy, even if it is just for the afternoon. All he needs now is a pistol, a spittoon and maybe a few tomahawk-wielding Indians to shoot at, and he's right there in the Wild West! Everyone knows he's a massive fan of John Wayne and he has all of his films in his cabin.

Eager as a beaver, Jock is the first to turn up at the passerelle, followed by Thrush and Tar. Thrush is his usual solemn self and there isn't a hint of humour in sight. The man couldn't cheer up a laughing hyena if his life depended on it.

'Here is some money from the slush fund,' Thrush says,

staring at Jock intently. 'I expect receipts for everything you spend and none of it is to go on alcohol. Is that understood?'

'Yep, no problem,' says Jock, lifting his hat.

'Tarquin, I want you to stay with him at all times. I want your best from both of you this afternoon. This is an unusual circumstance and it's not very often a guest of his stature goes away from the yacht on an excursion without their bodyguards.'

'This doesn't usually happen often, then?' enquires Tar.

'No, and especially not to someone like this guest,' says Thrush.

'What do you mean, if you don't mind me asking?'

Thrush tries to answer like he always does in his usual over-diplomatic and non-committal way: 'Let's just say that perhaps his wealth hasn't come from the more normal or legitimate ways.'

Tar is looking a little worried at this.

'I think what he's trying to say is his cash has probably been made illegally and he's probably pissed a few people off along the way,' explains Jock.

'I didn't say that young man, so don't put words into my mouth,' says Thrush.

'Well, that's exactly what you meant. You're trying to say he's a dodgy fucker.'

'Still you put the words into my mouth.'

Tar is now looking more worried. 'My God, I've just had a terrible thought. We could be in danger if he's made his fortune by illegal means and made a lot of enemies. We could get caught up in a vendetta.'

With no words of encouragement or without trying to

pacify Tar, Thrush turns and walks back inside. It's bloody typical of him but this is all new to Tar. *Life* is new to Tar. He's now working aboard a mega-yacht in an alien environment, away from home and completely out of his comfort zone. He wouldn't be human if he didn't feel at least a little bit apprehensive. Tar is being over-dramatic, much to Jock's amusement, but he plays along for the sheer entertainment value. It's becoming clear Tar can be a complete drama queen at times.

'Jock, I could be in trouble here.'

'Why's that, little man? Have you pissed your pants again?'

'Mr Big might have a price on his head from crossing some enemy back in Russia,' says Tar, frowning.

Jock is now quite enjoying the sight of Tar getting flustered. 'You might be right. Are you prepared to take a bullet for the man?' he says with a straight face.

'No, I'm not! Of course not,' Tar says with his eyes wide open.

'Ahhhh you see, you'll take tips off the guests but you won't put your arse on the line for them when the going gets tough, eh?'

Tar's voice is now getting even more high-pitched. 'Jock, there's a world of difference between doing a few extra hours a day for the guests' benefit and taking a bullet for one of them.'

'Would you take a bullet for £5,000?' asks Jock

'No.'

'£10,000?'

'No, I bloody wouldn't.'

'£15,000?'

'Jock, the point I'm trying to make here is you can't spend it if you are dead as a dodo.'

'Fair point, little man, just as long as you're prepared to get caught in the crossfire and back me up, that's all I can ask of you, I suppose.'

Tar is staring at Jock's poker face, unsure if he means it. Zecky puts her head through the porthole and tells Jock that their ride is just about to pull up at the yacht and Mr Big will be on his way down in a minute or two.

'No problem, gorgeous, I'll be ready with the door,' answers Jock. 'It doesn't look like we'll have a chance to go over the riding basics now, Tar, because we're leaving.'

'Brilliant... that's just brilliant. Now I might have to deal with you breaking your neck *and* possibly being caught in a revenge killing,' cries a flustered Tar.

Jock takes a coin out of his pocket and puts it in Tar's chest pocket.

'Here you are.'

'What's that for?'

'It's for you to go out and buy some testicles,' Jock says, trying to hold back a fit of the giggles.

'It's not funny, Jock. This could all be very real. Is it beyond the realm of possibility, I ask you that?'

'I think you should've seen Zecky for some Imodium before you came out, Tar.'

'Imodium? Why?'

'Because it's the only thing that will stop you from shitting yourself.'

'Very funny, Jock. Honestly, you should be on the stage,' says Tar sarcastically.

'Well, personally speaking I've always thought that. I reckon I've got hidden talent.'

'Well, I hope you find it one day.'

'Ha! You cheeky little sod. Anyway, quiet now because here's Mr Big walking towards us. If you see any red laser lights from rifle scopes passing over me, let me know, OK?'

The limo driver parks at the foot of the passerelle and opens the door as Mr Big, Jock and Tar walk down. Mr Big sits in the front whilst Tar and Jock sit together in the back. The driver speaks fluent Russian, which is unusual for around here. They start having a conversation between them, leaving Tar and Jock to talk quietly amongst themselves in the rear. Tar finally gives Jock a few very basic pointers on riding a horse.

'I don't know what you were bloody worried about, Tar. All of that seems fair enough. It's not exactly rocket science, is it?'

'Hang on a minute, Jock, because that's just some of the very basic theory we've gone through. The practice of it is much more difficult, and to top it all off, you never know what the horse will do. They all have minds of their own.'

At the stables they are met by a Corsican woman called Maria who shows them the eight horses that are available and provides them with a map of various routes and the distances of each. The horses are all large, muscular beasts in perfect condition. Her staff must spend hours a day grooming and caring for them, and it shows. She introduces each horse by name and tells them about their various personalities.

Mr Big is clearly impressed by a beautiful grey

thoroughbred male. His name is Sirius and Maria explains that he's a feisty one who loves to gallop. He is also the alpha male of the group and the other horses are happy to follow him. Sirius knows instinctively that he's about to go out; he's getting agitated and is starting to kick the door with excitement. One of the stable hands takes Sirius out into the courtyard with Mr Big to saddle up and get them acquainted. Mr Big clearly has lots of experience with horses. Maybe he made his money smuggling drugs over the Ural Mountains on horseback, or something equally mad. Whatever his experience is, it shows as he runs his hands over the horse and instantly calms him down.

Next, Tar and Jock choose their horses. Maria asks about their riding experience to gauge which of the animals each should have. Tar has the most experience and he talks for around five minutes about the rosettes he has won and equestrian friends, much to Jock's boredom. Jock just wants to get out and live the cowboy dream, so when Maria asks about his experience he just points at Tar and tells her 'same'. Mr Big is already on his horse, ready and waiting while Jock and Tar get saddled up.

'You get on first, buddy, so I can see how you mount,' Jock tells Tar quietly.

The horse seems to dwarf Tar, and when he's on he looks like an action man sat on a Shire horse – totally out of proportion. Now it's Jock's turn. He's got his back to Mr Big and he's stroking the horse's nose and telling it that if he doesn't hurt him, he won't hurt it. It seems like a fair deal. He follows Tar's lead and runs his hands along the horse's neck and along its back, then he puts his foot in the stirrup and climbs up. All appears to be well at this stage. Maria wishes them well, turns and leaves them to it.

'OK gentlemen, just try and keep up and follow me,' says Mr Big and with a click of his heels Sirius begins to walk out of the courtyard and down one of the bridle paths into a clearing in the wood. Jock follows whatever movements the others make ahead of him and it all seems to be working fine. Tar looks over his shoulder and has a word with him. 'Jock, if you don't want your horse to run fast, just make a bet on it in your head.'

'How's that going to help?' Jock whispers back.

'Well, judging by your past experience, betting on a horse slows it down,' says Tar, unable to resist a little piss-taking. But it's like water off a duck's back as far as Jock is concerned. He's dressed as a cowboy, he's riding a horse – or at least there is one between his legs – and he has the sun on his back. A big smile spreads across his face as he pulls out a big cigar from his chest pocket and sticks it in the corner of his mouth. The aroma from it is delicious and when Tar smells it wafting past him he turns around and sees 'John Wayne Jock' clearly in his element and living the dream.

'He's got to be kidding,' Tar mutters to himself.

After about half an hour of gentle trotting they reach an open field and Sirius starts to get restless. He's snorting and stamping his hooves and it looks like this is the place he usually burns off some pent-up energy. Mr Big stops to tell the boys that he's going for a gallop and that they should meet him at the ranch, which Maria suggested would be a good place to stop for lunch. Then he whips the reins and Sirius shoots off like he's been eating amphetamine rather than hay. It's magical to watch as all the horse's muscles become taught and Sirius accelerates from a standing start. The horse gallops down the field and they disappear around a wooden fence at the bottom of the meadow.

All is now silent and still, except for the whistling of the breeze through the tree branches and the gentle waving of the meadow flowers under the hot sun. Jock has the 'thousand miles stare' and his face is a picture of concentration as he gazes at the fence at the far end of the field. Tar can see what's going through his mind.

'Don't even think about it, Jock. You haven't done anything on that horse other than walk along. Galloping and leaping over fences is way out of your depth.'

There is no answer from Jock who is lost in the moment.

'Jock, are you listening to me?' repeats Tar.

After a moment of silence and quiet contemplation, a nugget of pure insight comes out of Jock's mouth, one that is far more philosophical than you'd ever expect from him. It's a moment of clarity and a defining one. 'I've just had an omen,' he says. 'Have you noticed how beautiful the landscape looks when you're standing at the edge of a cliff? Look at this place, it's beautiful.'

'An omen? Regarding what?'

'On how to live life. I'm going to gallop down this meadow on this horse and leap over that fence,' Jock says, pointing.

'No way, Jock, you'll kill yourself. It's far too dangerous, especially for someone of your limited experience. Anyway, it's a big fence and how do you know the horse will even try and jump it?'

'Faith. All you need is a little faith and belief, just like you need in life. Anyway, Tar, you came to sea to work, didn't you?'

'What's that got to do with it?'

'Well, you've no previous experience, and working at sea is the most dangerous place in the world to work,' says Jock.

'That's very different. I'm working with people who I trust and who know what they're doing.'

'You've only known us all a short time, though, so how can you be so sure you can trust us?'

'Because I can feel it.'

'Well, I trust this horse because *I* feel it. I'm going to trust this horse completely.'

'Jock, I still think you should take the safe option and go *round* the fence, because it's too risky to jump it.'

'Fuck the safe option, Tar. Life is a risk every day. Nothing ever worthwhile ever came from the safe middle ground. Life is only really satisfying and worth living at the extremes. Sometimes ships go to sea in really bad weather but that's never been a reason for them to stay in the safety of the harbour. Don't be a person who accepts mediocrity and the ordinary just because it's safe. You'll be amazed at the feeling you get by daring to be that person you've always wanted to be. When you put yourself in a position where you could lose everything, only then does your true nature show through. Be that intrepid spirit who strives to conquer. Live life without fear because it's only fear that holds you and everyone else back on this planet. At the end of the day, to deny your God-given feelings and emotions is to deny nature and your true self. The realisation of your true self is your prime aim in life.'

Tar is shocked and astounded at the words that have come out of Jock's mouth. He tries to think of something sensible to say to change Jock's mind but nothing comes. Everything Jock has just said is absolutely true and makes perfect sense. A life lived in fear is no life at all. Without comparison everything loses its meaning. Sometimes you *do* need extremes and risk to remind you of who you are and confirm that you are indeed alive. Tar takes a deep breath then looks back at Jock over his shoulder.

'I must be going out of my mind but I've just had déjà vu of this exact space and time. You on that horse, those words and this view,' says Tar.

'I'll see you on the other side of the fence, Tar.'

'Hang on Jock, *I'm* not jumping that.'

'Yeah, you are.'

'I'm not – no way!'

'OK, but you'll have to live with yourself and look yourself in the mirror every day knowing you could have been that person you've always wanted to be but then backed down at the challenge. Anyway, you've jumped obstacles on a horse before and I haven't, so you have the advantage.'

'Obstacles that were a couple of feet high, that's all. It's hard to see from here, but that fence looks around six feet and we don't know if the horses will jump. If they stop at the last moment we'll be off.'

'*Faith*, remember?' Jock tells Tar, looking him in the eyes.

No further words are spoken as Jock and a terrified Tarquin sit there on the backs of their horses. After a short period of contemplation Jock runs the palm of his hand gently between the horse's ears and down the side of his neck. The horse snorts loudly and stamps its hoof, as if it knows what is about to happen. Jock cracks his reins and digs his heels in. His horse momentarily rises onto its back legs and then bursts into a gallop down the field towards the fence.

Jock's posture is wrong and he looks really unsteady as he tries to keep his balance on the beast. He looks like he could fall off at any moment. As Jock and the horse speed down the field at full gallop and approach the fence Tar has his hands over his mouth. 'Shit... shit... shit... he's going to kill himself!' he mutters to himself.

A few moments later he sees Jock's horse rise as it launches itself over the fence. Somehow, Jock is still loosely on its back as it takes off, but as both of them reach the pinnacle of the jump there is a clear gap between them. The horse lands on the other side of the fence without stumbling and Jock can be seen lying flat on top of the horse with his arms around its neck. After a minute or so Jock rises steadily to a sitting position. He obviously needed a few moments for the realisation of what he's just done to sink in – either that or to thank a higher power for not breaking his neck!

Tar squints hard as he struggles to see Jock and the horse in the distance but he's sure he can discern a cloud of cigar smoke around his head. Jock shouts at Tar, who can't make out what he's saying. He can see him gesturing passionately with his arm, though, and it's clear what he wants him to do. Tar is battling with himself and he's trying to will himself forward but he can't make his body move to get the horse to shift. He's scared stiff and the feeling of self-preservation overlaps his inner need to step out of his comfort zone and be brave. He's just about to make his way down the meadow and apologise for not living up to expectations when he hears the words Jock spoke before the jump loud in his head, as if he was right next to him.

'Fuck it!' he squeals at the top of his voice before digging his heels into the horse's flanks.

The horse, already startled with the intensity of Tar's exclamation, is already on the move. Fearful but most definitely alive, Tarquin is well balanced and is taking the weight on his legs as he approaches the fence. He can see Jock on the other side willing him on with vigorously waving arms. He fights a natural reaction to close his eyes as the horse begins to leap, and keeps them open. The jump is graceful and the horse clears the fence with ease, helped by the small weight it's carrying. It lands with a thud and a small cloud of dust puffs up from the hooves. Jock is already yelling at the top of his lungs and he's clearly happy Tar had the balls to do it. Both of them leap off their horses and run toward each other to celebrate the feat. Jumping in the air and shouting with elation they give each other a hug.

'You took your bloody time!' Jock tells Tar good-naturedly while thumping him on the back. 'I thought I was going to get arrested for loitering.'

'It took me a while to pluck up the courage, I'll have to admit that,' says Tar.

'Well, you did it, mate, and that's all that counts.'

'I did, yes. I still can't believe it, really.'

'I can't either. I thought you were going to pussy out on me!'

'Well, it did cross my mind a couple of times.'

'All right now, Tar, that's enough hugging. If there are any women watching you'll convince them I'm spoken for, and we can't have that now, can we, little man?' says Jock through teeth clamped on a cigar.

'That was bloody amazing!' shouts Tar unable to control his excitement.

'It was a hell of a jump, mate. Let's put it this way, it was a lot more fluid than mine.'

'It did look like you separated from the horse at one point and I thought you were going to go one way and the horse was going to go the other.'

'Well, that makes two of us. I was hanging on for dear life! Have you ever seen those crazy motorbike riders on the TV? They go full throttle up a ramp then leave the bike in mid-air to do tricks but then get back on them before they land. Well, that was me, except my bike was that horse and I didn't mean to leave it!'

'Crikey, I bet that was a bit scary.'

'A bit scary?! I nearly shit my pants half way down the meadow even before the jump.'

'Maybe we should have taken some of that Imodium you mentioned.'

'I tell you, this fence-jumping is the best laxative I've ever had, mate.'

'What went through your mind when you were in the air?' asks Tar.

'Errrr… "You're fucked, Jock!"'

'Ha! No, really, what were your thoughts?'

'Live – just live to tell the tale.'

'Yep, that's about the same for me as well. I've never

wanted to live as much in my life as I did in that split second. I felt so alive I can't fully explain it.'

'It's called adrenaline. Now you tell me: what do you think is worth more, now you've done it – a life of mediocrity or even just a few seconds of what you've just had?'

'I don't really think you need to ask that,' says Tar. 'I've had at least a little horse-riding experience, Jock, even if it wasn't at that level, but you didn't have any! Seriously, Jock, you could have died young here today.'

'Yep, but look at it this way, little man – as I've always said, I'd have lived fast, died young but left a really good-looking corpse.'

'Well, there is always that.'

'By the way, Tar, you can give me back that coin I put in your pocket.'

'Why?'

'Because you no longer need to buy yourself some testicles.'

CHAPTER 21

INSPIRATION COMES
IN MANY FORMS

After their fence-leaping celebrations, Jock and Tar catch up with Mr Big and Sirius at the meeting place along the track. They have a light lunch, then Mr Big insists on introducing them to the merits of Stoli vodka – in large quantities. This spontaneous booze-up lasts much of the afternoon and after some initial language difficulties, proves to be much fun for all concerned. They spend quite a long time giggling hysterically at Sirius trying to shag the arse off Tar's horse. After a few more vodkas Jock even teaches Mr Big to moonwalk and shows him how to make a circumcised erect penis by carefully folding a beer towel in the right places. According to Jock, it's essential knowledge.

However, the afternoon of vodka drinking affects Tar a bit more than the other two. It is clear that he's had enough when Jock has to carry him over his shoulder and manhandle him onto his horse.

Back at the yacht in very good spirits – vodka, to be precise – they are greeted at the passerelle by Zecky and

Thrush. As Zecky opens the limo door to offer Mr Big a cool face towel she is met by a cloud of acrid cigar smoke. Jock and Mr Big are on either side of Tar in the back seat, propping him up and puffing on huge cigars.

Jock gets out and helps the still giggling and blind-drunk Tar. Mr Big climbs out the other side with a big grin on his face and slaps Jock on the back as he passes him at the foot of the passerelle. He clearly doesn't want to talk to Thrush, whose face is turning crimson with anger at the state of Tar. Instead he walks straight past him, then up the outside stairs to the sun deck where the girls are in the Jacuzzi.

'What the *hell* have you two been doing?' thunders Thrush.

'Looking after our guest,' answers Jock.

'I expressly told you not to drink alcohol!'

'That's not quite what you said,' says Jock, shaking his head.

'Don't you tell me what I did and didn't say, young man.'

'Well, you never said that.'

'Yes I did! I told you that I wanted your best this afternoon and to not spend any of the money I gave you on alcohol.'

'Hang on a minute,' says Jock as he helps Tar to sit down on top of a rope mooring bollard. He steadies him and puts him into a position of temporary stable equilibrium, then watches him for a second before continuing the conversation with the wild-eyed Thrush.

'What you said and what you meant were two different things. I didn't spend any of the money on alcohol.' Jock then pulls the cash out of his pocket and hands it back to Thrush. 'Every last penny you gave me is there.'

'Itsh allll therrrre,' slurs Tar, who is still sat on his bollard with eyes closed in a drunken stupor. He's starting to wobble from side to side so Jock holds his arm out to steady him.

'You knew what I meant when I said that,' says Thrush, jabbing a finger in Jock's chest.

'First of all, Captain, you'd better get your finger out of my chest before I rip it off.'

'Don't you threaten me, young man.'

'I'm not threatening you but if you keep jabbing me I'll have to stop you, that's all I'm saying. Secondly, if you meant otherwise, you should've been more specific.'

'Don't you tell me how I should or shouldn't talk to you, young man.'

'Look, we were just looking after the guest as you told us to.'

'Yes, but not by getting blind drunk, you idiot!'

'To be honest, Captain, I know I've had a few but I'm not drunk. I've still got all my faculties. Fair enough, Tar is a bit worse for wear, but the guest insisted. We couldn't let him drink on his own, could we?'

'Why not? You were on duty, for God's sake.'

'Well, he insisted, and it's bad form and rude to refuse when you're offered a drink. Have you ever drunk on your own when everyone else stays sober? It wouldn't have been much fun for him, so that's why we joined in.'

'Look, don't tell me about drinking. I used to drink.'

'Well, you should've kept it up, because you look fucking miserable!'

'Miiiisssserable,' mutters the still giggling Tar.

'How dare you speak to me like that! I can assure you this will be taken further. As for you, Tarquin, I expected much better from someone who has only been aboard a short time.'

There's no response from the swaying Tar. Thrush then pushes Tar on the shoulder to grab his attention, knocking him off balance so that the lad nose-dives like a Stuka into the teak deck. Amazingly he comes to rest in a wonderful position that is a pure comic moment – lying with the left hand side of his face on the deck, his arms by his sides, his knees under his chest and arse in the air. If he tried to do it a million times he wouldn't be able to repeat it. 'Oh, for God's sake, look at the state of you – that's pathetic!' winces Thrush.

Thrush is thinking 'pathetic' and Jock is thinking 'priceless'. Jock secretly wants to rush to his cabin and get his video camera. This is prime YouTube material.

'What have you got to say for yourself?' Thrush shouts at Tar.

There's a few seconds of silence whilst Tar's befuddled brain processes the question, but then comes his rather inappropriate response: 'Fuuuucking gooood afternoooon,' he drawls before vomiting green bile over Thrush's Italian leather shoes.

* * * *

Tar is taken straight to bed and spends the rest of the day in his bunk sleeping it off. Jock, on the other hand, has a couple of coffees and is fine after an hour or so. He decides to keep a low profile and disappears down the forward store to carry out an inventory. Mr Big has a Jacuzzi with the girls then has a sleep for a few hours to recuperate. Feeling a little shabby and hung-over when he wakes, he decides to powder his nose with some more coke to refresh himself. Zecky catches him doing two lines off the top of the glass table as she brings him a constant flow of strong filter coffee.

'Christ, it looks like he's been using the table for baking, judging by the amount of white powder,' Zecky tells Rob on her return.

The limo returns just before nine o'clock to take the guests to party at the Billionaire Nightclub, leaving just the crew aboard the yacht. Even Thrush manages to get ashore for a few hours to do what ever Thrush does ashore. Nobody knows what he gets up to. He doesn't drink or go down to the beach and he's too bloody tight to pay for a decent meal. Jock thinks he goes 'cottaging' or something equally sneaky. Rumour had it that he was suffering from cabin fever and so he needed a break. Not surprising, really. Before Thrush left he had told me and Zecky that the ship would be leaving at nine o'clock in the morning from Porto Cervo to head over to Ibiza, where eventually the guests would be leaving.

After the guests depart for the nightclub I lift the passerelle and raise it up to a forty-five degree angle. The end is about seven feet off the quay so nobody can get aboard without using their personal remote controls to lower it to ankle level. A buzzer will sound in the crew room to warn the crew that it is being lowered, so they can relax.

I invite everyone to gather in the crew room to break open a case of beer and to tell them about the sailing plans. And we all want to hear the story of Jock's afternoon with Mr Big. I'm anticipating that it wasn't a normal day, judging by the information I'd gleaned so far. Tar's vomiting has got rid of much of the alcohol but he's being drip-fed water by Zecky to make sure he's all right for the morning. He looks like shit but that's to be expected, because he's not used it.

Everyone is sat down around the communal table in the crew room waiting for Jock to finish showering and join us. After about five minutes he walks in with a beer in his hand. No change there then.

'All right, Jock, take a seat and tell us something we don't know,' I say.

Jock climbs over the seats and sits between Tar and me. He takes a swig of his Heineken and thinks for a moment. 'For some reason, I've been having really dirty dreams lately about Cherie Blair. It's bloody weird, because I don't even fancy her!'

The crew are instantly in fits of laughter whilst Jock sits there looking deadpan bemused. After I regain my composure I put my hand on Jock's shoulder. 'No, mate – I'm talking about today. What happened today with Mr Big?'

'Oh right, yeah, got you. Thought you were talking about something else then.'

'Clearly.'

'Just the usual really. Drove to the stables, leapt a fence, had an omen, watched Tar get wankered, watched his horse get reamed by Sirius and taught Mr Big how to moonwalk. Run of the mill day, really,' he laughs.

'How did you get on with riding a strange horse?' asks Zecky.

Tar relives the moment. 'Well, I wouldn't call it riding, really. It was more of a partially controlled free-fall. You know what I mean – when you jump out of a plane and skydive, you wouldn't call it flying, would you?'

'Well, yeah, he's got a point,' says Jock. 'I just about managed to stay on the horse as it was galloping and when he leapt over the fence.'

'You leapt over a fence?' asks Tom, incredulous.

'Yeah.'

'How big?'

'Not that big.'

'I beg to differ, Jock,' says Tar.

'How big was it Tar – truthfully?' asks Zecky.

'About as high as him but maybe taller.'

'Are you mad?' asks Rob.

'I think we all know the answer to that one,' says Tom.

'You could have killed yourself.'

'Tar and I have already had this conversation, mate. Besides, I've seen enough John Wayne movies to know the basics.'

'All except turn and stop,' laughs Tar.

'You told me you could ride, Jock,' I say, looking pained.

'Yeah, I can. I was just getting used to a different horse,' says Jock, squeezing Tar's leg under the table, prompting him not to say anything.

'How the hell did you get Mr Big to moonwalk, Jock?'

'You'd be amazed what vodka shots make people do. He was pretty good, actually.'

I point at Jock and Tar: 'I've got to tell you two that you might well be in some shit after today.'

'How so?' asks Tar innocently.

'How so?! You came back blitzed and puked on Thrush's shoes, for a start.'

'Fair point,' says Jock.

'I did what?! Noooo!' says Tar, looking astounded at the accusation.

'You don't remember?'

'I remember getting on the back of the horse but everything is a blur after that. What did Thrush say?'

'He was pretty pissed off and I'll guess you'll find out tomorrow what his response will be. Plus, you were both pissed while looking after the guest,' I say, biting my lip.

'He bloody loved it though, mate, and it was his idea,' Jock protests.

'Well, the only way you're going to get out of this is by getting Mr Big to tell Thrush that he insisted.'

'Look, I've taught him my cock trick with the beer towel. He loved it! I reckon I'll have no problems getting him to say it was his doing. I reckon me and him have a got a bit of a bond now.'

'Hope for your sake you have, mate.'

'What else did you get up to, then?' asks Zecky.

'The weirdest thing ever,' says Jock. 'Not sure if I believe it yet but I reckon we should all get our laptops and bring them in here.'

'Why?' asks Tom.

'Bit of a weird thing really. After a few vodkas Mr Big's English became a little better and he was a bit easier to understand.'

'That's weird because it usually goes the other way after drinking,' I say.

'Yeah, I know, but maybe he was relaxed and using a different part of his brain. I don't know, but anyway, he told me in pigeon English that he'd made his money back in Russia from making music and buying clubs.'

'We all thought he was dodgy.'

'Well, he is. He initially made his money through the usual illegal ways.'

'I thought as much. Anything specific?'

'Well, he looked at me dead in the eye, put his finger over one nostril and sniffed through the other. Then he smiled at me and winked. Take from that what you will.'

'Ohhhh, gotcha. No surprise there, then.'

'Then he came out with the weirdest thing. He said he got his inspiration for *everything* by sitting in the dark with his earphones on, turned up at full volume, staring at his computer screen.'

'His computer screen? Why? What's on the screen and what's in the earphones?'

'He said I'd think he was crazy if he told me but after I pressed him for a bit longer he told me.'

'What was that, then?'

'He told me but I couldn't understand it, so I asked him to write it down. He said in a roundabout way that you'll learn the secrets of the universe.'

'The secrets of the universe?'

'Yeah, and everything about yourself by having a couple of beers to relax then putting the screensaver on and listening to a particular song that you set on repeat. Once you've listened to the track three or four times and un-focus your eyes whilst staring at the screensaver *everything* just comes to you. He reckons you get these powerful random thoughts that surge into your mind like a juggernaut, a bit like a more visual meditation. He reckons he owes all of his great ideas, knowledge and resulting money to this.'

Everyone is staring at Jock, silently trying to comprehend what he's just told us.

'Are you bullshitting us, mate?' I ask him.

'Nope. Swear on my mother's life that's what he told me, and I know he was serious. I didn't detect a hint of bullshit. He was straight up.'

'Well, for all your faults you do have a fairly decent bullshit detector,' says Tom.

'How come I don't remember any of this?' asks Tar.

'Because you were sat down at the bottom of the steps, out of your box on vodka, watching Sirius trying to shag your old nag and wondering how Sirius's cock got to be the size it was.'

'I wasn't staring at his cock!'

'Yeah, you were. Mr Big and I were laughing at you.'

'All right, I'll admit I was in awe of it. It *was* massive!'

'You like a bit of cock, do you, Tar?' I add, unable to resist a little leg-pulling.

'No! I'm just saying I've never seen a horse's... you know... that big before, that's all.'

'That's probably why your nag was trying to get away from it, mate. If it was the size you say, you wouldn't really want that up your jacksy, would you?'

'I think we're getting off the point here,' says Zecky.

'Yeah, we are. What was the bloody screensaver and what was the track?'

'The track was called "Govinda",' says Jock. 'He said it's by a British band called Kula Shaker and it's on their album *K*.'

'What does "Govinda" mean?'

'Govinda is what the sages call Krishna,' says Tar,

suddenly confident. 'He pervades all the worlds, giving them power.'

'And who or what is Krishna?' asks Zecky.

'Krishna is a worshipped deity,' explains Tar. 'Many religious groups call him different names, but I guess he's recognised as the Supreme Being.'

'God?'

'Yes, if that's what you want to call it, but I prefer "the higher power", because when you say "God" it stirs up a lot of strange emotions and feelings in different religions.'

'And how do you know so much about this, Tar?' asks Rob.

'I had to study religion at school.'

'Oh, right.'

'What was the screensaver, then?' I ask him.

'It's in the Windows Media Player menu. Then you put the CD in or click on the download of the song from your hard drive until Windows Media Player pops up and plays the song. Once it does that you right click the screen, and then put the arrow over "Battery" in the sub menu and click on "The World" screen saver. Well, you do in Windows XP, anyway.'

'Then what?'

'Then just plug your earphones in, turn up the volume, watch the screen and have the mysteries of the universe unfold in front of your eyes... apparently. You have to have your mind clear and be relaxed when you start, though.'

Everyone takes a drink of their beers and we sit in silence for moment or two. Rob is the first to move. This is right up his street. He's kind of deep and soulful at heart. Eventually curiosity overwhelms him.

'Fuck it, I'm going to give it a go. Come on you lot, grab

your laptops and bring them in here and we'll put the lights out and give it a go,' he says.

Everyone fetches their computers and Rob quickly downloads the song onto their hard drive. After fifteen minutes or so we're all set.

'Right then,' I tell them. 'On the word "go" play the song and stick your earphones on. We'll listen to the track at least six times before we stop, put the light back on and take our earphones off. Now, is everyone sat comfortably?'

'Yep,' they all reply.

I then switch the light off and shuffle back to my seat, put my earphones on, and give them the countdown. The room is silent except for the music in our ears, and pitch black except for the faint swirling coloured light emitting from the screens. Everyone sits there in the darkness listening to the track again, again and again, and staring blankly at the screensaver with unfocused eyes.

After the sixth time of playing everybody takes off their headphones. There is a short silence before Rob switches the light back on. We all glance at each other, looking spaced out and thoughtful.

'Oh my God! That was AMAZING!!' says Zecky.

'Did you get any random thoughts spring into your mind?' asks Rob.

'Loads, I feel completely at peace with myself,' she says, wiping a tear from her cheek.

'I know! I thought it was just a load of bullshit at first but after the second or third play I just fell into a kind of trance and I forgot where I was. It was the weirdest feeling. What about you, Tom?'

'The same, mate – except I saw my childhood. I feel really calm now.'

'Is that all that came through, just your childhood?'

'No, that was just one part. I feel like I'm wiser, for some reason. Sounds crazy I know but I felt the presence of an immense calm force all around us. I feel more spiritually *aware*.'

'That's exactly what I was going to say – more aware of *everything*! It feels like I've taken a peek into the beyond and all the answers are within my grasp,' I tell them, not really knowing how this happened.

'Well, they say that God speaks to us in many forms,' says Zecky.

'Yeah, but come on! Through a bloody screensaver?' says Tom.

'What do you want – a burning bush?!'

'What about you, Jock? Did you feel anything?'

'I'm still tripping to be honest. It feels like I've taken a tab of LSD. Apart from that I felt pretty much the same as you've just said. It was almost hypnotic really. I feel different, for sure.'

'Bloody hell, that's weird how we all felt the same things.'

'Do you know what's *really* strange, though? You can get omens and pick up knowledge from seeing everyday things that speak a silent language that explains things to you,' says Rob.

'For example?' asks Zecky.

'I went for a walk one day in the woods and I was just walking along, thinking about where my life was going and what direction I should take with my job. I guess I just wanted a little inspiration from somewhere and I got it.'

'How so?' asks Rob.

'I just saw a tree. I saw the way its trunk rises up, then all the main branches come off it, then all the small branches and twigs came off them. I realised then that different branches leading off the trunk represented certain jobs and life paths I could take. If I took certain paths it would only allow me to go so far up the tree before I reached a dead end. It's hard to believe that a simple tree can really help you out and put your mind on the right track.'

Tar decides to share his experience: 'Something similar happened to me. I saw a tumbleweed blowing down a dusty old street. I was worried about coming here because it would be all new to me. I guess I felt a little bit apprehensive because you're all a lot more worldly wise than me because you're older.'

'So what did you get from the tumbleweed?' asks Zecky.

'As it rolled down the street it was getting bigger and stronger as it picked things up. I saw it as an omen that I shouldn't worry about coming here.'

'How so?'

'Because like the tumbleweed I'll grow from whatever I pick up as I cover new ground.'

'That's really philosophical, Tar!' says Zecky, smiling at him.

'Well, I didn't consciously think of it. Like Rob said, it spoke a silent language to me. It's true what Rob says – the most simple things can be the most helpful.'

Jock is nodding his head in agreement. 'Yeah, mate, I get them all the time as well.'

'Really? What was your omen, then?'

'I remember shagging this bird doggy-style over the back of my sofa.'

Everybody turns to Jock with confused looks on their faces.

'What thoughts did that inspire?'

'Well, I just remember looking down at her fat arse and thinking *fuck meeee*, I'm going to have to tell her to go on a diet!'

CHAPTER 22

WE ARE US

The guests' night at the Billionaire Nightclub was apparently a great success as they didn't get back to the yacht until nearly six in the morning. Zecky managed to get a little sleep for a couple of hours before the chauffeur called her to say they were leaving the nightclub and would shortly be back at the yacht. She met them at the passerelle and brought them some more drinks to finish their night. Everybody was a little worse for wear, as expected.

Earlier, Thrush and his partner Olga had come back from a very expensive meal ashore that she'd managed to claw out of him. She decided to come down to join the crew for a drink in the crew room to tell everyone how much the meal had cost and to brag about her new Gucci dress that she'd got Thrush to buy for her.

Tom couldn't hide his disdain towards her as he whispered in Jock's ear. 'That is some bloody woman, eh, mate? What a fucking gold-digger! How can Thrush *not* see what she's doing? If he lost his money you wouldn't see her for the dust she'd make running off into the sunset.'

'It couldn't happen to a nicer guy. The silly sod deserves everything he gets. Rose-tinted spectacles I think they call it.'

'I say "woman" in the loosest possible terms. She's more like a one-celled parasite that lives in his digestive track soaking up all the nutrients – bit like a tapeworm.'

'Ha! Tapeworm! I think we've just found a new nickname for her.'

'I think we have, mate. Growing bigger and fatter and with every mouthful.'

'Or every paycheck.'

It turned out to be a bit of an eye-opener for us all in the end. Thrush, as usual, didn't feel the need to socialise with his crew and went to bed when he stepped back aboard. We were all happy about that, but we couldn't help but wonder what was so wrong with coming in for one drink? Olga, on the other hand, had a few more glasses of wine. Zecky and the other girls were friendly to her but watched what they said. It was more through fear than anything, because if you're talking to her you're talking to Thrush in a roundabout way. It was very rare that she joined the crew for a drink, and that probably had something to do with Thrush.

However, last night was different. She was a little drunk when she got back and then carried on in the crew room. The conversation between her and the girls ended up revolving around men and their little foibles. This was after she'd talked at length about her Gucci and how Zecky's new top *wasn't* designer label.

In the course of the chitchat she let slip that Thrush likes to be called 'The Beast' in the throes of passion. Beautiful! It also came to light that they liked to dress up. She wasn't drunk enough to admit what he wore, but leather was insinuated. She eventually went to bed after a couple of hours and the rest of the crew kept quiet until they heard Thrush's cabin door close on the upper deck. Zecky crept up the stairway just to check that it was closed and then zoomed back down to the crew room. Jock, Tom, Rob and I had huge grins on our faces as she came in and closed the door.

Jock couldn't control his enthusiasm as the door slammed shut. 'Fucking hell! "THE BEAST" – that's priceless! We're going to get some mileage out of this one.'

Rob burst out laughing. 'I feel like I've just won the bloody lottery or something. From now on we have to bring the word "beast" into any conversation when he's around, and we can get away with it.'

* * * *

The time of sailing comes around far too quickly. Rob and I get up at around seven to do the usual cleaning routine. When we go down to the outside deck guest area we find Mr Big and his two girls crashed out on the sofa, still wearing what they had on the night before. The ashtrays are full of burnt joints and a big pile of coke is still on the glass table. We think it best to leave them to it so we don't bother cleaning that area until later. Then Thrush starts the engines to leave the port and the rumbling and the motion of the yacht wakes everyone. The guests manage to drag themselves inside and go straight to bed to catch up on their sleep.

Once the yacht is safely out at sea I instruct Tar to help Steve, the engineer, to fix the navigation light on the forward mast. The job is another complete piss-take.

I'm on watch in the wheelhouse, navigating the yacht clear of traffic, when I see a very worried-looking Tar concentrating on a bucket full of water that he's holding in front of him. He's really sweating and fidgety and his little arms appear to be shaking. A partly submerged margarine tub filled with white powder is floating in his bucket.

Steve had told Tar that to fix the light they needed to take some 'white sparks' up to the bow of the ship. He was also told that under no circumstances should he put the bucket down or let the margarine tub touch the sides because the powder in the tub was extremely unstable. If the tub touched the side of the bucket, Steve told Tar, it might knock the crystal powder and this would be enough to set off a very explosive chain reaction. What he didn't tell him was that the white powder was soap powder!

Steve had then disappeared out of sight and joined me in the wheelhouse to get a bird's eye view of the proceedings. We then spend the best part of fifteen minutes rapidly altering course to make the yacht rock from side to side. This made Tar more nervous and he had to try even harder to maintain his balance. After the first few alterations of course Tar is seen on the fore deck screaming at the wheelhouse, at the top of his voice.

Steve keeps out of view behind the radar as he's laughing and I gesture through the thick wheelhouse windscreen that I can't hear what he's saying. This makes Tar sweat even more and swear like a true sailor. What really breaks the camel's back is when I use the outdoor speakers to tell Tar that I'm going to sound the ship's horn to warn a vessel ahead that I'm going to alter course, and that he should put his hands over his ears.

I know he's been told not to put the bucket down, so there's no way he can cover his ears at the same time. The ship's horn is immensely powerful and in the right conditions can be heard up to two or three miles away. Steve and I can barely control our laughter as the horn blasts out. It is a sight to behold, watching a terrified Tar hold up the bucket in front of him, prancing around like an Irish dancer while trying to shield his ears with his arms. This is not helped by yet another alteration. After a while Steve goes down to the fore deck to end his misery, and it appears that Tar has forgotten his manners and decorum.

'WHAT THE FUCK KEPT YOU?!' he squeals.

Even though he expects Tar to be alarmed, the lad's fury catches Steve slightly off guard. 'Oh, I had to take a phone call from the owner, mate. It couldn't wait.'

'I nearly *dropped* the fucking thing! He sounded the horn and it's right above me. I thought my eardrums were going to explode!'

'Bastard, eh? OK, mate, you've done well. But the reason I ended the call was because I realised these are the *wrong* sparks. These are even more unstable than the ones I meant to bring.'

'*More* unstable!?'

'Yeah. Now hand the bucket to me and be fucking careful. If you knock these sparks and it goes off we're done for. Don't even breathe on them.'

Tar then slowly lifts the bucket with his tired arms and gingerly hands it to Steve. After a couple of seconds, Steve pretends he's about to sneeze. From what Tar has been told, this would clearly be fatal.

'Err... shit! Tar, get the... eeeeuuuur... I'm gonna snee...'

'WHAT? No, you can't!'

Tar is now looking even more terrified, prancing around on the spot with bulging eyes.

'Ahhhh... Ahhhhhhhh... AAAAAAAHHHHHHHH... CHOOOOOOOO!!'

Before the sneeze finished, Tar is already on the deck curled into a ball with his hands on his head. Steve can't help but look up to the wheelhouse. I now have tears rolling down my face.

After a few moments, Steve leans down and slaps Tar on the back. 'Come on numb nuts, it's time for a coffee,' he tells him before dropping the bucket next to his head on the deck and disappearing off the fore deck.

It isn't a very enjoyable day for Tar. After the bucket escapade he spends an hour searching for some tartan paint, and then Jock asks him to get a bucket of seawater. However, this *isn't* a joke. Jock had meant him to open a fire hydrant on deck and get the seawater from there, but Tar thinks he's meant to get it from the sea. He dutifully finds himself a big bucket and ties a rope around the handle, then ties the rope around his wrist and throws it overboard.

The only problem is the yacht is doing fifteen knots, so when the bucket hits the water the rope pulls tight and proceeds to pull the screaming Tar down the deck until Jock comes to the rescue with a knife to cut the rope. By the time he gets to him Tar is half way over the side and gripping on with his knees and the inside of his arm. Jock cuts the rope and pulls the flustered Tar back on deck and calms him down. After a couple of minutes Tar is pacified, at which point Jock gave him a couple of slaps around the head 'for being a dopey cunt!!'

The rest of the voyage to Ibiza is spent taking the piss out of Thrush in subtle ways and watching Olga act very sheepishly around the dinner table. The crew doubt that she can remember much, considering her low tolerance for wine, but it's fun to watch nevertheless. Even the usually stiff upper lipped chef sees the funny side of it and has to leave the room halfway through his main course to have a good giggle in the privacy of his cabin.

'This is one *beast* of a beef pie, chef! I wonder how many *beasts* it would take to make a hundred of these?' asked Rob, with a twinkle in his eye.

I walked in half way through dinner after a work-out and say that I've just *beasted* myself with the weights.

This is followed by Jock telling everyone around the dinner table that he felt like a sweaty *beast* working on deck in the hot sun. The ribbing continues for much of the day until everyone has had their mileage out of it.

* * * *

The voyage to Ibiza takes a day and a half and we sail elegantly past the harbour breakwater shortly after 4pm. Zecky had told us all earlier that all the guests are going ashore into Ibiza Town for cocktails, and then heading off to a very exclusive, private nightspot that doesn't appear in any guidebooks.

'If they don't advertise, then how do they get the custom and make money?' asks Tar.

Zecky puts her arm round his shoulders and smiles at his naivety. 'They obviously don't have to advertise, do they? Anything that is different or a niche market is usually sold by word of mouth and by personal recommendation. Some places have a cult following.'

'Yes, I understand that, but how many people would they be able to get through their doors to buy their product, so to speak, if they don't advertise?'

'Does it matter? If they have a niche market and a cult following, then whatever they sell will obviously be more expensive and sought-after.'

'Like what?'

'Well, you can go into a store in most town centres and buy a cheap mass-produced poster for your wall at home, but you can guarantee that it's probably hanging on thousands of walls all over the world. It isn't exactly personal and exclusive, is it?'

'No.'

'Or you could buy a Katherine Welsby oil painting of a landscape. Do you remember that really vibrant one I showed you the other day?'

'The one you said makes you feel like you've taken LSD when you look at it?'

'Me and everyone else, but, yeah, that's the one. They are really sought after. Well, that would be painted personally by her for you. It would be painted to your colour scheme and to your exact specification. When it's hung up on your wall you could rest assured that there's no other painting in the world like the one you're looking at. It's exclusive. Apart from posting a few of her pictures on an art gallery website and a Facebook page, everything she sells is by word of mouth. Those who know, *know*. Do you get it?'

'Yes, I think so.'

'Are you all set for a party tonight then, Tar?'

'Party? What party?'

'Once the boys have cleaned the yacht we're all going up the road for a bit of a knees-up. It's Saturday night after all and this is Ibiza in the summer.'

'I thought we were going to have to stay on board.'

'Well, two people will have to do the duty but it won't be us tonight, thankfully.'

'When will the guests be coming back?'

'Not until tomorrow evening around six. Mr Big has a friend here so they will be with him at his place in the hills until that time.'

'That's a cracking bit of luck.'

'Make the best of it because this doesn't usually happen on charter.'

'Who's going, then?'

'The usual crowd. If you've never been to Ibiza then you'll definitely have fun, I can assure you of that. It really is one of a kind.'

As soon as the guests have left, the boys immediately get on with washing down the yacht. It's amazing what the promise of a night out in Ibiza can do for your work motivation. The wash and leathering down takes an impressive two hours, and everyone is washed, changed and ready to go by 7.30pm.

The taxi arrives at the passerelle and everyone jumps in.

'Hola!' says the taxi driver with a welcoming smile.

'Hola! Cafe del Mar, por favor,' says Zecky.

An overpowering mixture of aftershave and perfume fills the interior of the car. 'It smells like a bloody perfume factory in here,' says Jock, winding the window down for some fresh air.

'Most of it's coming from you, Jock, so I wouldn't complain too much.'

Jock then puts his arm around Zecky and nudges up to her on the back seat.

'Well, I'm feeling lucky tonight, darling. I think this is our night,' he whispers, before biting her on the ear.

Zecky playfully slaps his face and then elbows him in the ribs with enough force to make him wince. 'Hey you, you don't have much chance, anyway, but slobbering in my ear like a basset hound will not increase your chances.'

'Ahhhh, playing hard to get again, eh? Don't you want me to give you something that you've never had before, then?'

'And what would that be, Jock? A micro penis or leprosy?'

Jock winks at Tar who's sat facing him in the taxi. After a few moments he unzips his jeans, leans over and slaps his dick on Zecky's lap.

'Ohhhh Jesus, man! Put it away,' Zecky screams at him in between giggles. She tries to flick it away with her finger.

The taxi driver has seen what is going on in the back in the rear view mirror and he's laughing.

'Sorry, mate. We can't take him anywhere!' I tell him with a wink.

The driver then says something in Spanish and Zecky laughs out loud.

'What did he say?' Tom asks.

'He said, "Does he feed that thing live rats?"'

Everyone finds this funny, especially Jock who then tells Zecky she doesn't have to worry about the micro penis thing.

'Looks like it's just leprosy I have to check for then.'

The taxi pulls up at Cafe del Mar and everyone gets out and heads straight to the bar to order some drinks. We then find ourselves a spot outside where we can slowly get drunk and watch the sunset. We sit and tell stories, laugh and joke as the sun sinks slowly into the shimmering ocean like a molten orange orb. Holidaymakers and locals sit around absorbing the atmosphere, chilling on the cushions and enjoying the vibe. The sound of music that started out as a murmur gets louder and funkier as the sun disappears and the place comes to life.

'Well, Tar, how does it feel, mate?' Jock asks.

'Bloody fantastic! How could it be any better? I'm in Ibiza in summer, getting drunk with my new family. It doesn't get much better, really. I feel like I've grown really close to you, even if it has been such a short time. I'd hate it if any of you had to leave the yacht for any reason.'

'Well, little mate, you're going to have to get used to it, I'm afraid.'

We all stop talking and stare at Jock. I put my pint down on the table. 'What are you talking about, mate? Do you know something we don't?'

'I didn't want to tell you this, but I can't think of a better time really. The vibe's good and this will probably be the last time I'll be ashore with you.'

Tom leans forward over the table with serious look on his face. 'What's happened, mate?'

Jock clears his throat then lights up a cigarette. He sits back and takes a long hard drag before answering. 'I got sacked this morning,' he says, raising his hands nonchalantly.

'What! Who? Why?' I splutter angrily.

'Who do you think? Thrush – that's who. He said he didn't like my attitude and I guess coming back after a few drinks with Mr Big didn't help.'

'Yeah, but come on!' says Rob. 'You were only doing what the guest wanted you to do and apart from that he doesn't know anything else that you've done. We do, but he doesn't.'

'Does that mean I'll be sacked as well, then?' asks Tar, looking worried.

'No, it doesn't, little mate,' says Jock reassuringly. 'He reckons you're too young to know any different and because this is your first boat he thinks that this is a learning experience for you. Anyway, I took the bollocking for you.'

'It's either that or he thinks he can bend you and mould you to what he wants,' says Rob.

'How can he sack you anyway?' asks Tar. 'Aren't there laws against this sort of thing?'

I shake my head. 'Unfortunately for Jock there aren't. The rules say that if the yacht is maintained under Section 8 of the Merchant Shipping Act 1995 then a crew member like Jock will only be able to access the UK Employment Tribunal for an unfair dismissal if certain criteria are met.'

'Well, hasn't he met those criteria? He's worked on here for months.'

'It's a shit state of affairs, but no he hasn't.'

'So, what you're saying is that Thrush can do virtually anything he likes to anyone in this situation.'

'As far as sacking is concerned, yes.'

Jock tries to lighten the atmosphere. 'Anyway, it's not the end of the world and I'm fucked if it's going to spoil our night. Let's just forget about it. The guests are leaving tomorrow night and he's given me a few days to sort something out. With a bit of luck we'll get a good tip. There are loads of yachts and work around here at this time of year, so I'm not really arsed. Now come on, forget about it and let's have a laugh. Besides, there's no way I'm leaving this yacht before you lose your cherry, Tar. Jobs come and go, but deflowering a ripe virgin like you – hell, that shit will stay with me for ever!'

Everyone has a laugh and we're all in awe at Jock's total lack pity for himself. Everyone puts on a brave face but we can't help but feel a degree of loss. It's like we're losing a big brother and your naughty little brother rolled into one. For all his faults, Jock is the joker of the pack and his coltish nature livens up any room he walks into. Everyone has time for him and he is going to be deeply missed.

The crew drink for hours and after a while we're all drunk and back to our happy demeanour. The place is bustling with holidaymakers – an eclectic mix of fashionable freaks, sexy street girls, local lads looking for an easy drunk girl, professional clubbers and a fair share of chavs. The streets are a monument to hedonism. We head from bar to bar, laughing at Jock's ingenious ways of getting rid of annoying bar touts trying to get them in for business.

As the touts approach, Jock sometimes uses reverse psychology to deal with them. Instead of trying to dodge them he leaps up to them. Hugging them tightly, crotch to crotch, he runs his hand down their back on to their arse. This is usually enough to send him or her running for cover. With others, he waits until he sees them coming over, then pretends he's about to vomit on them. Again the reaction is the same. Sometimes, if they're short, he'll take a run at them and put his hands on their shoulders before leap-frogging over them. He treats them like moving challenges in an obstacle course.

Around midnight we find a bar with a good crowd of people, the music sounds great and the vibe is good.

'Do you see anything you like then, Tar?' asks Jock.

'Not really,' says Tar, looking around.

'What do you mean, not really? It's wall-to-wall here!' I say, pointing at the girls all around the bar.

'It's true, Tar,' says Rob. 'This is definitely the place to pull. We just need to find someone who's about your age, but I think the schools are closed this time of night.'

'I'm really nervous because I'm not quite sure what to say,' says Tar, looking at Jock.

'Everybody is when they first approach someone, mate. Just feel the fear and go with it.'

'You should really just be yourself,' Zecky tells him.

'Be yourself? Unless you're Jock, you mean!' laughs Tom.

'Well, yeah,' she agrees.

'I don't really have much experience, though,' says Tar.

'Look, the journey of a thousand miles starts with a single step. Don't let the past dictate who you are. Just be a part of who you become.'

'I reckon you should just get over there with all guns blazing, Tar. Blaze a path for others to follow. Now, there must be someone you like the look of,' says Jock, scouting the girls.

Tar looks over at a young blonde girl who is sat down with a friend. 'Well, she's got a nice face,' he says.

'Not a bad rack as well,' says Jock, nodding his approval.

'Yes, she's very pretty.'

'Right, mate, they're drinking bottles of Stella so I'll take a couple over.'

'No, Jock – not yet. I'm not ready...'

'Bullshit, just wing it. You can't play the game of life with sweaty palms, mate. Remember, those who hesitate, masturbate!' says, Jock rubbing his hands together. 'If you waste all your time worrying about if you're going to pull, the bloody night will be gone! You'll end up back at your cabin, wanking over a *Playboy* centrefold and sipping your Horlicks. Action is what we need here, mate!'

No sooner has Jock finished his entertaining motivational speech than he orders a couple of beers and heads over to the girls. He gives the beers to the girls and stays over for five minutes or so before waving Tar over. All goes well for about ten minutes until Tar asks her to come to the bar and get a drink. When she pushes the chair away and stand up she is about six-feet-four. She politely tells Tar that he's sweet but she makes her excuses and leaves.

'Fucking hell! She was taller than *me*, mate. She didn't look tall when she was sat down. You'd have needed a step ladder,' says Jock, laughing.

'Oh well, plenty more fish in the sea,' says Tar, trying to keep positive.

'That's the ticket, mate. It's all about confidence,' says Jock encouragingly. 'Anyway, she'd have been no good for you, being the height she was. Can you imagine getting down to business with her?'

'How do you mean?'

'Well, look, you're around five-six and she's around six-four. You'd never get away from her fanny if you were both naked!'

'How so?

'Think about it, mate. When you're hugging her your *nose* would be in it. When you're kissing her your *toes* would be in it, and when you're fucking her you'd have nobody to talk to!'

Jock's joke makes everyone laugh, then we all hit the dancefloor as the bass kicks in and the strobe light flashes. Everyone's having great fun and for the next hour or so nobody is really thinking of anything else other than drinking, dancing and laughing.

Suddenly a girl approaches Tar from out of the dry ice surrounding the dancefloor. Tar is in the middle and having fun bouncing around with Jock and Zecky. The girl puts her hand on Tar's shoulder and drunkenly turns him around to face her.

'You're fucking mine tonight,' she says, wrapping herself around him and tasting his tonsils.

She's around 18, about the same height as him but weighs about fifteen stone. She's Chinese, caked in make-up and she has a strong Liverpool accent. She's dressed in tight spandex with a big sparkly silver belt around her stomach that draws attention to her ample girth. She's the queen of chav city!

'Oh bloody hell! The poor kid hasn't a chance!' Zecky shouts in Jock's ear.

'I know! Doesn't look like she'll be taking no for an answer.'

The girl is now getting amorous, pushing Tar against a dark wall of the bar and she's got her hands all over him. After a few minutes she tells her friends she's leaving and that she's going back to her hotel room. Jock strolls over to Tar to see how he's doing.

'You OK, kid?' Jock asks, grinning ear to ear.

'She's mental, Jock!' he says with an astonished look on his face. 'She's only known me two minutes and we're off to her room.'

'She's a man-eater, mate! I think it's safe to say that tonight's the night, buddy. She must love young boys. Anyway, it doesn't look like you have much of a choice.'

'I know, and I don't really want to upset her.'

'Don't forget, Tar, because she's Chinese her fanny runs horizontal, *not* up and down like white girls. So when you shag her you'll have to lay her down and stick it in from the side,' says Jock, keeping a straight face.

'How do you mean?'

'You know what I mean – if you're looking from above you'd look like a cross.'

'Oh, right, I've got you.'

'She's a big girl, so if you can't find it amongst the rolls just tell her to fart and give you a clue!'

Tar is looking a little worried as the girl comes back and pulls him towards the exit. He speaks quickly in Jock's ear: 'Jock, will you come with me and wait outside so I can find my way back to the boat?'

'Nothing surer, mate. Go have a blast – I'll follow you and wait outside.' Jock tells the group what's happening and says he feels a duty to look after Tar as it's his first time. 'Tar and I will see you back at the boat – well, if he's still alive. Catch you later,' he says before disappearing into the night.

Jock follows the pair, keeping around twenty metres behind them as the girl eagerly drags Tar through the busy crowds and into her hotel. Tar keeps looking over his shoulder to see if Jock is still following. She leads him through the main door of the hotel and into her room, which is on the ground floor. Jock notes which room it is and then goes out the front and sits by a tree outside. It is only a few metres from their balcony so he can hear what's going on. He has to hide behind the tree as the balcony doors open and the light shines through, but she's so drunk she doesn't notice. She grabs a half-empty vodka bottle on the balcony table, takes a swig and makes Tar take a gulp.

Then she pushes the nervous Tar against the wall and unzips his fly. At this point Jock thinks it best to turn away but he can still hear Tar making all sorts of strange whimpering noises.

'Errrr, wouldn't you like us to get to know each other first?' suggests Tar, barely managing to keep his voice even.

'What the fuck for, lad?' she says in a thick scouse accent before pulling him into the bedroom by his dick.

'Well, can I at least know your name?'

'Rita… it's Rita, now shurrup – ya' putting me off!!' she says, as she strips off and lies down on the bed.

Tar takes his clothes off nervously as he surveys the tattooed bobbling mass on the bed in front of him. 'Come on then, lad, what you waiting for?' she says, teasing him over to her with a beckoning finger.

He remembers what Jock said and slowly positions himself over her sideways, crotch to crotch with his body running across the bed. She is looking up at him, barely able to see him over the top of her ample boobs as he tries to insert his member into her.

'What the fuck are you doing, lad?' Rita says, bemused at his efforts. Jock can't help but have a look through the window at Tar's antics and he has to muster all his self-control not to laugh and give himself away.

Tar tries harder and harder until Rita loses her patience and throws him off her body. She manhandles him on to his back then mounts him with all the elegance of a Rottweiler. Back and forth she grinds on top of him, with Tar staring at the ceiling and her huge boobs bouncing and slapping against him.

After a couple of minutes of groaning and thrusting there is an almighty yelping noise from Tar as he climaxes. 'Oh for fuck's sake, lad! I've barely got started and you've shot your muck already! What about me, like?!'

'Oh, sorry. I don't do this very often. I...'

'Never mind that, lad – get down and eat me out,' she says, walking further up the bed on her knees and straddling his face between her huge, fat thighs. 'And for fuck's sake hurry up – my boyfriend will be back soon.'

Tar's eyes are now like saucers. 'WHAT DID YOU SAY?!'

'My boyfriend... he'll be home soon.'

'BOYFRIEND!! What the hell is this?' screeches Tar, trying to fight off her ample frame, but he's somewhat unsuccessful due to his arms being pinned by his sides.

'He screws around and I'm not bothered, and I fancy a young white boy for a change,' she says in between thrusts.

When Tar hears this it sends him over the edge. 'Ahhhh, I'd better go now… really… I'd better go now,' he says writhing around like an eel. Jock hears this and bursts out laughing. His laughter is short-lived though, as he sees a coloured boy walk through the hotel gates. Before entering the hotel he pauses, looks over to the balcony and hears what's going on.

'Fuck!' says Jock quietly to himself.

The young lad's face turns to a picture of anger as he runs towards the hotel entrance, shouting, 'Dirty fucking bitch!'

Jock springs into life, climbing over the balcony and bounding into the room like a springbok.

'Who the fuck are you?' gasps Rita, not missing a thrust.

'Tar! Get the fuck out NOW!' cries Jock, grabbing his arm and yanking him from underneath her.

'No time to explain, mate – just run!' he says, clumsily shoving Tar out the window and over the balcony.

Tar tries to run away with his trousers still near his ankles and he has to stop after a few strides to pull them up. 'Thanks for the rescue, Jock, but what's the matter?'

'Boyfriend, mate – he's just rocked up. He'll be walking through the door any second, so run like fuck.'

No sooner has Jock got the words out than Tar has his trousers up and is overtaking Jock, sprinting through the hotel grounds. They continue running and laughing for a few hundred metres until they are safely amongst the crowds, then Jock takes him to a bar for a nightcap to calm him down before making their way back to the yacht.

'Here you go, mate – get that down your screech,' says Jock, thrusting a beer into his hand and offering him a bar stool. 'So, stud, how was it?!'

Tar gulps down the beer almost in one go and turns to Jock with a big grin. 'I don't know what to say, really. It was scary, exciting and bloody intimidating all at the same time.'

'You didn't have much say in it really, did you, mate?'

'Not really. Shall I tell you what happened?'

'You don't have to – I heard everything and saw most of it.'

Tar is looking a little embarrassed now. 'You didn't see *everything*, did you?'

Jock winks at Tar and slaps him on the shoulder. 'You're OK, mate. I looked away at certain points.' There is a short silence before Jock asks his next question. 'Soooo, ya' big stud, how does it feel to finally lose your cherry? Was it everything you thought it would be, then?' he says, bursting out laughing.

Tar can't help but laugh with him. 'It wasn't *quite* the way I envisioned losing my virginity, or with the type of girl I thought it would be with, but I guess I won't forget it in a hurry.'

'Well, yeah, you definitely won't forget that. I must admit, when I saw her dragging you off I didn't know whether to tell you to fight it or fuck it!! She was some size, eh? I bet when she says it's Tuesday, it's fucking Tuesday!'

'I know. I didn't want to upset her so I just went with it.'

'What about her... you know?'

'What?'

'You know?'

'What?'

'Fuck's sake, Tar – do you want me to spell it out for you? What was her fanny like? Mouse's ear or Mersey Tunnel – excuse the pun.'

'What the hell am I going to compare it to, for God's sake? I was a virgin, remember?'

'Fair point, mate,' says Jock, shrugging his shoulders and grinning.

'Oh, and another thing – it doesn't go sideways like you said it would on Chinese girls,' Tar tells Jock seriously, as if he's just discovered a new continent.

'No shit, Sherlock! I can't believe you fell for that one, mate!'

Tar is laughing now and is crimson with embarrassment. 'Ahhhh, you bastard!'

'Very funny though, mate.'

'For you, maybe.'

'Anyway, how do you feel now you've done the deed?'

'LIKE I'M KING OF THE WORLD... KING OF THE FUCKING WORLD!!' shouts Tar, thrusting his arms in the air.

CHAPTER 23

NATURE HAS THE ANSWER

After a couple more beers Jock and Tar get a taxi back to the yacht and Tar goes straight to bed. Zecky is still awake, sitting on the side of the quay looking at the moon with her legs dangling down the harbour wall as the taxi pulls up. 'You know I'm really going to miss you, Zecks, don't you?' says Jock, shifting up the quay to sit next to her.

Zecky takes a deep breath as she looks out over the harbour before squeezing his hand and turning to look at him. 'I'll miss you too. This boat won't be the same without you.'

'Do you really mean that?'

'Yeah, of course I do. You're a good egg underneath, and believe it or not I've grown a real affection for you. I must admit you surprised me tonight, though.'

'Why's that?'

'I didn't think you'd be back until the morning.'

'How so?'

'You know what I mean. You're single, it's Saturday night

in Ibiza and there are lots of girls around. I thought you'd go and play, so to speak.'

'I looked after Tar and had a beer with him afterwards, but that's it.'

'Why? What's changed?'

'I don't know really. I guess it really drilled it home to me, watching Tar and everyone else.'

'In what way?'

'I guess I don't really want that promiscuous life any more. I don't know why, but I just don't. It's fun when you're growing up because it's exciting and you never know what's going to happen.'

'Well, yeah, I guess it is, otherwise no one would do it, would they?'

'Yeah, but looking back, how many of those girls did I actually respect and give a fuck about?'

'Not many, I guess,' Zecky laughs.

'None, actually.'

'Why did you then?'

'I've got needs, Zecks, and let's face it, if you aren't in a relationship with somebody aboard the yacht, you rarely get to have sex, do you?'

'Is that why you had that one night stand in Monaco?'

'Yeah, but I can't even remember her bloody name.'

'Well, she might not be able to remember yours. Did you ever think of that?'

'Yes I did. I've got to admit that it got me thinking.'

'About what?'

'About that. What's good for the goose is good for the gander and they could say the same about me. Is that the sort of life I want to live, going through life without ever really knowing and caring about anyone?'

'And vice versa.'

'Exactly, and vice versa. At the end of the day I don't want that for myself.'

'My God! Could this be the sound of Jock maturing?'

'I've felt that way for a while, to be fair.'

There is a silence for a few moments. Zecky stares into Jock's eyes to see if there is any sign of him bullshitting but there isn't. 'That's the most sensible thing you've ever said to me, Jock. I never knew you felt like that.'

'Neither did I. Would it have made a difference if I'd told you before?'

'A difference with what?'

'With us,' says Jock with a grin.

'It might have done, yes.'

That isn't the answer that Jock had been expecting. He'd been anticipating the usual flippant brush off.

'Really?!'

Zecky lights up a cigarette and takes a drag before answering. 'Look, Jock, you and I have always been great friends, even if it looks different to an outsider. There aren't many people I trust more than you if the shit hits the fan.'

'That goes for me as well. We do have a chemistry, don't we?'

'Yes,' she says, smiling.

'You've never told me that before.'

'Well, you've never asked. You've just tried to squirm your way in to my knickers – entertaining as that is. Anyway, the reason I stayed up tonight was to have a bit of a think.'

'About what?'

'Loads of things really, but I didn't want you to leave without knowing what is going on inside my head with regard to you.'

'Shit! Had I better dive for cover?' he says, giving her a playful nudge.

'We'll have to wait and see, won't we?'

'I'm really going to miss you, Zecks. I love you loads, you know that, don't you?' says Jock, looking down at his feet.

'I love ya' as well, Jock,' she says, slapping him on the back.

Jock then turns to face her with a serious look on his face. 'No… you don't understand,' he says nervously. 'I really love you and I have done for ages. I've just got a shit way of showing it and I've kind of been fighting the feeling, if you know what I mean.'

'I think it might be *lust*, not love, Jock.'

'Lust is definitely there as well but it isn't just that. When I was sat up in the bar with you tonight, all I wanted to do was take you to the beach and tell you how much I was going to miss you and how upset I'd be if we lost contact; how I sometimes lie awake at night wondering what you're dreaming about and if you're warm enough; how great you make me feel when I hug you, even if it is just in a friendly way; and how I feel completely at home when I look you in your eyes.'

There is another short silence as the two of them sit cross-legged on the edge of the quay, looking at each other.

'Well, what are you going to do about it, then?'

'I just needed you to know, that's all.'

Zecky leans over and cups his face in her hands, then kisses him softly but passionately.

There is a look of shock on Jock's face as he tries to come to terms with what's happening. He's waited so long for this moment. He gently cups the back of her head with his hands as he kisses her back. Together they share a perfect moment under the starry sky with the sound of the sea lapping against the quay.

'Do you want to come down to the beach with me?' Zecky asks him.

'When?'

'Now,' she says, kissing him again.

'You try and stop me,' says Jock.

* * * *

Next morning everyone meets for breakfast around the crew table. Jock and Zecky can't help but give each other little smiles and knowing looks across the table. They look a little tired and it wouldn't surprise me if they'd been up all night.

Thrush comes down for breakfast and is trying to get information on what time everyone got back last night, as well as moaning about lots of little things. He says that the guests will be collecting their luggage from the yacht earlier than expected and they should have it all packed up and ready for collection by 3pm. Their plans have changed and they will be leaving the yacht today, in Ibiza, as Mr Big is going to stay with his acquaintances on the island. Thrush also tells us that there is a problem with the yacht's gearbox. This will take about two days to fix, so the yacht will be staying alongside the quay until the job is done. This is also a factor why Mr Big is cutting short his charter, even if it is just by a day.

The morning is taken up with the usual cleaning and maintenance routine until the guests arrive to pick up their luggage and say goodbye to the crew. Everyone is lined up on the after deck in uniform, awaiting their arrival. They don't hang around long – just time to load up the limo and shake hands with all of the crew. Mr Big especially thanks Zecky. He also thanks the boys personally for looking after them when they did water sports. As he shakes Jock's hand he produces a folded bar towel in the shape of an erect penis – the trick Jock had shown him. The two of them joke for a few moments before he moonwalks back to the passerelle and says goodbye. Unsurprisingly he barely gives Thrush the time of day.

After the crew wave the guest's limo off and it disappears around the corner, Thrush asks everyone to go down to the crew room. Everyone turns up except Olga. Nobody knows where she is. Then he hands out the guest charter gratuity to everyone and, without so much as thanking the crew for all their efforts, stands up from the table and walks out of the room. As he leaves, he turns to Zecky and says, 'Could you come and see me in my cabin in ten minutes please?'

'Sure. What's it regarding?' says Zecky, looking puzzled.

'If you could just come up, please.'

Everyone looks at her, wondering what he wants to see her about. This definitely sounds strange.

'What's all that about, Zecks?' asks Rob.

'I wish I knew, mate. Haven't got a clue!'

'Have you upset him or something?'

'I don't think so.'

I look into my envelope at the gratuity Thrush has just handed us. I count it, then count it again to check. I'm a little confused so I attract the others' attention.

'Just have a look in your tip envelope and count what he's given you.'

'Why? What's up?' asks Tom.

'Well, it's not what I expected. I reckon it's hundreds short.'

'You're kidding!' says Tom.

'No, I'm not. Just check it would you?'

Everyone quickly opens their sealed envelopes. There are disappointed looks on all their faces as they all look around at each other. The room is so quiet you could hear a pin drop until Rob breaks the silence.

'That's fucking shit! All that time and effort we put into the charter, just for that!' he says, slamming the envelope down on the table.

'Hardly seems worth it, does it?' says Zecky, shaking her head.

Rob scratches his head. 'It seemed like Mr Big had a great time, though. He left happy and he wasn't exactly stingy with his cash, was he? I'm well surprised.'

Zecky stands up and lets out a big sigh. 'Oh well, I'd better go see what Thrush wants. See you all in a bit.'

As she walks out, the mood in the room turns even sourer. It seems like all our efforts have gone to waste. After a while we disperse until Rob and I are the only people left in the room.

'Are you thinking what I'm thinking, mate?' asks Rob.

'Bloody right I am.'

'What are you going to do about it?'

'What *can* I do about it? I don't know how much Mr Big tipped the yacht.'

'Why don't you go up to Thrush's cabin and have it out with him?'

'And say what? "Thrush, we all think you are a fucking thief – now cough up the rest of the tip and be fair!" I've got no proof and until I find it, we can't do a thing. That fucker can get away with it. He's the only one who knows how much we're tipped.'

'Why don't you ask to be kept abreast of the financial side?'

'I tried, remember? He politely told me to fuck off.'

'He told you to fuck off?!'

'Not in so many words but that's what he meant.'

'Well, why would he do that unless he was hiding something?'

'You tell me.'

There's the sound of a door slamming and Zecky comes down the stairs in tears. Rob and I look at each other and run after her to see what's wrong. We find her on deck sitting on a rope bollard with her head in her hands, in floods of tears. I sit next to her and give her a hug. 'What's the matter, sweetheart?'

It takes a few moments for her to regain her composure as she dabs away at her streaky mascara. 'The fucking prick has gone and sacked *me* now.'

Rob and I are astonished. If anyone's job on board was thought to be safe it was Zecky's. She was great at her job.

'Sacked *you*?! What the hell for? You've done nothing wrong.'

'I know!'

'What did he say to you, then?' asks Rob.

'He said that he thinks it's time we separated and moved on.'

'Did you ask why?'

'Of course I did. He said that sometimes he didn't agree with how I did things.'

'That's fucking bullshit, man!' says Rob angrily. 'Hang on a minute… I know what's going on here.'

'What's that?' asks Zecky.

'That fucker is trying to get rid of us all to split us up. He'll try and get rid of us one by one so a whole new crew can be hand-picked by him, so they'll bend to his whim.'

'Either that or he'll get his mates on,' I say.

'Another thing,' says Rob, getting angrier by the second. 'Where the fuck has Olga gone? Don't you think it's weird she wasn't around when the tips were being handed out?'

'You're right, Rob,' I say. 'Look at what's happening here. He treats us like shit so a few of us might think there are better yachts to be had elsewhere. The tips for the past two charters are short. He's already got rid of the Chief Engineer a couple of trips back to make way for his mate. Then he's got rid of Jock and now Zecks. Don't you see a pattern here?'

'You've got a point. If he gets rid of Zecky I bet you Olga will replace her as Chief Stewardess. That means she'll be in charge of the department and will get the extra cash. It will be a cushy little number for them both.'

'That's what I said to him,' says Zecky. 'I told him it doesn't take a genius to figure out what's happening here.'

'What did he say to that?'

'He just shrugged his shoulders and said, "That will be all."'

'How long have you got, then?'

'The same as Jock – until the gearbox is fixed and the yacht leaves.'

'Right, that's going to be at least two days.'

'What are we going to do? We can't let him get away with this,' says Rob, looking at me in a furious mood.

'Just let me think about it for a minute.'

I walk around the after deck biting my thumbnail and pondering the problem. Rob is comforting Zecky as best he can. She's in bits, and out of all of us, she doesn't deserve this.

After a few minutes I rejoin them. 'There is only one thing to do. I'm going to have to find out exactly how much Mr Big tipped.'

'How are you going to do that? Call him up and ask him?!' says Rob.

'That's exactly what I'm going to do. Zecky, have you still got his number?'

'You're kidding, right?' says Rob, pondering what he's just heard.

'Nope.'

'If Thrush finds out you've gone behind his back *you're* finished, mate,' says Rob.

'By my calculations we're all finished anyway. It's just a matter of time. Might as well go out in a blaze of glory. Anyway, we can't let the twat get away with this because it isn't right. I wouldn't treat my fucking dog the way he treats the crew. Who the fuck does he think he is? We've all got to stick together because he's only him and but we are us. Loyalty and looking after each other – it's as simple as that.'

Zecky hands me her mobile phone and Mr Big's number is already on the screen. I press the call button and await the answer. After a few moments Mr Big answers and I can hear loud music in the background. He shouts at one of the bodyguards to turn it down so he can hear.

'Hello?'

'Hello sir, I'm calling from aboard the yacht.'

'Yes... what's the problem?'

'Sorry to bother you but I just wanted to know if you'd had a good charter and to let you know that we've really enjoyed having you.'

'Great charter, and a great crew. I'm sure we'll be back.'

'That's great sir, it's good to hear. I'm just checking the final bill as well, sir. I wonder if you could put me right on a few items because we can't seem to find the paperwork.'

'OK... what do you want to know?'

'Yes, can you tell me what figure the total bill was and what gratuity you left? It's just for the records and office paperwork, you see.'

'Yes, hang on and let me check.'

After a minute or so Mr Big comes back on the phone and I write down what he tells me. 'Yes I can still hear you... yes, got that... yes... and what was the final gratuity? Right... well... that's great, and thanks for that. I'm sorry to bother you but paperwork is paperwork. Have a nice time here in Ibiza and we'll hopefully meet again.'

I get out my pocket calculator and do some quick arithmetic. I stand and stare at the figure and do the calculation again to double check.

'That dirty, sly, low-down, robbing, cunt!'

'I fucking *knew* he'd nicked some!' says Rob, standing bolt upright.

'How much are we short between us all, then?' asks Zecky.

'Fucking thousands!'

'Thousands! What are we going to do?'

'I'm going to call the owner and tell him exactly what's

gone on here with the sackings and the stealing and see what *he* can do.'

'You're calling the owner?! Mate, now you're really pushing the boundaries. Do you think that's wise?' asks Rob.

'Like I said before, we've nothing to lose now. It could be any one of us getting sacked next. Thrush can't be allowed to get away with this.'

'OK, it's your arse but if you're going to call him, calm down and sound professional.'

'Rob's right,' says Zecky. 'Don't go off all guns blazing. Just give him the facts. Now hand me the phone and I'll get the number up.'

The boss's phone rings and rings but nobody picks up. I'm just about to give up when a voice answers.

'Hi, Zecky. Are you looking after my beautiful yacht for me?' says the boss, sounding in good spirits.

'Oh, hi sir, it's me,' I say. 'I'm just borrowing Zecky's phone to call you.'

'Have you broken another one?! Christ, with people like you I should have my money in mobile phones! What can I do you for?'

'No... no, it's inside. Look, I know that this is pretty unusual for one of the crew to call you when it isn't via the Captain but I don't really have much choice.'

'That sounds a bit ominous, mate. What's up?'

'There's a few things happening on your yacht I think you should know about.'

'Like what?'

'Well, we've just finished the charter and the Captain's gone and sacked Jock and Zecky.'

'He's done what? What's he gone and done that for?'

'Nothing, plus the tips from the charter are really low again and we suspect he's taken some of it.'

The boss takes a few seconds to ponder the implications of what I've just said. 'You had the same thing last time, didn't you?' he says quietly.

'We did, sir, yes, but we took him at his word and didn't question him.'

There is a silence from the other end of the phone and I can sense the boss is beginning to fume. 'Have you got any evidence of this and are you telling me everything?'

'As a matter of fact I have. I've just got off the phone with the guest. I rang him to ask him for a run-down of expenditure, and it seems that what he gave as a gratuity is totally different to what we all received.'

'How much less?'

'Thousands, sir. I'm sorry to bother you with this but I thought you should know.'

'No, you did the right thing. Right, mate, listen carefully. You're pretty lucky because at the moment I'm not really up to much, so I'll call my pilot to get my plane ready for tomorrow morning. It won't take long to get to Ibiza from Monaco, so I'll be there about lunchtime, all being well.'

'You're coming down? Right... OK. Do you want me to mention it to the Captain?'

'No, don't say a thing. I want you to carry on as normal. Don't even mention it to the crew, except Zecky and Jock. I'm glad you called because there have been a few discrepancies over the past few months and I was going to check them out, anyway. You've just brought that forward.'

'OK.'

'Remember, not a word to anyone else because I want to catch him off guard.'

'No problem, sir.'

'I'll see you around lunchtime, then.'

'OK, sir...will do.'

I end the call and hand the phone to Zecky. I'm a little worried that the situation will now escalate. I look at the sky and take a deep breath before turning to Zecky and Rob.

'I'm not going to go into too much detail but the boss is flying in tomorrow lunchtime. He said that I should only tell Zecky and Jock, probably because they're the only ones who have been sacked. However, you've just overheard me, Rob, so that goes out of the window. He doesn't want anyone else to know, so you've got to promise me you won't say a word. OK?'

'Yep, no worries. My lips are sealed.'

'Right, let's get this yacht looking her best. Rob, you get the boys together because it's all hands on deck today. Zecks, you'd better crack on with your stuff. If Thrush asks you, just tell him that you should be all set to leave the day after tomorrow in the evening. That way he won't keep hassling you. Apart from that, just keep out of his way.'

'Yeah, OK,' says Zecky, jumping to her feet.

'By the way, I think we should all keep off the booze tonight to keep a clear head for tomorrow. And we should all stay on board tonight.'

The crew spend the whole day cleaning and detailing the yacht inside and out to make her look pristine. After a long, hard day everyone is tired and a night aboard the yacht is welcomed. Most of the crew except for Jock relax in the crew room watching TV. Jock is out catching more fish at the bottom of the quay. I wander over and sit next to him. Jock turns and smiles.

'How's it going, mate?' he says as I sit down.

'I'm OK, big boy. How are you?'

'Never fucking better, mate. Do you want one of these?' he says, offering me a cigar.

'Don't mind if I do, mate, but don't you only smoke these when you're celebrating something?'

'That's right.'

'Really? Considering everything with the tips and the sacking? I've known me and you to have better times, mate.'

'Don't you worry, it's all going to work out fine. I'm celebrating two monumental things.'

'What's that, then?'

'The first happened last night and the second will happen tomorrow.'

I smile knowingly at Jock. 'Oh yeah, and what would that be?'

'The first thing is, Zecky and I got it on last night.'

'I know, mate. I saw all the little sly glances at the breakfast table and I overheard you talking before slipping off to the beach together last night.' I put an arm around Jock's shoulders. 'Do me a favour though, mate. Don't go and hurt her. She's like a sister to me and she's a bloody good catch.'

'I've got no intentions of doing that, mate. I care too much about her.'

'I know, I heard what you told her.'

'Yeah, well, we really had a moment last night. It was electric. We really connected.'

'I'm glad and I really hope it works out for you. I had a feeling in my stomach about you two a while ago.'

'Really? I didn't. I thought I'd never get anywhere.'

'Just take it slowly, mate, one step at a time. So are you ready now for the pain?'

'Eh?'

'The *pain,* mate! This isn't going to be just a one night stand you know. If you're going to have a relationship with this girl, she's going to make you grow like you've never had to before. With growth there is always pain as you adjust and re-adjust. It goes with the territory.'

'Oh, right, that's one of the things I've been thinking about.'

'I'm glad you've thought about it. The rusty old edges will be smoothed out and this time next year I won't recognise you, mate!'

'She'll have a job on her hands. I've lived my single life the way I've lived it for so long, I'm going to need a bit of coaxing.'

'Well, Zecky is a strong-willed girl with a good head on her shoulders, so if anyone can do it, mate, it's her. She'll turn you into a S.N.A.G. before you know it.'

'A what?'

'A S.N.A.G… Sensitive New Age Guy.'

Jock looks at me with a mixture of horror and disbelief. 'This is *me* you're talking about, isn't it?' Jock says, bursting out laughing.

'Seriously, though, mate. How are you going to deal with it?'

'What the fuck am I supposed to do after all these years? What *is* normality? I don't know where it is any more. My life has been like a meal: my childhood was my shit starter that gave me a life-long ulcer to live with. It's made me grow a certain way.'

'Everybody is a product of their environment, mate.'

'Yeah, I know, but philosophically speaking I've lived an extraordinary life, eating fucking spicy chilli in an ordinary world where potatoes are the norm, and unfortunately life's dinner table doesn't serve my dish! Now I can totally see why the courts of this land give money to people when they divorce based on their past lifestyle to keep them in a lifestyle to which they have become accustomed.'

'How so?'

'Because it's fucking painful to step out of your comfort zone and live a life that you aren't used to.'

'Are you scared of change and being in love?'

'Fucking right I am! I feel naked and vulnerable for the first time in my life.'

'Yeah, well, so will the other person if they're in love, too. You'll sort it out; just stick with it. Do you remember what I told Tar. It's not the changes in life that are tough, it's just the *transitions*.'

'Yeah, I guess.'

'Talking of Zecky, has she told you what's happening tomorrow?'

'Yeah.'

'All of it? About the boss coming down in the afternoon to see if he can sort out this problem with your sacking and the crew tips?'

'Yeah.'

'Good. That saves me a job then. I just hope that Thrush

doesn't sweet-talk his way out of it. When his head is straight he can charm anyone and make them think black is white.'

'Maybe when his head is straight, but I doubt he can when it isn't.'

'What do you mean, Jock?'

'I mean exactly that. We'll just have to tip the scales in our favour, won't we?'

'What are you talking about? Getting him pissed so he makes a twat of himself? He barely touches a drop, and anyway there's no way on Earth he'll drink at that time of day. If you're thinking of getting him pissed for when the boss comes down, you've got no chance.'

'Who said anything about booze?'

I begin to feel a little uneasy. 'Jock, I hope you're not thinking what I think you're thinking. You'll get locked up for that and then your life really is fucked.'

'And what am I thinking?'

'Drugs? You're not thinking about drugging him?'

'Not with anything illegal.'

'Well, anything that's legal is shit and wouldn't do anything, so you must be talking about narcotics.'

'Take a look in the bucket behind you,' says Jock with a grin.

I lean over and see half a dozen gold and white coloured fish.

'What do you see?' says Jock.

'Fish?'

'Correct. That's what I'm going to use to tip the scales in our favour.'

'You're going to use *fish* to get him off his tits for when the boss turns up?'

'Yeah, that's exactly what I'm going to do.'

'What are you going to do with the fucking things? Beat him around the head with them and give him brain damage so he doesn't know what he's saying?'

'Nope, he's just going to eat them.'

I stare at Jock but nothing else is forthcoming about his plan. 'I'm not with you, mate. How is eating those fish going to get him off his tits?'

'These are no ordinary fish. These are *sarpa salpa* and they're a species of bream. If you eat the heads or some of the other body parts it's a bit like taking LSD. The Romans used it as a recreational drug. If you eat it, within a few minutes you get vivid hallucinations and you'll start hearing and seeing things. He'll be tripping his tits off for about a day and a half, and there's no antidote.'

'You're fucking kidding me, aren't you?'

'No, I'm not. I'm going to lace Chef's fish soup with it tonight, so if I were you, I wouldn't eat the soup tomorrow lunchtime.'

'How do you know about this?'

'Because I've had it myself, on holiday in Corfu, and I was off my fucking lord! I met some lads who used to fish off a peninsula where I was camping on the beach. They would be there first thing in the morning and about this time every evening. I couldn't understand why they went to so much effort, but they told me about it and they gave me some. They called it 'dream' fish and to top it all, it's completely legal.'

'How are we going to stop the rest of the crew eating it, though? We don't want everyone tripping their tits off when the boss arrives.'

'You've got a point. I haven't figured that one out yet and we don't want to tell anyone in case it gets out. The less people who know the better.'

'I couldn't agree more. Look, you're just going to have to lace only his meal with it, and the only way you're going to do that is help Chef serve it from the galley and make sure he gets it.'

'Sounds like a plan.'

'Jock, are you sure that this isn't going to do anything to him other than make him trip? I don't want him keeling over.'

'Yeah, I'm sure. Apart from tripping my tits off I was fine.'

'If anything happens to him I'll deny all knowledge of it. You know that, don't you?'

'Yeah, of course, but it's foolproof. I'm going to give the fillets to chef tonight and they are harmless. It's just the head and other parts that I'll grind up later and slip in his soup. If he figures out later that he may have been laced, there's no way to prove it. It would just look like some of the other parts found their way in to the soup and he must have eaten them accidentally.'

'Fucking hell, mate, this is perfect!'

'Yeah, I know. Nature always has the answer, doesn't it?!'

'Right, mate, are you coming in now? Most of the lads are in the crew room and the girls are going to have a slumber party around one of the cabins. It should be just the boys left in there and the footy is on in half an hour. I've got a little joke I want to play on Tar, because he's got away with it today. Just go with whatever I tell you, OK?'

'Cool. I'll see you in there in ten minutes.'

* * * *

Jock fillets the fish and puts it in the galley for Chef to put in his soup. Then he separates the heads and some body parts and grinds them up into a mush to lace Thrush's soup with, before joining me and the boys down in the crew room. As expected, all the girls are away at their cabin slumber party.

'Well, the footy isn't on for another twenty minutes, so what shall we do 'til then?' says Jock.

'I don't know really,' says Rob. 'What do you reckon?'

'There's not a lot we can do in twenty minutes, is there?' says Tom.

'Fuck it. Let's have a wanking contest. We've not done that in a while,' I say, like I've just suggested making a cup of tea.

Tar looks around the room to see if he's just heard correctly but everyone is looking completely normal. Tom, Jock, Rob, Steve and I are aware of the joke and we've done it to other young crew members before, with dramatic results.

'Did I just hear you right? Did you say we should have a *wanking* contest?' says Tar.

'Yeah, that's right,' I say, keeping a straight face.

'Here? Now? Are you crazy?'

'We do it all the time. It's just a bit of a laugh when we get bored.'

'You're kidding, surely?'

'No. Obviously we turn the light out so it's pitch black and we can't see each other.'

'Yeah, the lights are off when we do it. We're not fucking weirdos, for God's sake,' says Rob.

'Well, what's the point?'

'Money. We all throw in fifty euros in the pot, turn the lights off, lock the door, then jerk off into our hand. The first person to come shouts "bingo" then when you've tucked yourself away we put the lights on. Whoever comes first wins the money and it's as simple as that.'

Tar looks around at the five poker faces around the table. Nobody is cracking or giving anything away. 'So if all of you throw in fifty euros, that would be 250 euros profit for the winner?' says Tar.

'It sure would,' I say, 'but I reckon we should make it interesting. Let's make it a hundred each so the winner gets a five hundred.'

'Five hundred euros!' says Tar, who is now paying attention.

'That's nearly half a month's salary for a cadet, isn't it, Tar?' Tom says, reeling him in.

'Yes, it is.' Tar is slowly coming round to the idea that he could have a chance of winning a lot of money for a few minutes of pleasurable effort.

'Well, there's my hundred,' says Jock, slamming his money down on the table.

'And there's mine,' I say.

'And mine,' say Tom and Rob.

Everyone turns and looks at Tar to see if he's going to pluck up the courage and play. 'Are you in then, Tar?'

'No... no, I don't think so.'

'It's five hundred euros if you win... just for having a wank, mate!' says Jock.

'I know... I know and I'm tempted but it's a bit embarrassing. Anyway, I don't have a hundred euros. I've only got fifty in my cabin.'

'Oh fuck it, that'll do, since you're on a lower wage. Are you in, then?'

'Er, OK, then. But the lights will be off, right?'

'Yeah.'

'And you won't put them back on until everyone has tucked themselves away?'

'Yes, of course. You'll probably win anyway, mate. All you have to do is remember what you got up to last night,' chuckles Jock.

'Right, I'm in. Turn the lights off and lock the door then.'

Tom gets up and switches off the light, locks the door and finds his way back to his seat in the darkness.

'OK, everyone whip it out and I'll give you the countdown,' I say. 'The first one to come shouts "bingo". Is everybody ready?'

'Yeah,' they all chorus.

'OK then. Five… four… three… two… one… GO!'

After a few moments Jock, Tom, Rob and I start making little grunts. A few squelching noises can also be heard around the darkened room. Then higher-pitched sounds can be heard coming from Tar's direction and there is no mistaking who's making them. At this point Tom very slowly stands up and makes his way quietly towards the light switch.

The grunts and frequency of the squelches increase and the others continue to make their noises.

'Egggggh… euuuuurr… eeeeeurr… ahhhhhh…AAAAAHHHHH… BIIIIIIIIIIINGO!' shrieks Tar, as Tom switches the lights on, revealing Tar stood bolt upright in the middle of his orgasm, emptying the contents of his balls into the palm of his hand. Everybody is staring at him with huge grins on their faces, fully clothed and with their dicks safely in their pants. The squelching noises had not been coming from them all wanking, as Tar had thought – they'd been holding their face cheeks between thumb and forefinger and rapidly moving them from side to side. Everyone, except Tar, bursts out laughing.

'BINGO!!!!' we yell. Tar goes from a slightly pink sheen to beetroot red.

'Fuck off... FUCK OFF, would you?!' shrieks Tar, as he dives beneath the table to cover his embarrassment.

The rest of the night is spent shouting at the footy on the TV instead of shouting at Tar. At around midnight everyone goes to bed. It's been a long day.

CHAPTER 24

WHAT GOES AROUND COMES AROUND

Next day everybody is up at the crack of dawn. The shore-side engineer begins work on the faulty gearbox but has to wait for a part that will arrive by plane later tonight. The crew make sure the yacht is immaculate for the boss's arrival: stainless steel rails are gleaming, varnished wood polished, fresh flags are raised and the paintwork shines in the sun.

Lunchtime arrives and since there is no sign of the boss yet, Jock and I clear up, ready to go below decks and set his plan in action.

'Are you ready for this then, mate?' says Jock.

'Ready as I'll ever be. Where's the stuff to put in his soup?'

Jock takes a small, watertight plastic bottle out of his pocket and shows me the contents.

'All I've got to do is take the top off before I go in the galley to bring the plates down. Then, when I get the chance, I'll empty it into his soup.'

'There doesn't look much there, Jock.'

'There doesn't need to be – it's powerful stuff. It's just a few ground-up bits of body parts so he won't notice. He'll be off his lord.'

'How much does it take to trip?'

'One fish would do it if you ate the right parts.'

'How many fish did you use to make this little concoction then?'

'Seven.'

'SEVEN?!'

We head down below decks and take our seats for lunch. Jock sits at the seat closest to the entrance nearest the galley. I find a position so I can get a good view of Thrush. After a few minutes Chef calls down as usual: 'OK, lunch is ready – can someone give me a hand?'

'No problem, I'm on my way,' says Jock, standing up quickly.

He jogs up the stairs, his heart racing with adrenaline and nervousness.

'OK, whose is whose?' asks Jock.

'These can be anyone's. It doesn't matter, they're all the same. I've got Olga's and the Captain's,' says Chef, pushing past Jock.

Jock has to think quickly on his feet. The plan will fail if he can't lace Thrush's soup, and the boss could arrive any minute. It's now or never, he thinks. Just as Chef passes him in the doorway, Jock turns sharply with his elbows out and steps in front of him, knocking the hot soup over Chef's hands. The bowl smashes on the floor.

'Oh hell! Sorry, mate. That was bloody clumsy of me. Look, I'll take these down the stairs while my hands are full then I'll come back up, OK?'

'Shit! It's burning my hands,' says Chef, moving quickly to the cold tap.

Jock seizes the moment and turns the corner where he's out of sight for a few seconds. He pulls the small bottle out of his pocket and quickly empties it into Thrush's soup, then stirs the contents in with his finger before taking it down to the dinner table.

'What happened up there?' asks Thrush.

'We had a little accident with the soup and smashed a bowl. I'm just going up to sort it now.'

As Jock walks out of the room he gives me a sly wink to confirm the plan is in action. Now it's only a matter of time. Everyone is chatting away with their usual political correctness because Thrush is around. I am half way through my soup when Jock comes back. He gives me a little smile as he sits down to join us. After about twenty minutes, when Thrush is half way through his dessert, his eyes start to change. Instead of his usual intense vermin look they become impassioned and expressive. His journey has begun. Jock and I keep an eye on him as he begins to twitch and see things out of the corner of his eyes. He begins to inspect the pattern on the table closely, mumbling quietly to himself. The rest of the crew carry on their conversations and nobody really notices except us. The plan is working perfectly, so far.

Thrush is in the middle of carefully examining his reflection in the shiny cutlery when Olga asks him a question.

'How's your dessert?'

'What?' says Thrush, looking startled.

'Your dessert, how is it?'

'Dessert… fine… what?'

'What?' says Olga, looking confused.

'What did you say?'

There is a short silence before Olga repeats: 'I just asked you how your dessert was.'

Thrush is now getting confused and snappy. 'I *know* you asked me that! I'm sat next to you, for God's sake! What did you say after that?'

Olga is looking at him strangely. 'I didn't say anything after that.'

'I *heard* you.'

'Heard what?'

Thrush then sighs deeply and rolls his eyes at her before taking another mouthful of dessert. He leans over to Olga and whispers in her ear. 'I'm *watching you*!'

The crew finish their desserts then leave the room wondering at Thrush's odd behaviour. Most of them head up to the open deck to get some sunshine before starting work again. Shortly after 1.30pm I see Thrush resting his elbows on the handrail, looking out over the harbour. He's clearly in a world of his own.

I then turn and look down at the gate at the end of the quay, and I see two people walking through it. The boss has arrived, bringing somebody with him. I quickly go down to the after deck to let everyone know I've just spotted them walking along the quay. Zecky disappears inside and Jock and I stand at the gangway. As the two men approach I can see they are both looking serious, as if focused on doing a job. Jock and I meet them at the gangway and the boss greets us with his usual friendly expression.

'How are you, boys?'

'As well as can be expected, sir. It's good to see you.'

'Likewise, lads. This is Graham,' says the boss, introducing the other guy. 'He's coming aboard to check a few things and go over some paperwork with the Captain.'

'Pleased to meet you, Graham,' we say, feeling slightly nervous.

The boss then leans towards us conspiratorially and quickly briefs us on what's about to take place. 'I already know your side of things from our telephone conversation.' He says to me. 'I've checked out the story with the guests about the tip and it all adds up. Like I said, there are a few more accounting discrepancies Graham needs to talk to the Captain about, but I doubt he's going to be able to talk his way out of our questions and make any sense.'

'I doubt that very much as well,' says Jock, knowing a little more than them.

'By the way, Jock, as far as I'm concerned, your and Zecky's jobs are safe, so stop fretting, OK? And tell her straight away, so she doesn't worry.'

Jock relaxes visibly and it's clear a huge weight has been lifted from his shoulders.

'Right then, where is he?'

'I last saw him going in to his cabin,' says Jock. 'He looked a bit worse for wear, to be honest.'

'I see. OK, boys, I'll call you if I need you.' The boss and Graham then walk up the passerelle onto the yacht and disappear around the corner.

I look over at Jock, who has a huge smile on his face. 'I bet you're as happy as a pig in shit, mate, aren't you?'

'Fucking right I am, but not just because I've kept my job.'

'I know... I know before you even say it. Now you and Zecky can at least have a chance of staying together a little while longer.'

'Yeah, exactly. I feel like sparking up another cigar, mate.'

'Not yet, Jock. It isn't over till that spaced-out fucker walks down the passerelle for good.'

The boss and Graham find Thrush in the same state as at lunch. He's got his back to them and is having a conversation with himself.

'GOOD AFTERNOON!' Thrush almost jumps out of his skin as he hears the boss's booming voice behind him – among the many other sounds he's hearing inside his head. He turns around quickly and looks like he's just seen an apparition.

'Do you mind if I have a word with you in my lounge?' The boss says, leading him down the stairs.

After an hour or so Graham walks the deck to find Jock and I working on the jet ski at the back of the yacht. 'I've got a message from the boss and I'll quote him word for word: "Go into his cabin, empty his wardrobe, pack his and Olga's bags and order them a taxi for 3.30pm."'

Graham then disappears back into the lounge where we can see him going through paperwork with a very confused and aggressive Thrush. The boss looks like he would shoot him if only he had a gun.

Jock and I go upstairs to his cabin where his door is open. We find their suitcases and began packing.

'Where's Olga?' asks Jock.

'Don't worry, mate. She went ashore, so she won't walk in.'

As we go through the wardrobes Jock stops in his tracks. He can't really believe what he's seeing. 'I fucking well knew it – the warped bastard! Tell me I'm imagining this!' Jock can't take his eyes off what's in the bottom of the wardrobe.

'What's up?' I say, on hands and knees emptying Olga's wardrobe.

A big grin has crept across Jock's face. 'You know that conversation the girls had with Olga about men, sex and all that weird shit when she came back pissed that night?'

'Yeah.'

'And do you remember Zecky said Olga let slip that Thrush likes to dress up?'

'Yeah – she said leather was insinuated.'

'Well, fuck me sideways my old china – I've just found the *motherload*!'

I peer around the door and can't believe what I'm seeing either. 'I always knew there was something very strange about that guy,' I say as Jock reaches into the wardrobe and pulls out a pair of black leather shorts and a gimp mask fitted with a large snooker ball.

'It's like something off that scene in *Pulp Fiction*!' says Jock, examining the mask.

'I know! Who was that guy who was into all that gimp mask shit in the movie?'

'It was the owner of the shop that Bruce Willis and the big black gangster had a fight in. His name was Zed.'

'Zed, that's it. That's the Captain's new nickname from now on.'

'We'll hang on to these as a keepsake, mate,' says Jock.

The packing only takes around fifteen minutes, then Jock

and I drag the cases down to the bottom of the passerelle. When the taxi arrives Jock tells the driver to put the bags in the boot and wait.

'Where am I going to?' enquires the driver.

'Don't know yet, mate,' I tell him, 'but I think we're about to find out.'

As soon as the words are out of my mouth a commotion can be heard coming from the outside deck. Doors are being slammed and the boss can be heard arguing with Thrush. The voices are getting louder and louder and they are obviously in each other's faces as they walk towards the passerelle. Jock and I move onto the quay next to the taxi to get a better look of the outside deck where Thrush, in a world of his own, is barking at the boss as he walks away from him. At one point Graham has to separate the two and keep the boss where he is as Thrush walks down to the stairs then along the passerelle to the taxi.

'AND KEEP AWAY FROM THIS FUCKING YACHT, YOU THIEVING PIECE OF SHIT STONER!!' shouts the boss, as Thrush walks off.

Thrush stops momentarily and turns to look at Jock and me with his saucer-like eyes before he gets in the taxi. 'You two haven't seen the last of me – watch your backs!' he tells us, quietly and coldly.

Jock looks back at him equally coldly before answering him: 'Newton's Third Law.'

'What?' replies a flustered Thrush.

'Newton's Third Law is a law you should study. For every action there is an equal and opposite reaction. What goes around, comes around, you fucking sicko!'

Thrush snarls and mutters something before climbing into the back of the taxi, banging his head as he gets in. Just before the cab pulls away, I lean in through the window to have one last word.

'By the way, we absolutely loved the mask and the leather. I think you'd look absolutely lovely in it.'

As the taxi disappears the boss calms down a bit. He shouts from the deck to attract my attention: 'Get back on here, you!'

'You'd better answer him, mate,' says Jock.

'Are you talking to me, sir?'

'No – I was talking to the seagull behind you! YES, YOU!!'

'Oh, right...'

'Now get your arse on here, and Jock, you get the beers in. In fact get everyone up to the lounge. We're all going to have a drink or ten,' says the boss gleefully.

* * * *

For the rest of the afternoon and most of the evening the boss gets drunk with his crew. The music booms and everyone laughs and jokes and dances. The tension has disappeared as quickly as Thrush had. The boss flies back to Monaco the following day, but not before he orders me to store up the yacht as soon as possible. Another young captain has been found and we are to make the yacht ready for an Atlantic crossing to Barbados, where the boss is planning a surprise anniversary party.

The future looks rosy enough. We've all seen the last of Thrush, Tar has got laid, Zecky has kept her job and lowered her usually impeccable standards to let Jock into her life. The engineers have finished working on the gearbox and the yacht is quickly stored up for the crossing.

* * * *

As we head out of the harbour in the afternoon sun, Jock and I are on the top deck peering through the binoculars at a figure on the breakwater.

'Is that who I think it is?' I ask.

Jock starts to laugh. 'He's in the same clothes. He must be still off his tits!'

'How long do the effects last? It's been just over twenty-four hours!'

'One fish can keep you hallucinating for about thirty-six hours but it depends on your metabolism.'

'How much did you put in?'

'All of it.'

'That's *seven* fish. Fuck me, Jock! He'll be off his lord until the end of the month. Jock, run down and get the shorts and the mask from the crew room. You know what to do, mate.'

The paraphernalia have pride of place, hung up in the crew room next to Thrush's picture on the dartboard. Jock writes something on an elastic card tag which he fastens to the mask. The end of the breakwater is coming up fast and Thrush has spotted the yacht headed towards him close to the end of the pier.

As the yacht sails past, the new Captain sounds the ship's horn and Jock hurls the leather shorts at Thrush. Jock then shows me the gimp mask with the heavy ball at the front and I give him the nod.

'Go for it, mate!' I tell him, as I unfasten my trouser belt to show my arse at Thrush.

Jock takes aim and musters all his strength before hurling

the mask at Thrush. The heavy mask lands at his feet. Thrush bends down to pick it up and he notices the card tag with Jock's writing, which reads:

'*You've got no hope if you've got no soul.*

Lots of love,

Your dealer'

As Jock walks back up the deck, Thrush disappears in the distance behind the yacht.

'So mate, how was Zed?' I ask, grinning.

'To coin a phrase from *Pulp Fiction*... Zed's dead, baby... Zed's dead!